Data Structure Simplified:

Implementation using C++

JITENDRA SINGH, PhD
Assistant Professor
PGDAV College, University of Delhi
India-110065

Limits of Liability and Disclaimer of warranty

Author and the publisher have put their best to ensure that the programs, functions, description should be without error. However, publisher and the author does not make any warranty of any kind, expressed or implied with regard to these programs, function or other documentation used in the book. Authors and publisher shall not be liable for any kind of damage, incident, or performance issues that take place due to implementation of these programs.

ISBN-13: 978-1500949051

ISBN-10: 1500949051

Dedication

Dedicated to my beloved sister Anita, my respected father Sh. Jabar Singh Yadav and my mother Smt. R.B. Yadav

Acknowledgements

It was indeed a motivation and encouragement of my students who have inspired me for writing this book. Students were aiming for the text book that should enrich them both theoretically and practically at the same time it should be easy to read. In addition, it should engage them in more creative work where the learning from data structure can be applied.

This journey would have not been completed without the support of many of my colleagues. Indeed it is not possible to name all of them, however, it is worth naming few of them. First and foremost, I am extremely thankful to Dr. Vikas Kumar, who has taught me the art of representation of the text. He has also encouraged me to write few books after submission of my thesis. I am also grateful to my colleagues in PGDAV College (University of Delhi, India), Stratford University, USA (India Campus), who have always discussed me about data structure and the need of a book that should cover the case study aspect of data structure.

I am extremely thankful to my wife Ms. Nitu and son Varunjit Singh for extending their co-operation and sparing me for long hours that were needed for writing this book. Finally, I devote this book to my parents who are the constant source of motivation and inspiration. They have indeed encourage me to contribute in the field of computer so that it should benefit the entire computer fraternity and people below the bottom line in particular.

Jitendra Singh
Jun 2014

Preface

This book has been written to highlight the insight of data structure concept and programming needed to implement data structure. It has wide coverage on the various topics of data structure. We have started our book from Abstract data type and algorithm. We believe that knowledge of these topics before the implementation of other topics will enable the readers in writing as well as reading the effective and abstract code for the rest of the sections. We have discussed about the significance of Abstract data type in data structure. The second focus of this chapter is to highlight the significance of algorithm in designing and solving the computer problems. Mere writing the algorithm is not enough, instead writing the efficient algorithm is need of the hour. This can be accomplished with the help of efficient and effective writing.

Data structure has massive use of arrays and pointers. Familiarization of these topics in the early stage of learning facilitates in comprehensive understanding of the complex code written using points and array. This chapter covers the usage of array and pointers. To ensure that the student has grasped the concept completely, enough exercises along with the answers have been included within the chapter as well as at the end of the chapter. Strong understanding of arrays and pointers will be extremely helpful in understanding the advance topics, including the link list, stack, trees, etc.

Usage of link list enables the users in traversing the linear traversal. In link list, user can traverse with the help of next pointer that is stored in the each node of a link list. Various aspects of link list including insertion of the node at anywhere and deletion of a node is discussed in detail. Majority of the topics related to the link list are extensively covered. This topic is discussed before the stack to give the grasp of dynamic memory allocation and organizing the element in a dynamic data structure. This will also assist them in the creation of dynamic stack, which is widely used in the later stage of the book.

The next two chapters are related to the arrangement and accessing of the item. We have started it from the data structure that is opened from one end. This data structure is known as stack. The second data structure is also related to the arrangement of item. However, it is equipped with two ends and knows as queue. One end is utilized for insertion whereas the other is utilized for removal of the items. We are also widely utilizing this data structure in the other chapters of this book, wherever we need to store the element and access them in the order of insertion.

Linear data structure is followed by non-linear data structure and started with defining the trees and the need of the tree. Heading further, we have discussed the special case of tree known as binary search tree (BST). Major concepts pertaining to BST including insertion of a node, traversal in a BST, deletion of the nodes have been extensively covered. Extensive coverage to the basic of the tree has been enumerated in the chapter 7. In addition, we have also covered the programming of tree in detail. All the programs written in this chapter and the subsequent chapters are adequately tested (Turboc compiler) before including them in this text book.

Extending the topic of tree, we have considered the Advance tree in which the major limitations of BST have been discussed and the various trees that can be used to overcome these limitations of BST.

Consequently, threaded tree and AVL tree is discussed in detail. In the BST, AVL tree, threaded tree, etc. are of order 2, as a result, attaching more than two nodes was not possible. To accommodate more than two nodes multi-way tree have been discussed. In the multi-way tree, widely used Tree including B tree, B+ tree, B* trees have been described in detail.

Text book on data structure would not be completed without discussing the core concept of string and sorting. These topics are widely discussed in the chapter on sorting and strings, so that reader can get equipped themselves with various techniques of sorting, searching and the string manipulation.

Eventually, we have discussed the graphs that are needed in the wide variety of applications, for instance, during routing in a network. The key focus of this chapter is to cover the basics of graphs, their representations, traversal, etc. Finally, shortest path is determined from the source to the destination using prominent techniques existing.

Table of Contents

Chapter 1
Introduction

Chapter Objective

- Describe the abstract data type
- Usage of abstract data type
- Define the algorithm
- Characteristics of algorithm
- Types of algorithm
- Measuring the complexity of an algorithm

1 Introduction

Data structure is widely used in many areas of computer science. Although processing speed and memory are no more constraints for the computer system. However, for massive data, efficient program have significant impact in generating the instant results. Therefore, it is significant that the algorithm employed should be efficient and should require minimum time and space for execution.

It is equally important that the program written for one objective should be applicable to other similar objective with minimum or no changes at all. Necessary implementation details should remain hidden from the user. This chapter highlights the various aspects of algorithm that has the significant impact on the performance of a program.

1.1 Abstract data type (ADT)

In a language, data types have significant role in representation of data. Data type governs the various factor that include:

- Type of information accepted.
- Range of permitted value.
- Memory space needed.
- Operations permitted on the data type.

Primitive data type, for instance integer, real, character, etc. need to defines the basic operations. Consequently, complex operations cannot be used in these data types. To address this limitation, ADT is used. In abstract data type(ADT) users are provided the details that they need to know remaining information is inaccessible to the user.

ADT can be defined as a mathematical representation and determines the operations that are permitted, but it hides the implementation details. Hiding the implementation details permit the modification in the code that is needed due to bugs or other reasons. Consequently, user is not affected with the modification/inclusion of extra functionality.

Object oriented language has the capability to support the abstract data type. In object oriented language, complex and new /extra operations are required to be defined. ADT facilitates in defining the operations that can be performed on the data types. Even the hiding of internal details is widely supported in the object oriented language. In object oriented approach, to hide the members, they are declared as private. Usage of friend function is not allowed due to the accessibility of private member. ADT offers flexibility to implement the definition for complex structure, although it might have implemented for primitive data type.

1.1.1 Need of an ADT

User needs to implement the abstract data type due to variety of reasons. This is facilitated with the help of interface that is offered to the implementer. Abstract data type needs to implement various details. As a pre-requisite, code offered should be reliable and robust. Reliability can be attained with the help of data hiding. Consequently, user doesn't have the flexibility to access the defined variable.

1.1.1.1 Implementation of an ADT

Even though, ADT is widely used due to its various features. However, before implementation, readers need to learn many of the significant terms and their meaning associated to the object oriented abstract data type:

Constructor/Modificators- These are the methods that are capable to build or change the state of an object.

Accessors-Methods that can be accessed by the object are known are accessors.

Consider a case of a queue implementation. Since, the queue can be linear or circular, due to the usage of ADT; user does not need to know the implementation details. Instead, can concentrate on the usage of various functions offered. In the queue data are inserted from one end and is known as en-queue whereas items are removed from another end known as de-queue (Readers who are not aware of the queue, please refer section 6.1, basic definitions, for more clarity). We can also determine the item that is available at the front of the queue without removing it.

During the implementation of ADT, we need to know the various input, output and changes that are caused due to these inputs. Eventually, to determine the final output after the changes. In ADT, these can be accomplished as described in the table 1.1.

Table 1.1: Queue interface

Name	Description	Input	Output	Changes
Enqueue	Places the item at the at the end, if queue is not full	Queue and item		Item added, rear will move one position back
Dequeue	Removes an item from the front of the queue, if queue is not empty	Queue		Front item is removed and the front will point to the next element
Empty	Examines whether the queue is empty or not	Queue	A Boolean value	
item	Returns the first element without making any changes in the front	queue	Front of the queue	

	position			

Axioms-Axioms are the mathematical representation of the various operations that need to be carried out by utilizing ADT. Consider a case, if the queue is q1 and the item to be inserted is 'e' then the axioms are:

Enque(q1,e)=e //Element inserted

Dequeue (Enque(q1,e))=e //Element removed

Empty (Enque(q1,e))=Boolean //status flag

Item(Enque(q1,e))=e //first element of queue

Once the axioms have been written, they pave the fertile ground to denote the prototype of the functions that can be used to accomplish a specific task.

Prototype of the above axioms can be the following:

```
Template<class T>
T enqueue(Q q, T t1); //insert the items in the queue.
T dequeue(Q q); //returns the item removed.
Bool Empty(Q);      // To check whether the queue is empty
T item(Q);     // to determine the first element of the queue
```

Above functions signifies that the usage of ADT makes the programmer life simpler. Any error or complexity can be analyzed well before time. Correspondingly, it saves a lot of time during the testing stages.

1.2 Algorithm

In computers, we need to solve wide varieties of given problems, majority of them fall under the category of simple or complex. Given problems can be solved by applying various steps/sequence. The complete set of statements needed to solve a given problem is known as algorithm. In majority of the cases, algorithms are written using pseudo code. Coder/Developer we translates pseudo code used in the algorithm into specific code of a needed programming language.

Good algorithm is a pre-requisite for good procedure. To solve a given problem, sequential set of statements are grouped together, and may be categorized into simple statements, conditional statements, loops statement, etc. It requires careful thought for writing efficient and cost effective code by utilizing these language construct. For instance, the written logic should not allow the loops to continue, once search is already accomplished. Consider an example of searching from an array, if the element is already found then the looping effect must terminate. A faulty algorithm to search an element has been discussed as follows:

Problem 1.1. Write an algorithm to search an item from the given array

```
int search(a[],element)
{
found=false;
k=0;
while(not end of a)
{
if(a[k]== element)
```

```
found=true;
}// end of while
increment k;
 }// end of search
```

In the above algorithm, even though the element may be found at the first location despite that searching will continue up-to the end of the loop. However, it is undesired; since loop continue to execute without any objective. For effectiveness, the above code needs to be modified in a manner so that any possible unnecessary cycle of loop can be avoided.

```
Problem 1.2. : write an algorithm to search an item from the given array
search(a[],element)
{
found=false;
k=0;
while(not end of array a[])
{
if(a[k]== element)
{
found=true;
break;  // come out of the loop
}
k++;    //increment the value of k
}// end of while
 }// end of search
```

Algorithms have their significance in problem solving.

Consequently, writing an efficient algorithm has major role in polarizing the program based on latency, throughput, space needed, etc. Correspondingly, an algorithm needs to have some specific properties that include:

Input- An algorithm should be capable to accept the input from the external world. This input guides an algorithm for further processing.

Output-Algorithm should able to produce the verifiable output after processing the given input.

Unambiguous- Language used to write an algorithm should have explicit meaning. Ambiguous words leads to more than one interpretation. Consequently, it leads to errors in the resultant code.

Termination- All the algorithms are written to accomplish specific task. Algorithm should be capable to accomplish the task in finite steps. Once the objective is achieved, an algorithm should be capable to terminate.

Feasibility- Algorithm written to solve the specific problem should be feasible for the language considered so that it can be implemented in real world with the assistance of contemporary languages.

1.2.1 Types of algorithm based on Call

To solve the specific problem, we can apply various types of approaches. Broadly, algorithm based on call/flow can be categorized into:

- Non-recursive
- Recursive

1.2.2 Non-Recursive

In the non-recursive algorithm, we use conditional statement(s) or the looping statement(s) to solve the specific problem. This approach is considered as simple and widely utilized by the developers in their coding. Debugging the recursive algorithm is simple and needs less time.

Problem 1. Program 1.3: To find out the sum of numbers

```
int sum_array(int x[])
{
int total=0;
while(x[i])
 {
total=total+x[i];
i++;
}
return total;
}
```

Non-recursive algorithm has less overhead relative to recursive approach that utilizes the stack to store/save it various states. However, there are number of instances where solving the problem using the non-recursive approach is complex, for instance, traversal in a tree, Tower of Hanoi, factorial, etc. In such situation, applying the recursive approach makes the programmer life simple.

1.2.3 Recursive Approach

A problem that is solved by non-recursive approach can also be solved with the help of recursive Approach. In the recursive algorithm, thing are defined in its own term. For instance, consider a case for the sum of all the elements of an array.

```
int sum(int x[], int n)
{
if(n==0)          // base condition
return 0;
return total=sum(x,n-1)+x[n];
}
```

In the above example, the entire problem has been solved in terms of sum. Whenever, we are writing a recursive approach, it is imperative that two conditions should be essentially included as:

- Base condition (Condition at which the function terminates).
- Condition that leads to the base condition in subsequent calls.

In the above program, if n==0 is the base condition, whereas sum(x, n-1) is the condition that is leading the function towards the base condition. To accomplish this objective, decrementing is carried in the n with the usage of expression 'n-1'.

1.3 Complexity analysis

To solve the given problem, there are number of methods (algorithm) can be employed. Programmers code the solution as per their perception and understanding. Due to the existence of various solutions, it becomes extremely challenging to select the solution that best describes the given problem.

Selection of a proposed solution is governed by various factors, for instance, computation cycle needed to solve the problem, need for memory, storage requirement, etc. Solution that needs minimum time to compute, minimum space for memory is considered as the optimum solution.

Algorithms which are selected based on time and space requirement are known as asymptotic. In such types of algorithm we compute the Complexity. Analysis is one of the major components of any algorithm written. In best cases, an algorithm can solve the given problem in the few cases, however, in worst cases it can solve in last step or penultimate step. However, amortized, considers the average time needed to solve a given problem.

Complexity of an algorithm is governed in terms of:

- The maximum time needed.
- Minimum time needed.
- Equal time needed.

Accordingly, they are categorized into lower bound, upper bound, equal bound, etc. In this book, we have considered big (O) that represent the upper bound.

1.3.1 Big Oh

Big Oh: Big Oh for a function having n number can be defined as f(n)<=c*g(n) for all n, n>=n0;

Big (Oh) acts as upper bound that means it represent the complexity in the maximum terms. However, algorithm in real time may need lesser time than the one denoted by the Big(O).

Mastering the big 'O' complexity is the major challenge to the students who have left the mathematics or could not remember many of the formulae. In big Oh, the major complexities results are O(1), O(n), $O(n^2)$, $O(2^n)$, O(log n). This section enumerates the Big Oh in profoundly simple terms and substantiated with the help of number of examples.

A. **O(1)**

Big (1) is the simplest among the other complexities in the Big Oh notation. O(1) denotes that only one comparison is needed. Many times the program itself is of single statement. Consequently, complexity is resulted in O(1). In the O(1) notation computational time always remains same. Since, the item has been searched in the first step itself.

For instance, consider the following example:

Problem To find out the maximum of two numbers

```
// Solution to find out the maximum of two numbers
bool max_value(int a, int b)    // function that accept two numbers
{
```

```
if(a> b)          // Compare the two numbers
return true;      // if first is greater return true
else
return false.     // otherwise return false
}
```

In the given example, only one comparison is needed therefore, overall performance will remain the same, irrespective of any other factors. So the complexity of this algorithm is O(1). Correspondingly, complexity is not dependent on the number of elements.

B. **O(n)**

O(n) is also known as linear complexity. Since, in O(n) we start from the first element and then second element and continues till the last element or the item to be searched is not found. However, it may also happen that the item to be searched has been found before the nth element but we consider it as n^{th} only. Consequently, the complexity is represented as O(n). Same has been depicted in the following example.

```
// Program to search a number from the given list of numbers
bool search( int arr[], int number, int n)
{
bool found=false;
for(int i=0;i<n;i++)
{
if(arr[i]==number)
{
found=true;
```

```
break;
}        // end of if
}        // end of for
return found;
}        // end of function
```

In the above example, element to be searched may be in the first position in that case it will be O(1). However in the majority of the cases it will be in the second position, third position or may be n^{th} position. However, we consider its complexity as O(n).

C. **$O(n^2)$**

O(n2) type of complexity is known as quadratic. O(n2) result due to the nested loop involved in the algorithm. Consequently, for the 1st iteration of the external loop, the inner loop execute for n times. Same has been depicted in the following example.

```
Problem: Write a program to sort out the numbers

Solution: Bubble sort method to sort the given array
void array(int arr[], int n)
{
int i,j;
for(i=0;i<n;i++)          // start of outer loop
{
for(j=1;j<n-i;j++)        // inner loop
 {
if (arr[j+1] > arr[j])    // comparing the elements
  {                       // swapping if the adjacent is larger
temp=arr[j+1];
```

```
arr{j+1]=arr[j];
arr[j]=temp;
}        // end of if
}        //end of inner for loop
}        // end of outer for loop
```

Above example signifies that for the one iteration of outer loop, the inner loop executes n-i times. Therefore, total number of iteration can be computed as:

n[n-1+n-2+n-3+..........3+2+1].

=n(n+1)/2

$=n^2$ [we have considered that the value of n is high (Here high signifies the value of n that is at-least five digits i.e. 10000), in such cases value of n will be negligible in comparison to n^2].

It is apparent from the above example that the power of n will increase with the increment of loops nesting. Consider a case that have three nested loops, correspondingly the complexity of this algorithm will be $O(n^3)$. If four nested loops are used then it will be $O(n^4)$.

D. **$O(2^n)$**

$O(2^n)$ is known as polynomial and will result if the consecutive terms are double to that of the previous terms.

No. of steps needed	2	4	8	16	32	64	128	256	512

In the above example, we can observe that the consecutive terms are double of the previous terms. Therefore, the complexity of such series will also result in $2(2^{n-1} -1)$ i.e. $O(2^n)$.

E. **O(log n)**

Logarithm type of complexity results due to the split of the given series into two halves. Consequently, from the two halves we select only one half. The half that is selected again divided into two halves i.e. left and right halves. This process continues till the objective to divide the series is not accomplished. This approach is also known as divide and conquers method.

Consider the binary search, where we follow the approach discussed above. To solve the binary search, firstly we compute the mid by adding the index of lower and the upper (last) element and dividing the result obtained by 2. If the number to be searched is greater, in that case we follow the right half else we follow the left half. This process continues till the number is not found or the series is not exhausted. Algorithm for the binary search is discussed as follows:

Program: Write an algorithm to search the element from the series by using the binary search techniques.

```
bool bsearch(b[], n,low,upper)          // return Boolean(True/false)
{
while(low<=upper)
{
mid=(low+upper)/2;           // find out the center
if(b[mid]==n)
break;
```

```
if(n < b[mid])
{
upper=mid-1; // Select the left half
}
else
low=mid+1;              //Select the right half
}
```

In the above series, we divide it into two halves. Depending upon the value of the number found at the center of the series, we select the left half or the right half. Here the series of searching will result in:

n + n/2+ n/4..............4+2+1.

Consequently, the algorithm will result in O log(n)

Exercises

A. Descriptive answers

1. What is the significance of data type in programming language?
2. ADT is complement to data type and not the substitution, justify.
3. How ADT is related to object oriented language?
4. What is an algorithm? How it is different from program?
5. Efficient algorithm is the prerequisite for efficient program, justify?
6. Write an algorithm for binary sort?
7. What is asymptotic notation? How it computes the efficiency of a program?
8. How to define big O?
9. How to define the upper and lower bound in complexity analysis?
10. What will be the effect on the value calculated with the help of Big Oh, if the base of log is changed?
11. How complexity may differ for best case, average and worst case? Justify with suitable example?
12. What will be the complexity of the following algorithms:
    i. Insertion sort.

ii. Linear search.

iii. Binary search.

13. In the above question (12), how the efficiency will differ for each method? Which is best? Prove mathematically.

B. Multiple choice Questions.

(Answer the most appropriate answer, in cases where more than one options are true.)

B.1 Abstract data type, allows defining:

i) New data type
ii) Extend the feature of existing type.
iii) Both i and ii
iv) None of these

B.2 Abstract data type is widely utilized in modern programming:

i) True for all the language
ii) False for all the language.
iii) Both i) and ii)
iv) None of these.

B.3 In asymptotic notation, we compute

i) Time complexity.
ii) Space complexity.
iii) Running complexity.

iv) None of these

B.4 Big O is the

i) Upper bound of the algorithm.
ii) Lower bound of the algorithm.
iii) both i) and ii)
iv) None of these.

B.5 Big O of quicksort is

i) log n.
ii) n^2.
iii) n log n
iv) None of these.

B.6 In Big O, if the base of log is changed

i) It will change the resultant value.
ii) It will not change the resultant value.
iii) It will change the value, however that change is negligible, therefore can be neglected.
iv) None of these.

Chapter 2

Arrays and pointers

Chapter Objective

- Define array
- To describe the type of arrays.
- Usage of single dimensional and two dimensional array
- Defining pointers.
- Describing the single pointers and its usage
- Describing the pointer to pointer and its usage

2 Arrays and Pointers

Arrays are extremely useful in cases where we need to store the similar set of elements. It helps in reducing the program complexity at the same time increases the programmer's productivity. Depending upon the element organization, arrays can be categorized into the following:

- Single Dimensional array.
- Double Dimensional array.
- Multi-Dimensional array.

For this text book Multi-dimensional array is out of scope and here it has been discussed for the sake of completeness only. Remainder of the topics have been described in the upcoming sub-sections.

2.1 Single Dimensional Array

Consider a case that we need to store the marks of five students; in this case we need to declare five different variables. Due to the homogeneous information that needs to be stored, variables declared should be of the same type. Program to store five elements has been depicted below:

Program 2.1: To accept marks of five subjects and display them (without an array)

Solution:-

```
int main()
{
int marks1, marks2, marks3, marks4, marks5;
cout<<"enter marks1";
cin>>marks1;
cout<<"enter marks2";
cin>>marks2;
cout<<"enter marks3";
cin>>marks3;
cout<<"enter marks4";
cin>>marks4;
cout<<"enter marks5";
cin>>marks5;
return 0;
}
```

In the above program, we have observed that to store the marks of 05 different subjects, we have to create five distinct variables. Complexity of the above program will further grow with the increase of subjects. Correspondingly, to input the details of 100 students or more, there will be phenomenal growth in the complexity of the above program. In such situations, to reduce the complexity and to improve the programmer's productivity, we can use arrays. Once array is declared, space needed for an array is allocated contiguously. This space is allocated at the time of compilation.

Array can be defined as:

- Set of similar data types.
- In an array, elements are stored in continuous memory locations.
- Index, or subscript starts with 0.
- Character array terminates with the special symbols '\0', known as null.

Index also known as subscript starts from '0' is the first location of any array. At index '0', first element is stored. Same has been illustrated in the following figure.

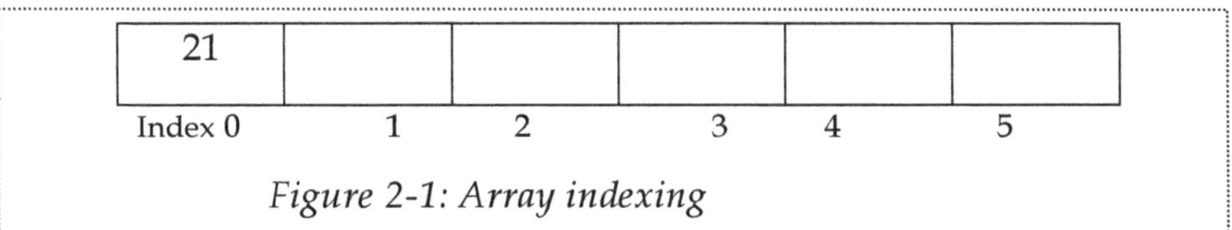

Figure 2-1: Array indexing

2.1.1 Declaration of an array

If we are intending to create an array that should be capable to store 10 elements and the elements that need to stored are of integer type. To declare this array, following syntax can be used.

int number[10];

In the above statement, number is acting as an array identifier. Here an array of integer type is created, that is capable to store 10 integer type numbers. If we assume that the size of integer is 2; also assume that first address of an array is 3000 then we can compute the address of subsequent elements. Address computation of various elements of an array has been illustrated in the figure 2-2.

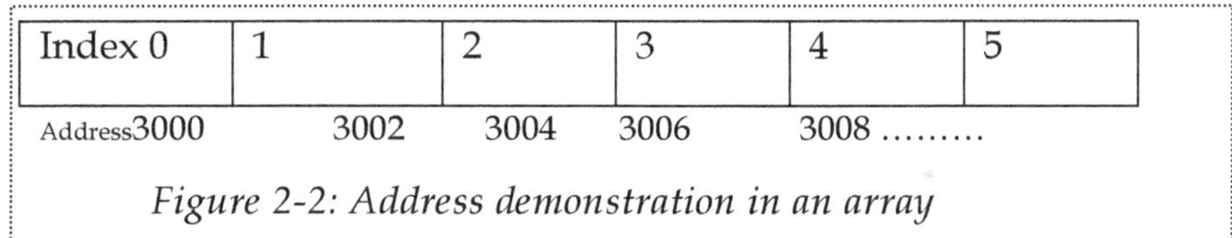

Figure 2-2: Address demonstration in an array

In array, elements are placed one after the other; however, storage at any index/subscript is possible. For instance, if the order of arrival of elements is 15, 10, 7 then it is not mandatory that they have to be stored in the index 0, 1, 2 respectively. We can store them in any order in the first three locations. For instance, the first element can be stored in the array index 2, 10 at index 1 and the element 7 at the index number 1. Initialization of these elements is as follows:

array[2]=15;

array[0]=10;

Array[1]=7.

However, it is suggested to use the contiguous address for storage. Correspondingly, to access an array element stored at 4th index, syntax array [4] need to be used. It is worth mentioning that the element which we will be stored at 5th location of an array(Since index starts from 0). For instance, if the array={4,9,12,67,90,45}, in this case, array[4] will be 90, which is 5th element of an array.

Array eliminates the need of creating many variables. Consequently, complexity of the program is reduced to a great extent. Program 2.2 demonstrates the array usage.

```
Program 2.2: To accept and display five marks using array

int main()
{
//Creation of an array to store five elements
int marks[5];
int i;
// input of five elements
cout<<"enter marks for five students";
for(i=0;i<=4;i++)
cin>>marks[i];
cout<<"marks entered for five students are:"<<endl;
//Display of marks for five students
for(i=0;i<=4;i++)
cout<<marks[i]<<endl;
return 0;
}
```

Similarly, we can determine the element having the maximum number from the given set of elements. We would use an array to store the elements.

```
// Program 2.3: To input 5 random numbers and to find out the
maximum.
int maximum(int a[])
{
int i=0;
// assume that the first element is the maximum element
int m=a[0];
```

```
// Check all the element of the array, one by one
while(a[i])
{
if(a[i]>max)    // if array element is more than the max
max=a[i];       // Make this element as maximum
i++;    // increment the index
}
return max;     //return the max
}
```

2.1.2 Initialization of an Array

Array can be initialized at the time of creation. Once array is initialized at the time of creation, there is no need to declare the size of an array.

int A[5]= {45,6,7,8,12};   (1)

int A[]={45,6,7,8,12};   (2)

The above (1) is redundant, since the array is initialized at the time of creation. Therefore, it is suggested to use the syntax depicted in (2), since compiler allocates the size considering the number of elements initialized.

```
Program 2.4: Initializing of an array at creation itself
void array1()
{
int arr[]={12,5,67,98,54};
int i=0;
while(arr[i])
```

```
{
cout<<arr[i]<<endl;
i++;
} //end of while statement
} //end of function
```

In the above program, the array is initialized at the time of creation. Here the size of an array will be five, if user is attempting to initialize the size of an array say arr[3] then also it will be overruled by the compiler and the new size will be 05. It will be helpful in the occasion where we are aware of the values to be enumerated.

```
Program 2.5: Initializing of an array at creation time
void array1()
{
int arr[]={12,5,67,98,54};
int i=0;
while(arr[i])
{
cout<<arr[i]<<endl;
i++;
} //end of while statement
} //end of function
```

A. Special cases of initialization

Beyond, the above methods of initialization, there is one more method of initialization that is worth discussing at this point of time. In this method, instead of initialization all the index individually, we are initializing only one and other indexes are initialized by the compiler. Syntax for the program will be as shown in the (1).

int arr[8]={0}; (1)

In the above statement, all the array index will be initialized with 0 (arr[0] to arr[7])

But consider another example:

int arr[7]={4}; (2)

In the above case, all the indexes are not initialized with data 4; instead first index will have the value 4, whereas others will have the value of 0 only. Method (1) is significantly helpful in cases where we need to initialize all the index of an array to 0.

B. Problems based on integer array and their solutions

In this section, we will discuss some of the significant problems related to the integer array and their solutions.

Program 2.6: Searching the element from an array.

```
void array1(int arr[],int element)
//arr[] is the array consisting of the elements whereas element is the
//number to be searched
{
int i=0;
int found=0;            //initially, item is not found
while(arr[i])   // Run till item exist in the array
{
if(arr[i]==element)     //Element found
{
```

```
found=1;
break;          // terminate the loop
}
i++;
}       //end of while statement
return found;
} //end of function
```

Explanation 2.6: In this program, user is intending to search an element from an array. To accomplish this objective, array has to be scanned from the first index up-to the last index. During the search, there are two probabilities, i) element exist in the array. ii) It does not exist in the array. In the second case, found should return false value. In case element is found in the array, instead of continue to go up-to the end, loop should terminate at the point of search. Value of found to be changed to 1 that signifies the success. Eventually, the value of false is returned to the caller.

Problem 2.7: Program to count the number of elements having value more than the given number

```
//Function to count the number of elements having values more than the
given number n.
int countNumbers(int array[], int number)
{
int count=0;
int i=0;
while(array[i])
 {
if(array[i]> number) // check if array element is more than number
```

```
count++;        //increment the count
i++;    //increment the index of array
}
return count;  // return the count
}
```

Explanation 2.7: In this program, we intend to count the number of elements in the array which are more than the given number (n), in this case we have to scan the array from the first element and continued up-to the last element. On each run, array element need to be compared with the given number, if it is more than the given number then the variable count is incremented each time.

Program 2.8: Program to increment the array element by the given multiple. For instance, if multiply is 5, then it should increase in the multiple of 5.

```
void increase(int array1[],int mul)
{
int i=0;
while(array1[i])
{
//multiply the element with the given multiple
array1[i]=array1[i]*mul;
i++;
}
}
```

Explanation 2.8: In this program, we intend to increase the value of array element by multiplying it with specific multiple. This can be achieved by accessing each element and multiplying them individually with the given multiple. Once the elements are accessed and multiplied by the given multiple, numbers need to be stored back in their respective locations.

Program 2.9: to find out the average of given numbers of an array

```
int average(int num[])
{
int i=0,sum=0, avg = 0, count=0;
while(num[i])
{
sum=sum +num[i];
count++;
}
avg=sum/count;
return avg;
}
```

Consider a case in which we are not knowing the total number of elements available in the array. However, we have to determine the average of all the numbers stored in the array. To accomplish this task we have computed the sum of all numbers by using the variable Sum. At the same time, number of elements in the array is also computed with the help of count variable. Eventually, total of all the numbers is divided by the count (that represent all the elements).

2.1.3 Character Array

In a single dimensional array, character elements can also be stored. Character elements are terminated by the special symbol '\0' also known as NULL. This special character have significant impact in determining the size of an array. **Character array is also known as String in C++**.

Program 2.6: To find out the length of a string.

```
int length(char name[])
{
int len=0;
while(name[len++]!='\0'); // From beginning to end
return len;                          //return length.
}
```

In the above program, array is started from the first index and we increment the index till end of an array is not encountered. Once the end of an array is reached the length of the array is returned to the calling function.

These functions help enormously in the other function of string. Correspondingly, we can determine whether a given string is palindrome or not. A string is known as palindrome if reading from left or right gives the same result. For instance, madam, Malayalam, nitin, pop, etc. are some of the widely used string palindrome.

To determine whether the string is palindrome or not first element is compared with the last element, second element with the penultimate element, so on and so forth, till we don't reach to the mid element. If all these elements are same then the given string is known as palindrome otherwise it is not palindrome. Function to determine the palindrome has been given below.

```
// Program to determine the string is palindrome
int palindrome(char str[])
{
int l=length(str);        // finding the length of the string
int i=0, flag=1;
while(i<=l)     // executing the loop up-to center element
 {
if(str[i]!=str[l])
{
flag=0;          // setting the flag value to false and breaking the loop
break
}
i--;
l--;
}
return flag;     // returning the value of flag to the calling function
}        // if flag is 1 then it is palindrome else it is not palindrome.
```

In the above function, we have considered that the given string is palindrome, correspondingly flag has been set to true. In the while loop, we check the first element with the last element, if it is same, we check the second element with the penultimate element. If it is also same then next element is checked. This will continue till the string is not exhausted. At any point of time, if the characters that are matched are not same, then the flag is set to false and further checking of the element is terminated. Eventually, flag is returned to the caller function where the status of flag is evaluated to flash the appropriate message (true or false).

2.1.3.1 Program on String

In addition to the above discussed string program, there are many other interesting array program. Many of them have been discussed in detail.

A. Program to concatenate the string

In our daily usage, we require that second string should be concatenated with the first. For instance, in a database that is storing the first name and the last name, here the need is to concatenate the second name into first and then display.

```
// Program to concatenate second string into first
// function to concatenate the string2 with string1
void concate(char s1[],char s2[])
{
int i=0;
int j=0;
// Running up-to the end of the string
while(s1[i]!='\0')
i++;
// concatenate the second into first from the end
while(s2[j])
{
s1[i]=s2[j];
i++;
j++;
```

```
}
s1[i]=s2[j];      // copying the null character into the first string
}

int main()
{
clrscr();
char str[40];
cout<<"Enter string "<<endl;
cin>>str;
char str1[]="singh";
concate(str,str1);
cout<<"String after concatenation"<<str<<endl;
getch();
return 0;
}
```

B. Program to copy one string into another

In this program we copy one string into the another; here we consider that first string is copied into the second string. To copy the string one(str1 into the string two (str2), we have to copy the characters of str1 into the string str2 till str1 is not exhausted. After completion of the copy, NULL character of str1 is also copied into the str2. Otherwise the string will not have the NULL character. Consequently, it will pose the problems in further operations, such as display, checking, length, etc. Same has been depicted in the following program.

```
//function to copy first string into second
```

```
void strcopy(char s1[],char s2[])
{
int i=0;
while(s1[i]!='\0')
{
s2[i]=s1[i];
i++;
}
s2[i]=s1[i]; //copy the null character
}
```

2.2 Two Dimensional Array

In the two dimensional array, elements are arranged in row and column order. Indexing in two dimensional arrays starts with 0. Statement to create two dimensional arrays has been depicted below:

int A[row][column]; //declaration

int A[5][4]; // should have constant type parameters

In the above statements, a matrix having 5 rows and each row will have 04 columns will be created. In computer, elements will be arranged in a single row and their indexing will start from 0. Same has been illustrated in the following figure.

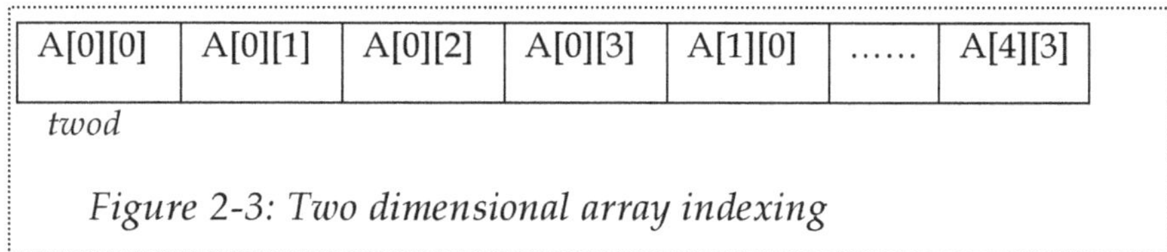

A[0][0]	A[0][1]	A[0][2]	A[0][3]	A[1][0]	……	A[4][3]

twod

Figure 2-3: Two dimensional array indexing

Once the index of the columns reaches to the maximum value then only index for second row will start. In the above example, total numbers of columns that have been declared are 4 therefore, row 1 will start after the row '0' have exhausted its column's upper limit, i.e. 3. However, in the random storage, we can store the elements anywhere within the two dimensional array, without the completion of any column. It signifies that the statement like A[3][3]=90 is permitted irrespective of the state of element in the previous indices.

2.2.1 Two dimensional integer array

Two dimensional arrays are also known as matrix. Similar to one dimensional array, two dimensional array can be initialized at the time of creation. Initialization of the matrix at the time of creation has been depicted as follow.

```
Int x[3][4]={
            {1, 2, 3, 4},
            {5, 6, 7, 8},
            {2, 4, 6, 3},
        };
```

The above matrix is having three rows and four columns. Correspondingly, we can also create the two dimensional array by:

- Declaring the two dimensional array
- Input the elements of the two dimensional array.

The following sub-section describes how to accept and display the matrix.

A. **Program to accept the matrix**

As described earlier, in the case of two dimensional array the first statement is to declare that the array is two dimensional at the same time declare the type of values it will accept. To accomplish this objective, we can use the syntax:

```
int mat[3][4];
```

Afterwards, we can use the nested loop to accept the elements of the matrix. The outer loop will denote the row whereas the inner loop will denote the column. The entire program has been depicted as follows:

Program 2.4: Program to accept the matrix and to display it.

```
void matrix(int mat[3][4])
 {
int i,j;
cout<<"enter the element of the matrix";
for(i=0;i<=2;i++)
  {
for(j=0;j<4;j++)
  {
```

```
 cin>>mat[i][j];
  }
}
void display(int mat[3][4]}
 {
int i,j;
cout<<"element of the arrays are :"<<endl;
for(i=0;i<=2;i++)
 {
for(j=0;j<4;j++)
 {
 cin>>mat[i][j];
  }
}
}
```

B. Program to sum two Matrix

We have already learn during our mathematics course that the sum on two matrix can be performed by considering one element of the matrix with the corresponding element of the other matrix. Result obtained after adding is stored in the third array. In our case, we have named it with result.

```
Program 2.5: To sum two matrix
void sum(int matrix1[2][3],int matrix2[2][3])
{
int result[3][4];
for(int i=0;i<3;i++)
 {
```

```
  for(j=0;j<=3;j++)
        { //storing the sum of matrix1 and matrix2 into result matrix
        result[i][j]=matrix1[i][j]+matrix2[i][j];
        }
}
}
```

C. **Program to transpose the matrix**

In a matrix, if we change the row of a matrix into the corresponding column, this is known as transpose of matrix. In the transpose of matrix, we exchange the first row with first column, second row with second column, so on and so forth.

We can accomplish the transpose of the matrix by exchanging the row into column and column into row. To achieve this objective, we have created the function transpose that exchange the row into column by creating a temporary matrix named tp. Once the matrix is transposed into the tp matrix, it is copied back to the original matrix. Same has been demonstrated in the following program.

1	2	3		1	4	7
4	5	6		2	5	8
7	8	9		3	6	9

Figure 2-3 X: Transpose of a matrix

Program 2.6: To transpose the matrix

```
//In matrix transpose, element of row is transformed into column and
column into row;
void transpose(int m[3][3]);
int main()
 {
 clrscr();
 int matrix[3][3]={{3,4,5},
                    {6,7,8},
                    {9,10,11}};
                    int i, j;
                    cout<<"Matrix output"<<endl;
        for(i=0;i<=2;i++)
        {
        for(j=0;j<=2;j++)
         {
        cout<<matrix[i][j]<<"\t";       // display of matrix element
        }
        cout<<endl;
        }
        transpose(matrix);      //transposing the matrix
        cout<<"Matrix after transpose"<<endl;
        for(i=0;i<=2;i++)
        {
        for(j=0;j<=2;j++)
         {
        cout<<matrix[i][j]<<"\t";
        }
        cout<<endl;
        }
        getch();
```

```
return 0;
}
//program to transpose the matrix
void transpose(int matrix[3][3])
        {
        int tp[3][3];
        int i,j;
for(i=0;i<=2;i++)
{
for(j=0;j<=2;j++)
 {
tp[j][i]=matrix[i][j];    // transposing and storing in tp matrix
}
}
         //cout<<" Matrix after transpose"<<endl;
for(i=0;i<=2;i++)
{
 for(j=0;j<=2;j++)
        {
matrix[i][j]=tp[i][j];    // Re-assigning the tp back to the matrix
// cout<<tp[i][j]<<"\t";
}
          cout<<endl;
         }
        }//end of the function
```

D. Program to multiply two matrices

We know that when we intend to multiply the two matrices, it is significant to determine the feasibility of the multiplication.

Possibility of multiplication can be determined by the number of column in the first row to that of number of rows in the first column of the second matrix. If both of them are same, then only the multiplication is possible, otherwise multiplication is not possible. From the above rule of multiplication, we can determine the number of rows and columns in the resultant matrix.

Program 2.7: Program to multiply two matrices

```
void multiply(int a[r1][c1], int b[r2][c2])
  {
 int c[c1][r2];
int sum=0;
if(c1!=r2)
{
cout<<" multiplication not possible"<<endl;
getch();                    // wait for the key to be pressed
return;            // return to the calling function
}
for(int i=0;i<=c1;i++)
 {
  value=1;
for(j=0;j<=r2;j++)
  {
for(k=0;k<c2;k++)
sum=sum+a[i][k]*b[k][j];
}
c[i][j]=sum;
sum=0;
}
```

Two dimensional arrays have significant role in character array, as they can only be stored in two dimensional arrays.

char name[number][length];

Above are the statements that are used in creating the two dimensional array.

```
Program to display the forward diagonal of the matrix
void fordiagonal(int matrix[][])
{
int row,col;
for(row=0;row<n;row++)
{
col=row;        // diagonal can be accessed if both row and
                //column index are same
cout<<matrix[row][col];
}
}
}
```

2.3 Pointers

Pointer is the variable capable to hold the address of another variable. Holding of address is needed in various instances that include:

- To access the array element
- To change the value of variable from function
- In dynamic allocation of memory.

- In complex programming, such as link list, tree, etc.

To denote that this variable is acting as pointer, they are preceded by the symbol *. For instance, int *x, Here the pointer is integer type. It means this pointer can hold the address of integer variable.

2.3.1 Declaring pointers

As already stated that pointer holds the address of another variable, correspondingly, we need a variable whose address can be stored in the pointer and consequently, we can access the variable with the help of pointer. To declare the pointera variable name is preceded with asterisk (*) symbol.

```
int x=8;
int *p;// variable that is pointer of int type
p=&x; //p now holds the address of x
cout<<p;        // print the address of x;
cout<<*p;       // print the value pointed by p;
```

Working of the above statements has been illustrated in the figure 2-4. Initially, the variable is declared as x and considers that it has been allocated the address 1000. Similarly, once int *p is declared, it is also allocated the address like any other variable. Here we have considered that the pointer p is allocated at the memory address 1010.

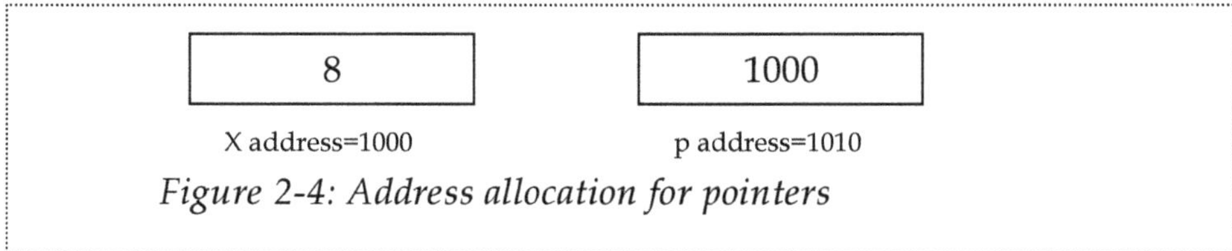

Figure 2-4: Address allocation for pointers

2.3.2 Accessing the pointer variables

Pointer is also a variable but instead of holding the value it holds the address of another variable. We are considering that it is holding the address of variable x that is having the address 1000. Now, it will have the address of 1000 in its value part, as demonstrated in the figure 2-4. Once user is printing the value of this pointer, he will get this address as value. However, it facilitates to access the variable whose address is held by the pointer. To access the value stored in the address held by the pointer we use de-referencing. To denote the de-referencing the statement *p is used. Consequently, it displays the value stored in the address. Usage of pointer has been depicted in the following program.

```
// Program to display the use of pointer
int x=8;
int *p;
p=&x;
cout<<" value of x "<<x        // 8
cout<<" value of p="<<p        //1000
cout<<" value pointed by *p"<<*p;  // 8 will be printed
*p=30;
cout<<" value of x"<<x;        // 30
```

```
cout<<" value of p="<<p;            1000
cout<<" value of *p="<<*p;  // 30
```

Pointer is widely used in the character array (string). Correspondingly, it is used in integer array. Pointer usage in array has been depicted in the subsequent sections.

2.3.3 Pointer to pointer

Sometime, we need to store the address of a pointer this can be accomplished with the usage of pointer to pointer. It is a variable that holds the address of another variable that is pointer type.

Declaring pointer to pointer

Declaring pointer to pointer is different from the normal pointer type. In pointer to pointer notation two asterisk (*) are preceded before the identifier.

int **pp;   (2.4.1)

int *p;   (2.4.2)

pp=&p;   (2.4.3)

In the line 2.4.1 the variable that is declared is pointer to pointer type. It is capable of storing the address of another variable that should be pointer type. Notation to store the address of pointer in the 'pointer to pointer' has been given in the line 2.4.3. Usage of pointer to pointer type has been depicted with the help of following example.

```
// Program to display the use of double pointer
#include<iostream.h>
#include<conio.h>
int main()
{
int v=20;
int *p;
int **pp;
// Assigning address to pointer
p=&v;
pp=&p;
cout<<"value of v=:"<<v<<endl;
cout<<"Address of v=:"<<&v<<endl;
cout<<"Address held by p=:"<<p<<endl;
cout<<" Address of p=:"<<&p<<endl;
cout<<"Valued de-referenced of p=:"<<*p<<endl;
cout<<" Address of pp=:"<<&pp<<endl;
cout<<"Address hold by pp=:"<<pp<<endl;
cout<<"Valued de-referenced of *pp=:"<<*pp<<endl;
cout<<"Valued de-referenced of **pp=:"<<**pp<<endl;
getch();
return 0;
}
```

Output

```
Value of v=20;
Address of v=0xfc1fff4

Address of *p=0xfc1fff2        // Now address of p
Address held by p=0xfc1fff4  //Address hold by p (i.e. of v)
```

```
Valued de-referenced of p=20          //de-referencing the value of p (i.e. of v)
Address of pp=0xfc1fff0               // Now address of pp
Address held by pp=0xfc1fff4          //Address hold by pp (i.e. of p)
Valued de-referenced of pp=20 // de-referencing the value of pp(i.e. of v)
```

2.3.4 Use of Pointers in an Array

Pointers are widely used in array. To access the array element we can initialized the index of the array. For instance, in the array 'a', we have initialized it with list of numbers. Accessing of array element with the help of pointer has been depicted in the following program.

```
// Program to access the array element with the help of pointers
int a[]={10,50,20,40,70};
int *x;
x=&a[0];
cout<<x<<endl;
cout<<*x;            //output 10
cout<<*(x+2);        // output 20
cout<<a[2];          // output 20
cout<<*(x+3);        // output 40
cout<<a[3];          // output 40
```

In the above program, pointer is initialized with the base address of the array. Consequently, statement *x displays the element stored at the index '0'. Correspondingly, when the statement *(x+2) is used. It signifies that the 2 is to be added at the base address which results in x[2]. Consequently, the element accessed by the *(x+2) and x[2] gives the same result. In the same line, the statement *(x+3) will result in 0+3 i.e. 3rd index. Correspondingly, the element stored at the 3rd index will be visible.

2.3.5 Dynamic Array creation

Array can be created and the needed space can be allocated at the time of at compile time or the runtime. Accordingly, it can be classified as:

- Static array
- Dynamic array

Array whose size is allocated at the time of compilation is known as static array. Arrays that have been discussed in the previous sections are known as static array.

Other type of array is dynamic array, which are allocated the needed space at run time. In C++, creation of runtime array is accomplished with the help of new operator. For array, as well as pointer, address can be allocated at run time. Same has been depicted in the upcoming example.

Program: Create the dynamic array and their various ways of initialization.

```
#include<iostream.h>
#include<conio.h>
int main()
{
```

```
int *x;
int *y;
y=new int(45);
x=new int[4];
clrscr();
x[0]=90;
x[1]=55;
x[2]=32;
x[3]=67;
int i=0;
cout<<"Dynamic array elements are"<<endl;
while(i<=3)
{
cout<<"x[i] i="<<i<<"  "<<x[i]<<endl;
i++;
}
cout<<"y ="<<*y<<endl;
getch();
return 0;
}
```

```
// Program to initialize the dynamic pointer.
#include<conio.h>
int main()
 {
int *y;
clrscr();
```

```
y=new int(45);
int i=0;
cout<<"y ="<<*y<<endl;
getch();
return 0;
}
```

2.3.6 Array of pointers

Array of pointer is an array that holds the pointers (addresses). Usage of array pointer is significant in cases where we need to store the addresses of various pointers and all of them can be easily accessed. Array of pointers improves the efficiency of the program written. Primarily array of pointer is used to deal with double dimensional type of problems. For instance, if we intend to store the 2 or more array, then we can use pointer arrays. Example to access three array using array of pointers has been depicted in the following program.

```
// Program: Create a program to access integer arrays using array of pointer.
#include<iostream.h>
#include<conio.h>
int main()
{
int a[]={26,89,4};
int b[]={98,5,42};
int c[]={78,6,23};
int *arrp[4];
```

```
arrp[0]=a;      // Storing the base address of array a
arrp[1]=b;      // Storing the base address of array b
arrp[2]=c;      // Storing the base address of array c
cout<<"Output of the array is"<<endl;
int i=0;
for(i=0;i<=2;i++)
 {
 for(int j=0;j<=2;j++)
  {
  cout<<arrp[i][j]<<" ";
  }
  cout<<endl;
  }
getch();
return 0;
}
```

In the above program, we have used array of pointers to store the address of three arrays. Since, naming the array denotes the first base address; therefore, these array pointer holds the address of the first address of the given arrays. Using the array of pointers we can access the individual element of the array as depicted in the above program.

The other potential use of pointer of array is in character array (also known as string), here the details of n entities can be stored, and these details can easily be accessed using array of pointers.

In the following program, we have demonstrated how the various arrays holding the values can easily be linked with array of pointers and their values can easily be accessed.

```
Program : Accessing of character array(string) using array of pointers
#include<iostream.h>
#include<conio.h>
int main()
{
char ca[]="first";
char cb[]="second";
char cc[]="third";
char *cp[3];
cp[0]=ca;
cp[1]=cb;
cp[2]=cc;
cout<<"Output of the array is"<<endl;
int i=0;
   cout<<" Output of character array"<<endl;
   for(i=0;i<=2;i++)
   cout<<"output of array "<<i+1<<cp[i]<<endl;
getch();
return 0;
}
```

Output

```
Output of array 1      first
Output of array 2 second
Output of  array 3      third
```

In the character pointer, statement cp[0]=ca holds the base address of character array ca, correspondingly, cp[1]=cb hold the base address of character array cb, and cp[2]=cc holds the address of character array cc. In the for loop, it first address of the character array is represented, it continues to move till it does not encounter the '\0' character. Consequently, the output of each word is displayed.

2.4 Exercises

2.4.1 Descriptive type questions

1. How array is different from other variables.
2. What are the advantages of array?
3. An array is consisting of 10 elements. Delete the 4th element; correspondingly move the remaining element, so that now array should consist of 9 elements.
4. In the above array, insert the element at 3rd position and move the third to n^{th} element to the right side. So that there is no overlapping.
5. Write a program (WAP) to find out the minimum element from the given array.
6. Write a program to increase the each element of the array by 2. For instance, if the array element were 2, 3, 9, and 4 then after adding 2 they should become 4, 5, 11, and 6.
7. WAP to find out the maximum and minimum from the given array. Use only one function, these minimum and maximum should be accessible from any other function.
8. Write a program to swap the first element with the second, third with forth, till the end of the array.
9. Write a program to swap first element with the last element, second element with the penultimate element and so forth. After making change see the changes by the display function.

10. Write a program to merge the element of two arrays into the third array.
11. Write a program to store the string into the array without initializing it or accepting from the keyboard.
12. Write a program that eliminates the immediate repetition. For instance, if the string is 'jiitiiee' then the resultant string should be 'jitie'.
13. Write a function to copy the string into another array.
14. Write a program to capitalize the first element of the string array.
15. Write a program that accepts numbers, character and special characters. Your program should count the number of characters, numbers and special characters.
16. Write a program that accept the string in small case and converts it into upper case.
17. Character array is of size 20; write a program that extracts the character from 4th position to 9th position.

2.4.2 Predict the output of the following

1.
```
int x[]={3,8,5,90,12,34};
int y=2;

cout<<x<<endl;

cout<<*x<<endl;
```

```
cout<<*(x+3)<<endl;

cout<<*(x+y)<<endl;
```

2. ```
   `int *x=new int[4];
   int *y=new int(4);
   ```

3. ```
   char x[]= "jitendra";
   cout<<x;

   cout<<*x;

   cout<<*(x+1);

   cout<<(x+1);

   cout<<*(x+3);

   cout<<(x+3;

   cout<<x+3;

   cout<<*x+3;

   cout<<(*x)+3;
   ```

2.4.3 Find out the error(s), if any in the following given codes.

Problem 1

```
int x[5]={4,6,1.89,8};
cout<<x;
cout<<*(x+5);
```

```
cout<<*x+4;
```

Problem 2

```
int x[4]={67,9,2,78,45,54};
cout<<x;
for(int i=0;i<4;i++)
cout<<x[i];
```

Problem 3

```
int x[4]= {67,9,2,78,45,54};
int y=2;
cout<<*(x);
cout<<x;
cout<<*(x+y);
x=x+y;
cout<<x;
cout<<*x;
```

Problem 4

```
int x[2]= {67,9,2,78,45,54};
int y=2;
cout<<*(x);
cout<<x;
cout<<*x+y;
```

Chapter 3
Link list

Chapter Objective

- Describe link list
- Creation of link list
- Display/ Traversal of a link list
- Insertion into a link list at various position
- Deletion any node of a link list
- Reversing the link list
- Operator overloading in a link list
- Application of a link list
- Limitation of a link list and defining circular link list
- Benefits of circular link list

3 Link List

Array is having major limitations related to size specifically, if the number of elements to be stored in the array is not known in advance. In such cases usage of array is inefficient. Consider a case in which if the size allocated is more but items to be inserted are less. This will lead to wastage of array space. On the other hand, if size of an array defined is less and elements to be stored in the array are more, in that case many elements would not be placed inside an array. To address the variable need of data storage, a new data structure known as link list is used.

This chapter highlight many significant features of the link list that include:

A. Defining the structure of a node.
B. Creating the link list.
C. Display of the link list.
D. Inserting the node in a link list.
E. Deleting the node from a link list.
F. Usage of operator overloading in a link list(+operator
G. Searching the item from a link list.
H. Orderly link list
I. Reversing the link list.
J. Circular Link list
K. Link list using template

3.1 Creation of link list

The complex part of the link list is its creation. It can be accomplished by creating the nodes and then connecting them immediately after creation. In a link list, the smallest entity is node and is created dynamically. Each node consists of two parts

- Data Part
- Address part

Data part consist of data that need to be stored in the node. This data may be simple or complex type like structure or any other data type created by the user. Whereas, address part represent the address of next node. Initially, the node is one therefore, it links will be NULL. Structure of a node is illustrated in the figure 3.1.

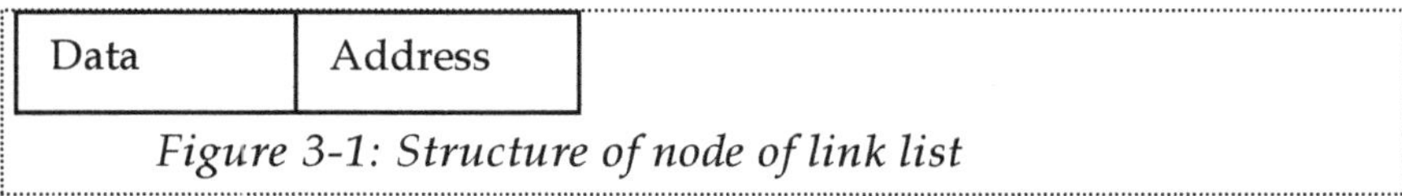

Figure 3-1: Structure of node of link list

In the figure 3-1, data part will hold the user' data, whereas address part consist of address of a next node.

Structure of a node can be defined as:

```
class node
{
public:
int data;
node *next;
};
```

Once the first node is created the next pointer will point to the NULL, since it does not have any next node. To create a node, we can use the syntax as given below:

```
node *one;
one=new node;// node created
one->data=10;
one->next=NULL;
```

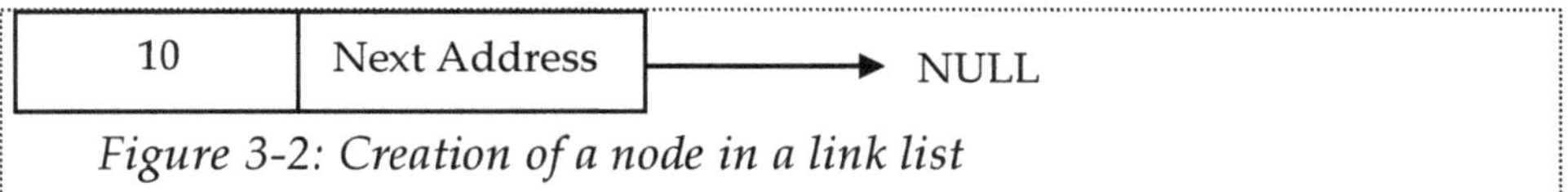

Figure 3-2: Creation of a node in a link list

A. **Creation type**

During the creation of a link list, it can grow in forward or the backward direction, it is known as creation type. This is entirely governed by the method of inserting the new node in a link list. Correspondingly, the nodes insertion include:

I. At the end

II. At the beginning.

In the insertion from the end, a new node is placed at the end of existing link list. For instance, inserting the node at the end having the data 20, in the link list already having the node 10 is illustrated below.

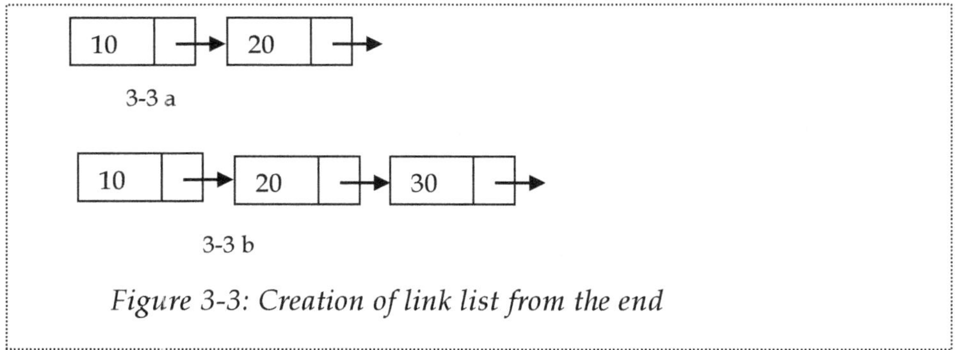

Figure 3-3: Creation of link list from the end

After inserting 20, consider that we have to insert 30 into the existing list. Same is illustrated in the figure 3-3(b). This is known as backwards growth of a link list. Since new node is attached at the end. Correspondingly, we can create a link list that can be forward growing list. In forward list, the new node is inserted at the beginning instead of at the end. Same has been illustrated in the figure 3-4.

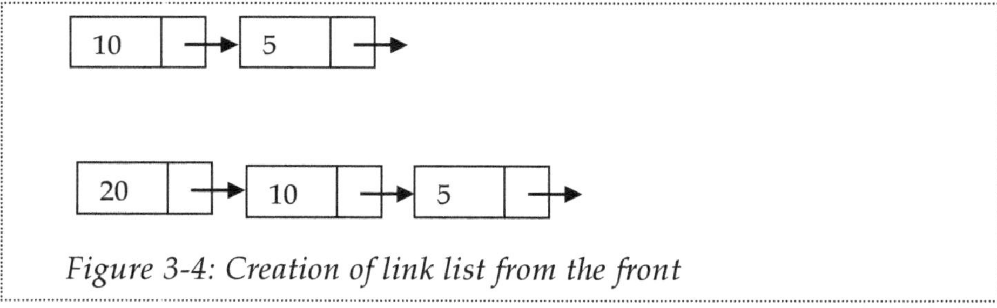

Figure 3-4: Creation of link list from the front

Consider the case of figure 3-4. In this case, a node with the value of 5 already existed. The new node having value 10 is created; correspondingly it will be inserted at the beginning of the existing link list. Similarly, the new node has arrived is 20. It will be positioned at the beginning of 10 (refer figure 3-4). This type of growth in a link list is known as forward growing link list.

B. **Display the node**

Once the link list is created, irrespective of the forward growing or the backward growing, we would like to view the data of the link list node. To display the node element, we begin from the start i.e. first node and move towards the end. Next pointer of the last node points to the NULL, that can be used to stop the traversal. Logic for the traversal has been depicted in the following program:

```
node *current;
current=first   //initialize the first pointer
while (current!=NULL)          // moving up-to the end of a list
{
cout<<"current->info"<<current->info; //displaying info part
current=current->next; //move to the next node
}
```

The complete program for creation and display function of a link list has been depicted as follows:

```
Program1: Create and display the node of a list. In the program, node is to
be inserted from the end.
// class to define the structure of a node
class node
{
public:
int info;
node *next;
```

```
};
// class of a link list
class list
 {
node *first, *end;        // creation of first and end pointer
public:
list()
 {
first=NULL;
}
void create(int);
void display();
};


// function to postion the new node at the end and connecting it
void list::create_end(int el)
          {
          node *current,*temp;
           if(first==NULL)        // if first node does not exist
            {
             first=new node;
             first->data=el;
             first->next=NULL;
             end=first; //initialize the end with first (as now both are same)
             return;
             }
             //if first node exist, follow the line given below
             current=new node;
             current->data=el;
```

```
current->next=NULL;
end->next=current; // connecting end with the current
end=current;        // making the current as end node
} //end of create_end
```

```
//function to display the content in a linked list
void list::display()
{
        node *current;
        current=first;
        cout<<"Linked list:"<<endl;
        while(current!=NULL)
        {
          cout<<current->data<<" -> ";
          current=current->next;
        }
}
```

C. Creating the list by inserting at the beginning

Link list can also be created by inserting the element at the beginning. The new node that is attached becomes the first node of the list. For instance, if list is to be created for the series of item 10, 20, 30, 5, 9, 100, then the list will grow as illustrated in the figure 3-5.

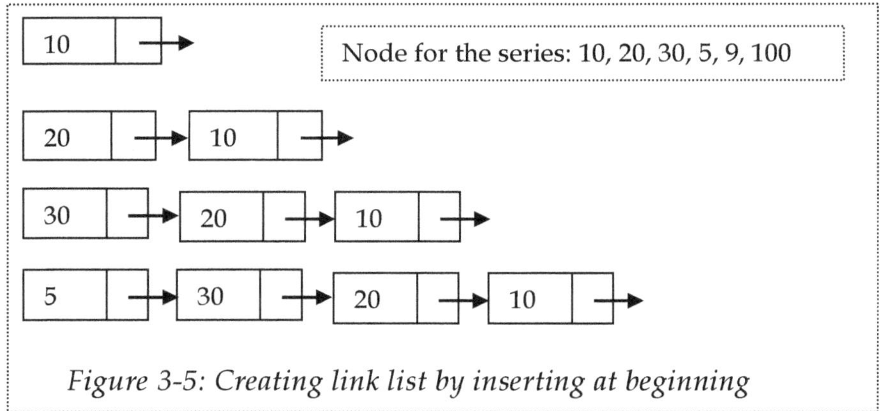

Figure 3-5: Creating link list by inserting at beginning

Once the new node is created then it will be connected at the first position, as a result the existing first node will move to the second position. Therefore, the new node should become the first node. The complete program for the insertion of a node in a link list has been depicted below:

```
//function to create the list from the beginning
        void list::create_beg(int el)
         {
          node *current,*temp;
         // if the list does not exist
          if(first==NULL)
           {
            first=new node;
            first->data=el;
            first->next=NULL;
            end=first;
            return;
           }
```

```
// If the link list exist then program will start from here
current=new node;
  current->data=el;
  current->next=first; //link current to first
  first=current;          // make the current node as first node
 } //end of create_beg
```

3.2 Inserting the node in an existing link list

In an existing link list, node can be inserted anywhere as intended by the user. During the insertion of a new node the probable locations can be:

1. At the first position
2. Position, other than the first.

All these cases along with the method of connecting them has been depicted in the following sub-section.

3.2.1 Inserting at the first position

Consider a link list as illustrated in the figure 3-6. In this list, a new node is to be placed (inserted) at the beginning. To accomplish this objective, first we have to create the new node and attach it to the existing first node. This operation is illustrated in the figure 3-6.

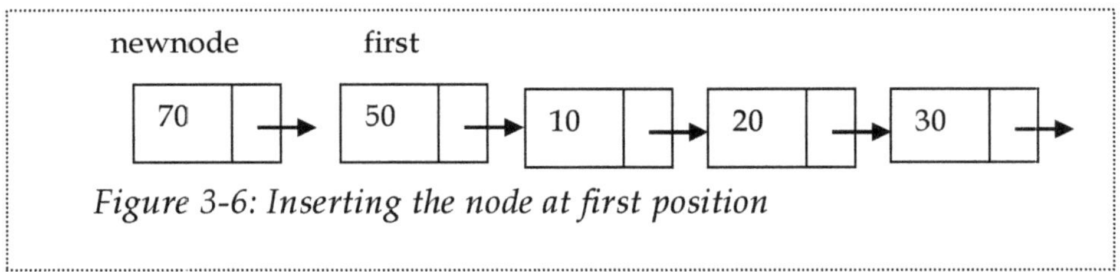

Figure 3-6: Inserting the node at first position

Due to insertion of a newnode at the beginning will change the first node. As first node will become the second node and the newnode will result into first node. Consequently, the first pointer has to be moved to the newnode. The complete sequence has been described as:

Method of inserting at first position

To insert the node at the first position, the following sequence needs to be followed.

I. Create the newnode

II. Link it to the first node

III. Change the position of first node with the newnode.

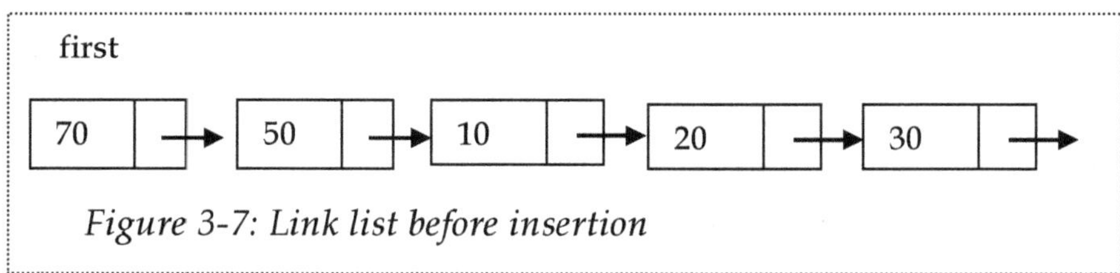

Figure 3-7: Link list before insertion

The resultant link list has been illustrated in figure 3-7. The first node is now moved to the newnode that is inserted just now, having value 50. Code to connect and shifting the first node is depicted below.

```
newnode=new node;
newnode->data=el;
newnode->next=first;
first=newnode;
```

Inserting the node other than the first position

To insert the node in between, we will determine the two nodes whom which new node is to be inserted. The node that will be before this node will be known as previous node and the node after this node will be known as next node. In our program, we have defined as current node. Same is illustrated in the following figure 3-8.

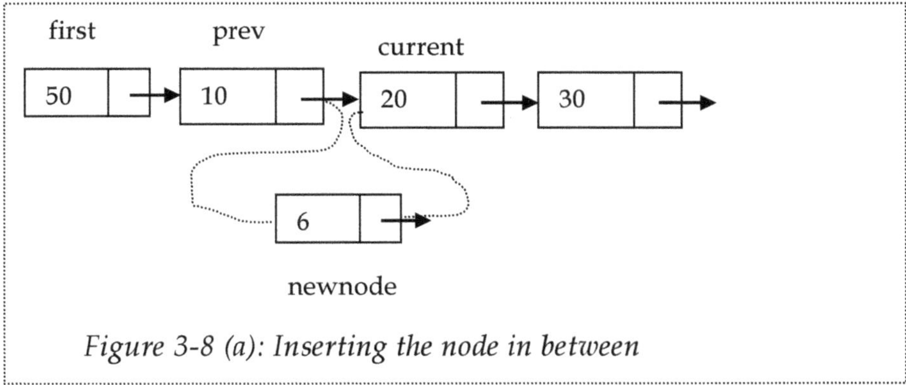

Figure 3-8 (a): Inserting the node in between

In the existing link list, pointer of previous node needs to be connected to the newnode, whereas pointer of the newnode to be connected to the current node.

```
prev->next=newnode;
newnode->next=current;
```

The complete method of inserting the node in a link list has been depicted in the insert function. In the discussed function, we accept the position, that is passed as an argument and check it with the number of nodes that a link list is consisting at that specific point of time. Users intended position should not be more than the existing list size (number of node) by 1. For instance, if the total numbers of nodes are n, then the position given should not be more than n+1.

```
Program of inserting the element in a list
//function to insert at particular position
        void list::insert(int el, int pos)
          {
         node *current,*newnode,*prev=NULL;
         int cnt=count();//count number of nodes
         if(pos<=cnt+1)
           {
           current=first;
       // Create a new node
           newnode=new node;
           newnode->data=el;
           newnode->next=NULL;
           int i=1;
           //moving to the appropriate position
           while(i<pos)
            {
               prev=current;
               current=current->next;
```

```
            i++;
            }//end of while
            if(prev==NULL)// to be inserted at first position
            {
             newnode->next=first;
             first=newnode;
             return;
            } //end of inner if
    // if node is to be inserted is other than the first node
       newnode->next=current;
       prev->next=newnode;
       } //end of out if
         else
         cout<<"Size of list is less than position, Try again...\n";
       }//end of function insert_beg
```

The above program is also applicable for the insertion at the last position. Since, during insertion at the last position involves position the newnode at the last this is followed by connecting the last node with the newnode and eventually, connecting the last node pointer NULL to the next of the newnode. Insertion of a newnode is illustrated in the figure 3-8 (b).

Code written for the in-between will also support the insertion of the last node.

```
prev->next=newnode;         (1)
newnode->next=current       (2)
```

However, the prev node will point to the last node, whereas the current will point to the last node. Since the code of (1) will connect the last node to the newnode therefore one objective will be completed. Whereas the code (2) will connect the newnode to the current node which is already resulted in NULL, as illustrated in the figure 3-8 (b). Consequently, the code will work for inserting the node at any position other than the first position.

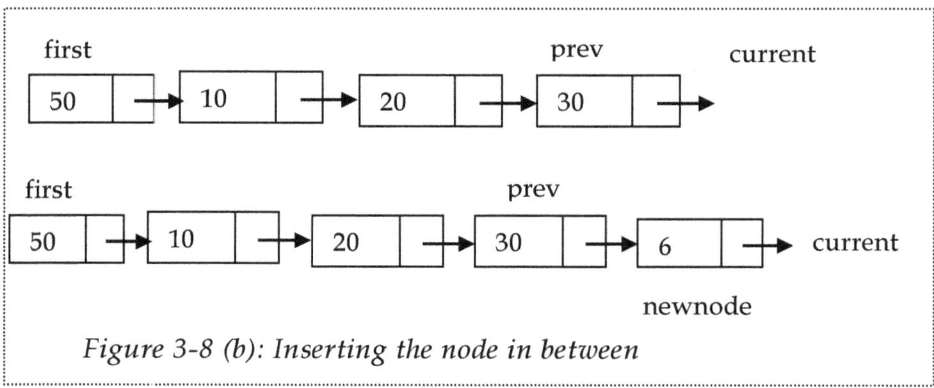

Figure 3-8 (b): Inserting the node in between

3.3 Deleting the node in a link list

Corresponding to insertion operation, there is another operation known as deletion. In the deletion operation, a node can be deleted from the existing link list. During deletion of a node, the following possibilities need to be considered.

- Deleting First node.
- Deleting other than the first node.

3.3.1 Deleting the first Node

Once the user is aiming to delete the first node in that case pointer of first node will be lost. Therefore, to delete the first node the following sequential steps need to be followed.

- Hold the first node.
- Find out the second node.
- Store the first node into temp.
- Assign the second address to the first node.
- Delete the temp (the previous first) node from the list to free the resources.

Code to delete the first node is given here as under.

```
node *temp;
temp=first; //storing the first node into temp
first=first->next; //moving the first pointer to the next node
delete temp; //delete the temp node and free the space
```

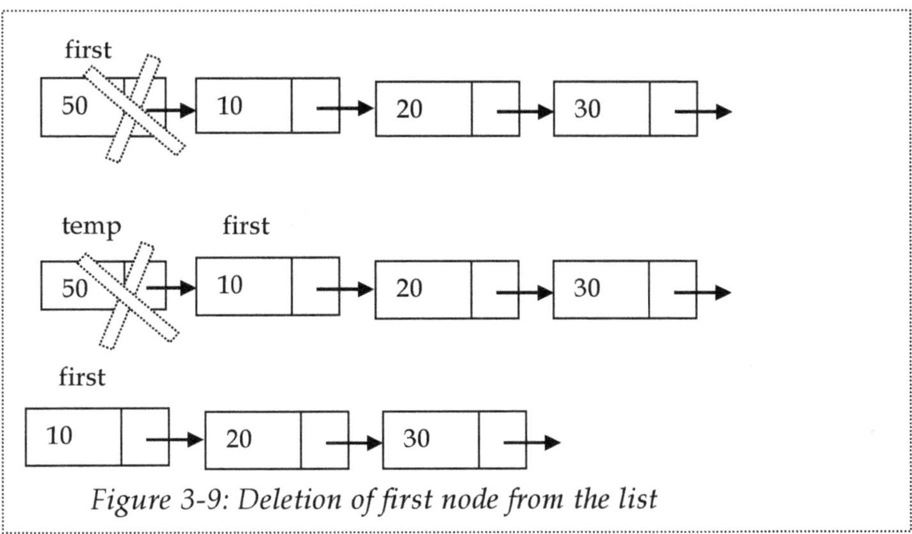

Figure 3-9: Deletion of first node from the list

The complete method of deleting the node has been illustrated in the following figure 3-9.

3.3.2 Deleting the node other than first node

Suppose users need to delete the third node that has the value 20. To delete this node, following steps need to be followed.

1. Traversing up-to the target node, at the same time holding pointer of the previous node.
2. Store the pointer of target node (current node, node to be deleted i.e. 20) into temp.
3. Connecting previous node to the next node of the current node.

To delete the node, users need to traverse up-to current node by maintaining the pointer of the previous node. In case next pointer is NULL, then previous pointer will point to the NULL. Similarly, if the node to be deleted is the first node, in that case previous will be NULL. In such cases first is moved to first->forward. The node that is left previously is deleted. Finally, to delete the node in between, previous next is connected to the current next. At the same time, current is deleted to release the free space to the heap.

```
temp=current;
prev->next=current->next;
delete temp;
```

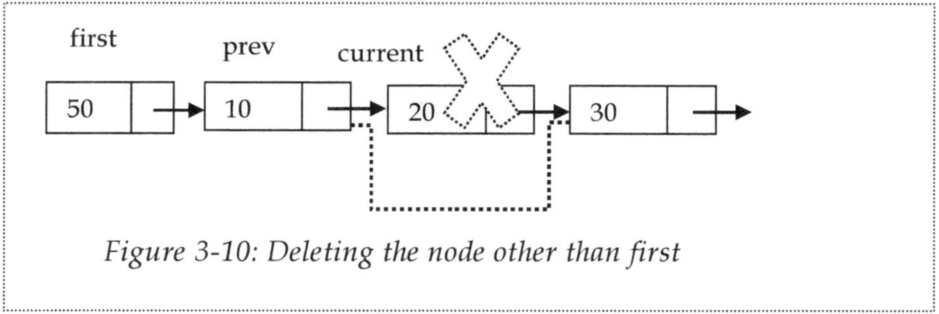

Figure 3-10: Deleting the node other than first

The complete program is discussed in the following program.

Program to delete the node from a link list

```
void list::deletenode(int element)
    {
    node* current,*prev=NULL;
    int found=0;
    current=first;

    while(current!=NULL)
        {
        if(current->data==element)
         {
         found=1;
         break;
         }
        prev=current;
        current=current->next;
        }
        if(found)       // if node to be deleted is found
```

```
        {
        if(prev==NULL)        // if first node
         {
         prev=current->next;
         first=prev;
        }
        else    // for other than the first node
        prev->next=current->next;
        delete current;
        }
        else
        cout<<"element not in the list"<<endl;
    }//end of deletenode
```

3.4 Searching the element from a link list

Link list is a linear data structure; therefore elements need to be searched from the beginning. In the list, elements are searched starting from the first node. This is followed by visiting the subsequent nodes till elements is not found or the list is not exhausted. In the best case, element to be searched may be found at the first position. In worst case, element to be searched may be found at the last position. Therefore, in best case, complexity will be O(1). In the worst case the complexity will be O (n). Program to search an element has been depicted in the following program.

```
Program to search the element in a link list
//search function
        int list::search(int el)
```

```
    {
        int found=0;
        node *current=first;
        while(current)
         {
          if(current->data==el)
          {
           found=1;
           break;
           }
          current=current->next;
    }
     return found;
    }//end of search function
```

3.5 Ordered Link list

In the orderly link list, items are arranged in order, i.e. in ascending or descending order. In orderly link list, overhead is involved at the time of creation. However, it offers excellent performance during searching, finding out the minimum, or the maximum element, etc. Since during search, all elements are not to be searched instead as soon as elements with higher value is encountered loop needs to be terminated. Therefore, orderly link list gives better performance relative to ordinary link list.

In an orderly link list, items are arranged in ascending order from the beginning itself. Whenever a new node to be inserted in an orderly link list, logic of insertion need to be applied. For instance, consider a list for the numbers 20, 5, 13, 90, 100, 25 has to be created. Also assume that in this orderly link list, items are to be arranged in ascending order. Detailed steps have been described as follows:

- If the link list is empty, insert the item at the first position.
- In all other cases, keep on moving to the right till element having more value is not encountered.
- Once the larger element is encountered, terminate the traversal.
- Insert the element into the link list, by connecting the previous node to this newnode, whereas connect the nextnode to the next of the newnode. that is following this node.

Orderly link list for the items 20,5,13, 90, 100, 25 has been illustrated in the figure 3-11.

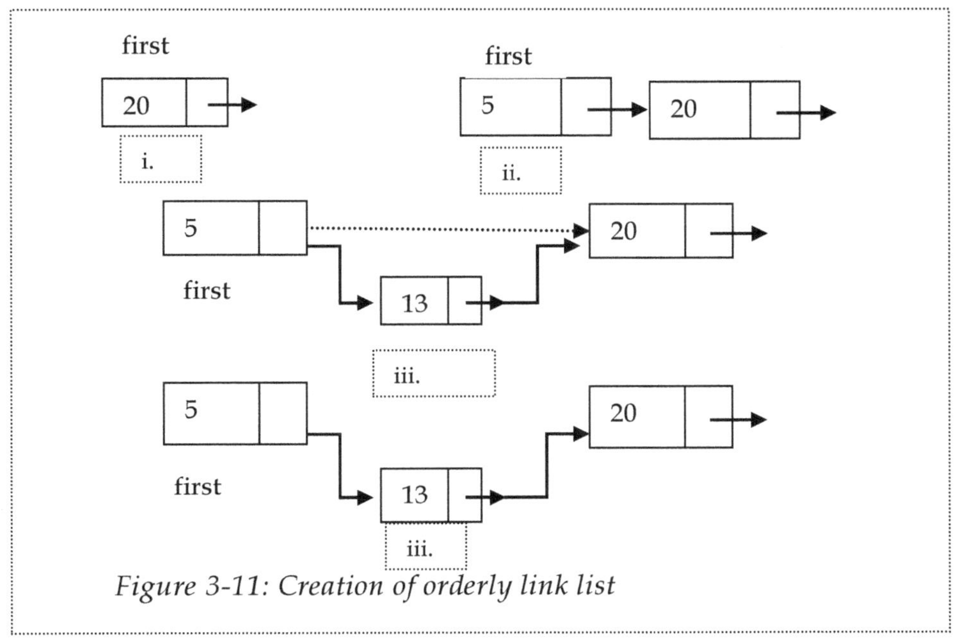

Figure 3-11: Creation of orderly link list

```
//Program to create and insert node in an orderly link list-
#include<iostream.h>
#include<conio.h>
class node
{
 public:
 int data; //data part of the list
 node *next;// address of next node
};

class list
{
```

```
//creating the first pointer of the list
node *first,*end;
//public part of class
 public:
 //linked list constructor
  list()
   {
        first=NULL;
   }
   void order_list(int);
   void display();
};
void list::order_list(int element)
 {
 //if list is empty
 if(first==NULL)       // if link list is not existing
  {
  first=new node;
  first->data=element;
  first->next=NULL;
  return;
  }
  //if list is not empty
  node *temp,*prev=NULL,*current;
  temp=new node;
  temp->data=element;
  //temp->next=NULL;
  current=first;
  while((current->data < element)&& (current!=NULL))
  {
```

```
    prev=current;
    current=current->next;
    }
        if(prev==NULL)        // if node to be inserted at first position
        {
        temp->next=current;
        first=temp;
        }
        else
        {
        prev->next=temp;
        temp->next=current;
        }

}// end of function

//function to display linked list
            void list::display()
            {
                    node *current;
                    current=first;
                    cout<<"Ordered Linked list:"<<endl;
                    while(current!=NULL)
                    {
                      cout<<current->data<<" -> ";
                      current=current->next;
                    }
                    cout<<endl;
             }
int main()
```

```
{
list l1;
clrscr();
cout<<"Creating ordered list"<<endl;
l1.order_list(29);
l1.order_list(14);
l1.order_list(70);
l1.order_list(12);
l1.order_list(30);
l1.order_list(121);
l1.display();
getch();
return 0;
}
```

3.6 Reversing a link list

Reversing link list is a complex operation and requires deep understanding of the pointer. Losing any pointer result in the lost of node and information. During the reversing a link list, we traversed from the front towards the last node. During this traversal, the node that is accessed will be attached at the beginning of a new link list, similar to the insertion from the beginning operation.

A link list is illustrated in the figure 3-12, it need to be reversed. In the considered link list, the first node is. 50 it will be attached at the beginning. On the arrival of newnode i.e. 10, it will be attached at the beginning of the 50 as illustrated in the figure 3-13(b).

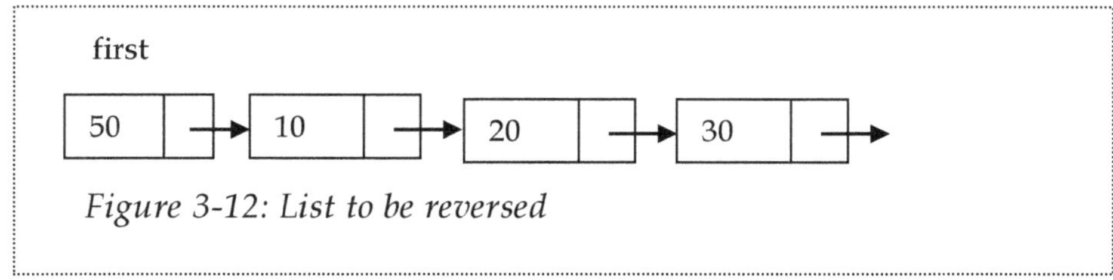

Figure 3-12: List to be reversed

Reversal is demonstrated in the following figure in step by step.

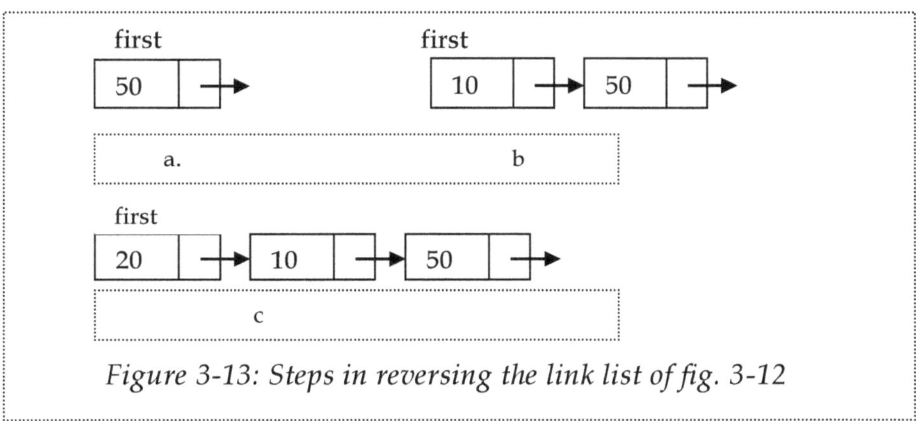

Figure 3-13: Steps in reversing the link list of fig. 3-12

Program to reverse a link list:

```
void list::reverse()
        {
        cout<<" Reverse of the list is ::"<<endl;

             node *current,*forward,*back=NULL;
             current=first;
             forward=current->next;
             while(forward!=NULL)
             {
              current->next=back;
```

```
                back=current;
                current=forward;
                forward=forward->next;
                }
                 current->next=back;
                 first=current;
}               }
```

3.7 Merging two link list

Due to the variety of reasons, we need to merge the link list so that data available in more than one link list can be accommodated in a single list. During merging, due care need to be observed to ensure that items of the both the link list that are merged into third remain in the shorted order. This would result in better performance and management. Method and program to merge the two link list has been described in the following program.

```
list list:: merge(list l1,list l2)// To merge list 1 and list 2.
          {
          list l3;
          node *one,*two,*current;
          one=l1.first;
          two=l2.first;
           if(one->data < two->data)   // if the first list is having smaller
          element
           {
           l3.first=current=one;
```

```
            one=one->next;// move to the next node
            }
           else
           {
           l3.first=current=two; // otherwise initialize with the first node
of second list
           two=two->next;
           }
           while((one!=NULL) && (two!=NULL))
            {
            if(one->data < two->data)
            {
            current->next=one;  // connect current to the one
            current=one;     // move one to the current
            one=one->next;  // move to the next node
            }
            else
            {
            current->next=two; // connect current to the two
            current=two;      // move two to the current
            two=two->next;  // move to the next node
            }
            }// end of while
            if(one)         // if list one is not exhausted
             {
             current->next=one;
             }
             else if(two)   // if list two is not exhausted
                  {
                  current->next=two;
```

```
            }
        return l3;
    }
```

3.8 Use of operator overloading in a link list

Operator overloading allows the programmer to define the operators to function as per their own way instead of the one defined for the primitive data type. However, use of the overloading is restricted at the place and scope of definition, beyond which it can be used as per its normal definition. For instance '+' operator is defined to sum two integer number. However, it can also be used for two concatenate the two string or to join the two link list. Similarly, ++ operator can be used to move to the next node of the link list. Operator '=' can also be used to compare the number of nodes in two link list are same or not.

In our discussion, we would like to explain the operator overloading by joining the two link list using the '+' operator. In our case, we would like to write the statement, List3=list1+list2, this should result in list2 that should consist of both list1 and list2. To accomplish the above objective, the code is written below:

```
list operator +(list l2)
{
while(first->next!=NULL)      // Move to the last node of the list1
first=first->next;
first->next=l2.first;     // connect the last node to the first node of list l2
return *this;     // return the first list
```

```
}
```

To achieve the above task, first we need to create the list l1 and the list l2. Afterwards, we can call them using the + overloaded operator. Code for the main function is described below:

```
int main()
{
list l1, l2, l3;
l1.create_beg(10);
l1.create_beg(20);
l2.create_beg(6);
l2.create_beg(33);
l3=l1+l2;
```

Using the same method, readers are advised to use the operator overloading for instance ==, >, <, etc.

3.9 Self-Organizing list

Link list is the linear data structure, whenever user needs to carry out any operation, he has to start from the first node and traverse the subsequent node one by one. Therefore, efficiency of the list is dependent on the size of the list. If the list is large at that time, efficiency of the link list reduced. To overcome this limitation a new version of link list known as self-organizing list is used. Self-organizing list is capable to re-organize the node based on usage criteria. Consequently, yields better performance relative to the normal link list.

Due to our daily experience, we know that in a given list some items are more frequently used relative to others. Self-organizing list draws the advantage of this trend and organizes the node according to the accessibility. Possible method by which list can be organized are:

A. Ordered based.

B. FCFS based.

C. Count method.

D. Shift based method.

3.9.1 Ordered List

In the ordered list, items are arranged based on their values. This signifies that items are arranged in ascending or descending order. In the event of new item arrival, it is inserted in the existing link list based on its value. Correspondingly, it can be placed at the beginning, at the center or at the end.

Positioning of the node in a link list is entirely governed by its value. Orderly link list has been illustrated in the figure 3-14.

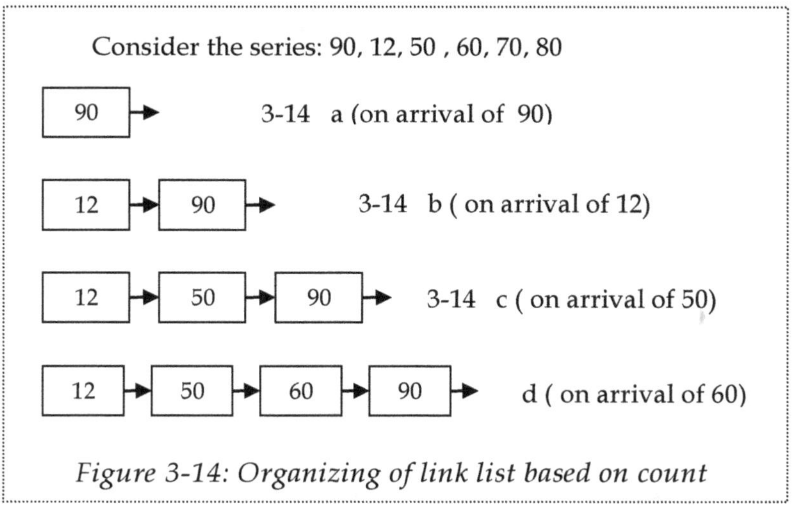

Figure 3-14: Organizing of link list based on count

Ordered link list has the following advantage over the simple link list.

- During insertion of the node, we traverse till a node having more value is not encountered or the list is not exhausted.
- During removal again traversal is taking place till the node consisting of the value is not found or nodes are less than the node to be searched, after which searching terminates.

Consequently, it yields better performance relative to simple link list.

3.9.2 Count based link list

In the count based link list, additional data member count is provisioned. Value of the count is governed by the accessibility of the node. On each accessibility the value of the count increases by adding the value 1 to the current count. During organization node having the maximum count is placed at the first position whereas, the node that is having the minimum count is placed at the end.

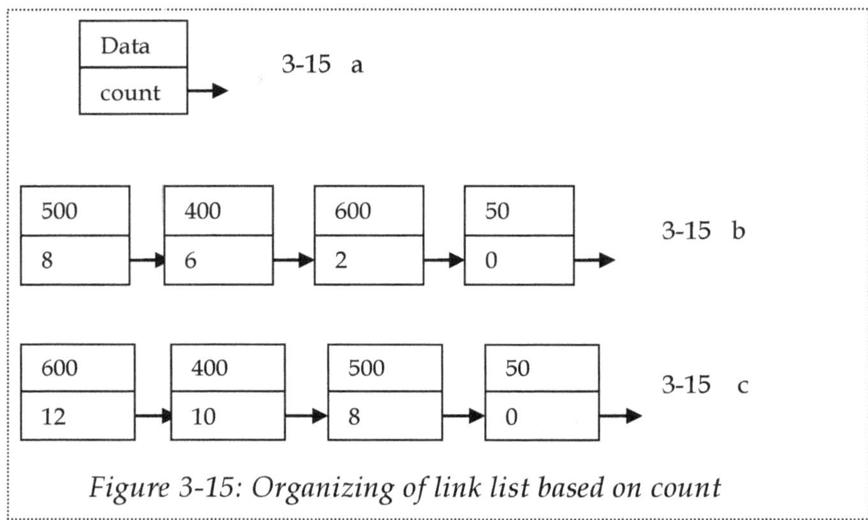

Figure 3-15: Organizing of link list based on count

In the 3-15 a, structure of the list has been demonstrated. In the figure 3-15 b , nodes are organized based on the count. Node having the maximum count is placed at the first position. In the 3-15 c, if the count changes, consequently, the nodes are rearranged based on the count. Same has been illustrated in figure 3-15 c.

3.9.3 First come first serve (FCFS)

In the first come first serve method nodes are arranged on the order of their arrival. Nodes coming later are arranged are placed at the last. Creation of a link list based on the FCFS has been illustrated in the figure 3-16. Initially, 500 is arrived, since there is no element therefore, it is placed at the first position. It is followed by 400, correspondingly, it is placed after the existing nodes, here it is 500. Refer figure 3-16 b. Eventually, the last time 12 is arrived, correspondingly, a new node is created and attached at the last of existing link list, refer figure 3-16 c. The same sequence will be followed for the other elements.

It is apparent from the above description that the FCFS follows the sequence similar to that of insertion at the end. FCFS base algorithm is immensely useful in the scenarios where we are aiming to serve the element based on their arrival. For instance, in railway reservation.

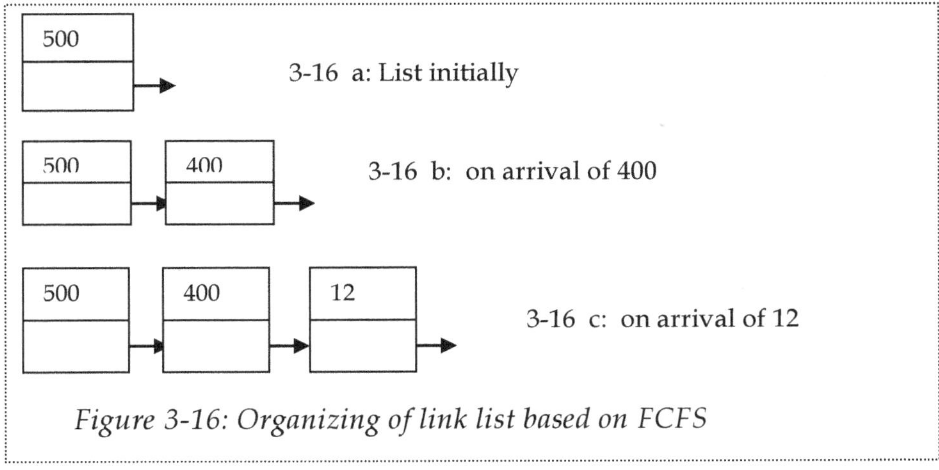

Figure 3-16: Organizing of link list based on FCFS

3.9.4 Shift based method

In the shift based method, node accessed is shifted one position ahead. It is having much similarity with the count based method. Working of shift based method has been demonstrated in the figure 3-17. However, in count based method, position is primarily decided by the count method, but in the shift based method it is decided by the accessibility. For instance the node which is available at the first position might have been accessed 5 times that's why it is in the first position whereas the second node might have not been accessed even once then also it is in the second position. As soon as second node is accessed it will replaced the first node irrespective of the time it has been accessed previously.

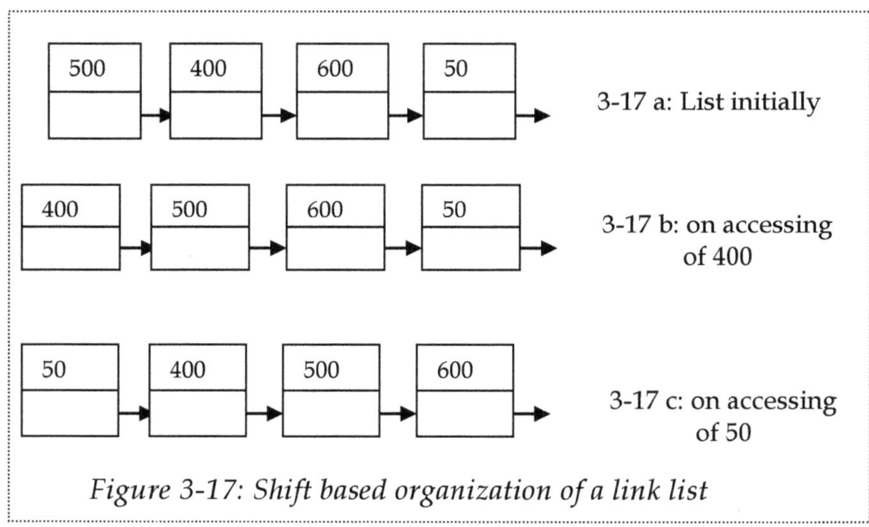

Figure 3-17: Shift based organization of a link list

3.9.5 Skip List

All type of link lists that have been discussed above is not yielding the significant performance. To address this bottleneck, a new type of list known as Skip list has been created. Skip list is the special case of orderly link list in which while organizing and traversing we are skipping some of the node. In this type of list, instead of traversing node by node, a number of nodes are skipped to improve the traversal. This type of link list has the substantial advantages over other type of link list described earlier. Two major types of skip list are used:

- Even skip list
- Random skip list

3.10 Calling from the Main function

Various functions are defined to conduct the various link list activities. These functions need to be called from the main function. Various parameters and method of calling the function has been defined as follows:

```
// Calling the function from the main


int main()
{
int el;
list list1,list2,list3,list4;
clrscr();
```

```
//creating the list from beginning calling
list1.create_beg(40);
list1.create_beg(2);
list1.create_beg(14);
list1.display();
cout<<" inserting 100 at 1 position"<<endl;
list1.insert(100,1);
list1.display();
cout<<" inserting 34 at 3 position"<<endl;
list1.insert(34,3);
list1.display();
cout<<" inserting 200 at 6th position"<<endl;
list1.insert(200,6);
list1.display();
cout<<" Total number of nodes now:\t"<<list1.count()<<endl;
cout<<" List after deleting 200"<<endl;
list1.deletenode(500);
list1.display();
cout<<" List2 inserting from the end"<<endl;
list2.create_end(1);
list2.create_end(7);
list2.create_end(3);
list2.create_end(4);
cout<<" List2 Now :"<<endl;
list2.display();
cout<<" Inserting the node in list2"<<endl;
list2.insert(70,1);
list2.display();
list3=list1+list2;
cout<<" List3 after list1+list2"<<endl;
```

```
list1.display();
if(list2.search(30))
cout<<"Element found"<<endl;
else
cout<<"Element not in the list"<<endl;
if(list4.emptylist())
cout<<"List4 is empty"<<endl;
if(list1.emptylist())
cout<<"list1 is empty"<<endl;
else
cout<<"list1 not empty"<<endl;
getch();
return 0;
}
```

3.11 Creating the link list using template

In the example discussed above we have considered the integer list to insert the items. Similarly, if we need to create the link list for the character, a new link list for the character needs to be created. This results in rewriting of the existing code. In the new written code, error may creep in that result in re-testing of the program that was already tested. To overcome this limitation, we can create the link list using template. Complete logic need to be written once, and will work for the all types of data. (Readers not aware of the concept of template are requested to refer the appendix A)

```
Link list using template
//Singly Linked List Using Template
```

```
#include<iostream.h>
#include<conio.h>
template<class T>
class node
{
 public:
 T data; //data part of the list
 node<T> *next;// address of next node
};
template<class T>
class list
{
  //creating the first pointer of the list
  node<T> *first,*end;
  //public part of class
   public:
   //linked list constructor
    list()
     {
          first=NULL;
     }
     // create the link list by inserting at beginning
     void create_beg(T);
     // create the link list by inserting at end
     void create_end(T);
     // Insert the element at specific position
     void insert(T,int pos);
     //To delete the node consisting the value
     void deletenode(T el);
     //To search the element in the list
```

```
int search(T);
// To count number of nodes
int count();
 //function to traverse the list
void display();
//function to reverse the list
void reverse();
//To find out list is empty
int emptylist();
// To concatenate the two list
 list operator+(list);
};
template<class T>
int list<T>::emptylist()
       {
       int empty=0;
       if(first==NULL)
       empty=1;
       return empty;
       }//end of emptylist
       template<class T>
void list<T>::deletenode(T element)
 {
 node<T>* current,*prev=NULL;
 int found=0;
 current=first;

 while(current!=NULL)
       {
       if(current->data==element)
```

```
      {
      found=1;
      break;
      }
     prev=current;
     current=current->next;
     }
     if(found)
     {
     if(prev==NULL)
      {
      prev=current->next;
      first=prev;
     }
     else
     prev->next=current->next;
     delete current;
     }
     else
     cout<<"element not in the list"<<endl;

  }//end of deletenode
  //function to create the list from end
     template<class T>
     void list<T>::create_end(T el)
      {
      char ch;
      node<T> *current,*temp;
      if(first==NULL)
       {
```

```
        first=new node<T>;
        first->data=el;
        first->next=NULL;
        end=first;
        return;
        }
        current=new node<T>;
        current->data=el;
        current->next=NULL;
        end->next=current;
        end=current;
       } //end of create_beg

//function for creating linked lists from
template<class T>
void list<T>::create_beg(T el)
      {
      char ch;
      node<T> *current,*temp;
      if(first==NULL)
       {
        first=new node<T>;
        first->data=el;
        first->next=NULL;
        end=first;
        return;
        }
        current=new node<T>;
        current->data=el;
        current->next=first;
```

```
  first=current;
 } //end of create_beg
//function to insert at particular position
template<class T>
void list<T>::insert(T el, int pos)
 {
node<T> *current,*newnode,*prev=NULL;
int cnt=count();//count number of nodes
if(pos<=cnt+1)
  {
   current=first;
   newnode=new node<T>;
   newnode->data=el;
   newnode->next=NULL;
   int i=1;
   //moving to the right position
   while(i<pos)
    {
        prev=current;
        current=current->next;
        i++;
        }//end of while
        if(prev==NULL)
        {
         newnode->next=first;
         first=newnode;
         return;
        } //end of inner if
 newnode->next=current;
 prev->next=newnode;
```

```
} //end of out if
  else
  cout<<"Size of list is less than position, Try again...\n";
}//end of function insert_beg

//search function
template <class T>
int list<T>::search(T el)
{
        int found=0;
        node<T> *current=first;
        while(current)
         {
          if(current->data==el)
          {
           found=1;
           break;
           }
          current=current->next;
}
 return found;
}//end of search function


//overloading + operator
template<class T>
list<T> list<T>::operator +(list<T> l1)
{
        node<T> *current;
        current=first;
```

```
        while(current->next!=NULL)
        current=current->next;
        current->next=l1.first;
        return *this;
}

//reverse function
template<class T>
void list<T>::reverse()
{

        node<T> *a,*b,*temp;
        a=first;
        b=a->next;
        temp=b->next;
        a->next=NULL;
        while(temp!=NULL)
        {
                b->next=a;
                a=b;
                b=temp;
                temp=temp->next;
                //this->display();
        }
        b->next=a;
        first=b;
}

//counting nodes in a linked list
template<class T>
```

```
            int list<T>::count()
            {
                    node<T> *current;
                    int c=0;
                    current=first;
                    while(current!=NULL)
                    {
                            c++;
                            current=current->next;
                    }
                    return c;
            }

            //function to display linked list
            template <class T>
            void list<T>::display()
            {
                    node<T> *current;
                    current=first;
                    cout<<"Linked list:"<<endl;
                    while(current!=NULL)
                    {
                      cout<<current->data<<" -> ";
                      current=current->next;
                    }
                    cout<<endl;
            }
int main()
{
int el;
```

```
list<int> list1;
clrscr();
//creating the list from beginning calling
list1.create_beg(40);
list1.create_beg(2);
list1.create_beg(14);
list1.display();
cout<<" inserting 100 at 1 position"<<endl;
list1.insert(100,1);
list1.display();
cout<<" inserting 34 at 3 position"<<endl;
list1.insert(34,3);
list1.display();
cout<<" inserting 200 at 6th position"<<endl;
list1.insert(200,6);
list1.display();
cout<<" Total number of nodes now:\t"<<list1.count()<<endl;
cout<<" List after deleting 200"<<endl;
list1.deletenode(500);
list1.display();
//list<int> list3;
list<char> list2;
cout<<" List2 inserting from the end"<<endl;
list2.create_end('A');
list2.create_end('Z');
list2.create_end('B');
list2.create_end('C');
cout<<" List2 Now :"<<endl;
list2.display();
cout<<" Inserting the node in list2"<<endl;
```

```
list2.insert('I',1);
list2.display();
//list3=list1+list2;
cout<<" List3 after list1+list2"<<endl;
list1.display();
if(list2.search('I'))
cout<<"Element found"<<endl;
else
cout<<"Element not in the list"<<endl;
if(list2.emptylist())
cout<<"List4 is empty"<<endl;
if(list1.emptylist())
cout<<"list1 is empty"<<endl;
else
cout<<"list1 not empty"<<endl;
getch();
return 0;
}
```

3.12 Circular link list

In the link list user can traverse only in one direction that is from first towards the last. Reaching to the last node, there is no method to traverse towards the first node. To overcome this limitation a modification can be incorporated in the link list by connecting the last node to the first node. List in which last node is connected to the first node is known as circular link list.

3.12.1 Creating the link list

In circular link list, special attention is needed on the first node. First node in a circular link list will not be pointed to the NULL instead it will be connected to itself as illustrated in the figure 3-18.

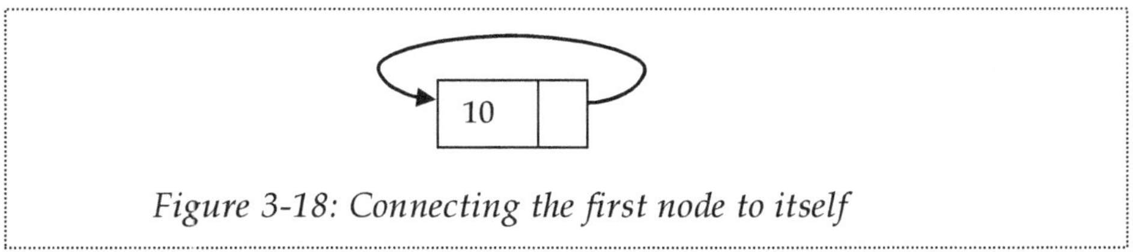

Figure 3-18: Connecting the first node to itself

To accomplish this task, code of the first node can be modified as follows:

```
first=new node;
 first->data=el;
 first->next=first;
 end=first;
```

At the time of adding a new node, next pointer of the last node needs to point the new node, whereas the next pointer of the last node will be connected to the first node. To accomplish this objective, we store the next address of the last node (which is pointing the first node) to the next node of newnode. It is followed by connecting the last node with the newnode. Same is illustrated in the following figure 3-19.

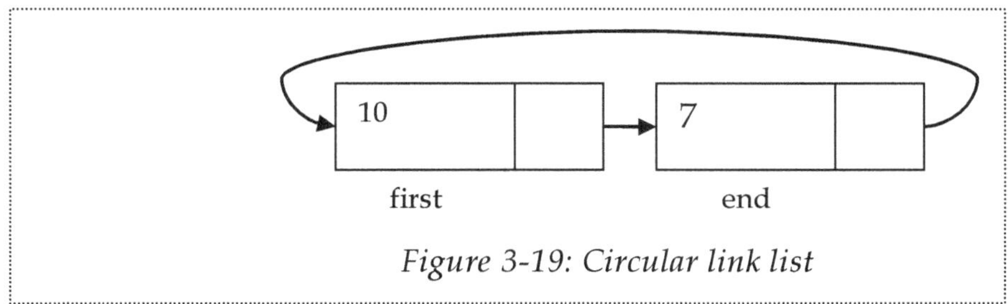

Figure 3-19: Circular link list

Attaching more node at the end will have to follow the same sequence of steps that are already enumerated.

3.12.2 Inserting the node in between the circular list

Inserting the node in between the circular link list is not different than the simple link list till it does not disturb the first and last node.

Once node to be inserted at the first position the following changes need to be incorporated:

a) Connecting the new node to the first node.
b) Connecting the pointer of the last node to this new first node.

Correspondingly, if the node to be inserted is the last node in that case, following changes need to be carried out.

a) Connecting the next pointer of the previous last node to the next pointer of new last node.
b) Connecting the existing last node pointer to the next node of this new last node.

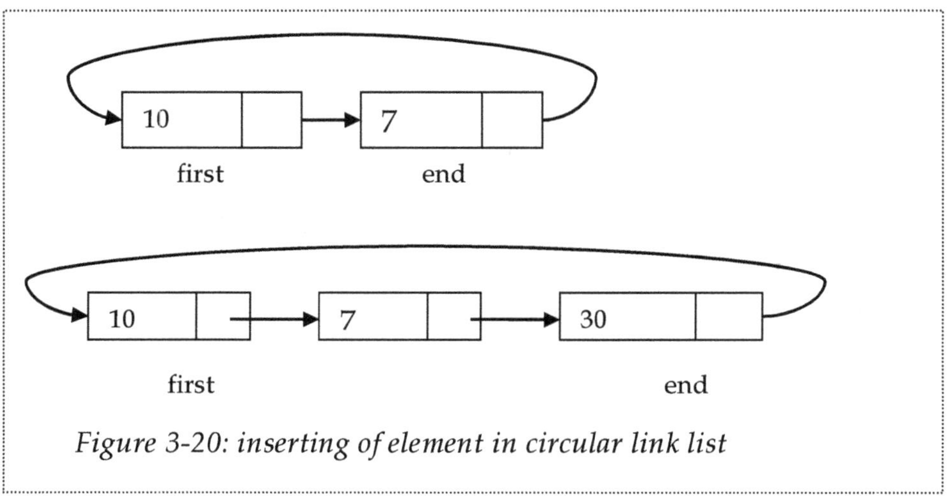

Figure 3-20: inserting of element in circular link list

The complete code to achieve the entire above objective has been described as follows.

```
// Program to attach the last node to the circular link list.

node *temp;
// create a new node.
temp=new node;
// assign data to the new node
temp->data-20.
//Connect the next node to the first node.
temp->next=end->next;
//connecting the node to the last node of the circular link list.
end->next=temp;
```

```
Program to attach the new node at the first position of a circular link list.
node *temp;
```

```
// create a new node.
temp=new node;
// assign data to the new node
temp->data-20.
//Connect the temp node to the first node.
temp->next=first;
//connecting the last node  to the new first node (temp).
end->next=temp;
```

3.12.3 Traversal in circular link list

In a circular link list due care need to be observed during traversal of the list, since the last node is connected to the first node. Correspondingly, there is no end of the list. In our code, we have started from the first node and traversed till the next node of the list is not pointing to the first node of the list. Since last node remained unvisited therefore provision is made to visit this last node.

```
    while(current->next!=first)// Till next node is not the first node
            {
              cout<<current->data<<" -> ";
              current=current->next;
            }
            cout<<current->data<<" -> "; //visit the last node
```

```
//Creation of Circular link list
#include<iostream.h>
#include<conio.h>
class node
```

```
{
 public:
 int data; //data part of the list
 node *next;// address of next node
};

class list
{
  //creating the first pointer of the list
  node *first,*end;
  //public part of class
   public:
   //circular list constructor
    list()
     {
          first=NULL;
     }    // create the link list by inserting at end
     void create_end(int);
     // Insert the element at specific position
     void insert(int el, int pos);
     //To delete the node consisting the value
     void deletenode(int el);
     //To search the element in the list
     int search(int);
     // To count number of nodes
     int count();
      //function to traverse the list
     void display();
     //function to reverse the list
     void reverse();
```

```
//To find out list is empty
int emptylist();
// To concatenate the two list
 list operator+(list);
};
int list::emptylist()
     {
     int empty=0;
     if(first==NULL)
     empty=1;
     return empty;
     }//end of emptylist
void list::deletenode(int element)
{
 node* current,*prev=NULL;
 int found=0;
 current=first;

 while(current!=NULL)
     {
     if(current->data==element)
      {
      found=1;
      break;
      }
     prev=current;
     current=current->next;
     }
     if(found)
     {
```

```
        if(prev==NULL)
         {
         prev=current->next;
         first=prev;
        }
        else
        prev->next=current->next;
        delete current;
        }
        else
        cout<<"element not in the list"<<endl;

    }//end of deletenode
    //function to create the list from end
        void list::create_end(int el)
         {
         char ch;
         node *current,*temp;
         if(first==NULL)
          {
           first=new node;
           first->data=el;
           first->next=first;
           end=first;
           return;
           }
           current=new node;
           current->data=el;
           current->next=end->next;
           end->next=current;
```

```
        end=current;
       } //end of create_beg

 //function for creating linked lists from
/* void list::create_beg(int el)
      {
      node *current,*temp;
      if(first==NULL)
       {
        first=new node;
        first->data=el;
        first->next=NULL;
        end=first;
        return;
        }
        current=new node;
        current->data=el;
        current->next=first;
        first=current;
       } //end of create_beg  */
      //function to insert at particular position
      void list::insert(int el, int pos)
        {
       node *current,*newnode,*prev=NULL;
       int cnt=count();//count number of nodes
       if(pos<=cnt+1)
         {
          current=first;
          newnode=new node;
          newnode->data=el;
```

```
newnode->next=NULL;
int i=1;
//moving to the right position
while(i<pos)
 {
      prev=current;
      current=current->next;
      i++;
      }//end of while
      if(prev==NULL)
      {
       newnode->next=first;
       first=newnode;
       end->next=first;
       return;
      } //end of inner if
newnode->next=current;
prev->next=newnode;
} //end of out if
  else
  cout<<"Size of list is less than position, Try again...\n";
}//end of function insert_beg

//search function
int list::search(int el)
{
        int found=0;
        node *current=first;
        int i=0,cnt;
        cnt=count();
```

```
            while(i<=cnt)
            {
             if(current->data==el)
             {
              found=1;
              break;
              }
             current=current->next;
             i++;
    }
     return found;
   }//end of search function
    //counting nodes in a linked list
    int list::count()
    {
            node *current;
            int c=0;
            current=first;
            while(current->next!=first)
            {
                    c++;
                    current=current->next;
            }
            return c+1;
    }

    //function to display linked list
    void list::display()
    {
            node *current;
```

```
                    current=first;
                    cout<<"Linked list:"<<endl;
                    while(current->next!=first)
                    {
                      cout<<current->data<<" -> ";
                      current=current->next;
                    }
                    cout<<current->data<<" -> ";
                    cout<<endl;
              }
int main()
{
int el;
list list1,list2,list3,list4;
clrscr();
//creating the list from beginning calling
list1.create_end(40);
list1.create_end(2);
list1.create_end(100);
list1.create_end(14);
list1.display();
cout<<" inserting 5 at 3 position"<<endl;
list1.insert(5,3);
list1.display();
if(list1.search(20))
cout<<"Found"<<endl;
else
cout<<"Element not in the list"<<endl;
/*cout<<" inserting 34 at 3 position"<<endl;
/
```

```
getch();
return 0;
}
```

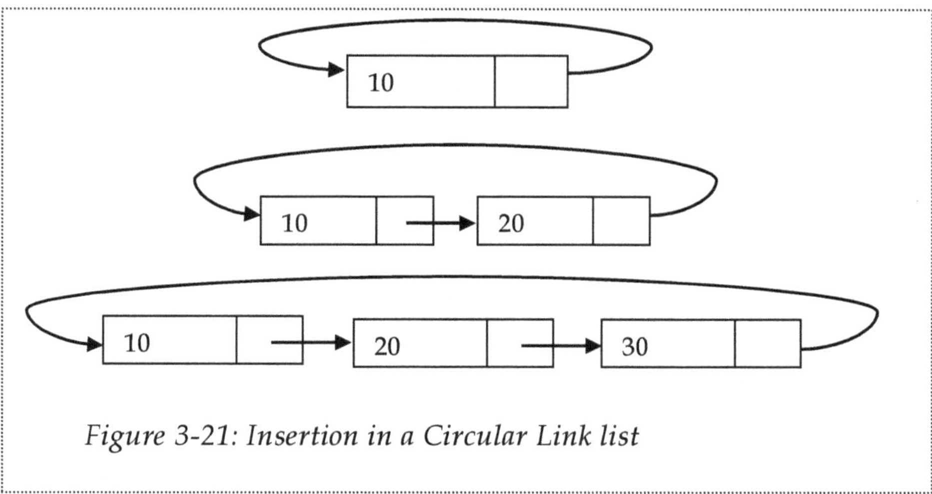

Figure 3-21: Insertion in a Circular Link list

Case study based on link list

A financial institution utilizes the storage device for the storage of its data. Various information related to the client is stored that include clients basic details, stock own by them, value of their portfolio, etc. Necessary information, their fields along with the short description has been given as follows:

Table 3.1:Client file

S.no	Field	Description
1.	Name	Name of the client
2.	Id	Unique id of the client
3.	Address	Unique address of the client
4.	DoB	Date of birth of a client

Table 3.2: Stocklist

S.No	Field	Description
1.	Stockid	Unique id of the stock
2.	Stock_name	Name of the stock
3.	Market_price	Current market price of the stock
4.	Total share	Total number of share of particular company

Table 3.3: Purchase table

S.No	Field	Description
1.	Stockid	Unique id of the stock
2.	Stock_name	Name of the stock
3.	Market_price	Current market price of the stock
4.	Qty_purchased	Total number of share purchased of a particular company

Table 3.4: Stock sold

S.No	Field	Description
1.	Stockid	Unique id of the stock
2.	Stock_name	Name of the stock
3.	Market_price	Current market price of the stock
4.	Qty_purchased	Total number of share sold of a particular company

User is engaged in stock trading business and need to store the data as described in the above table. He intends to store the record of his client once he opens the account to purchase or sale the shares with him. Based on the above table, create the node of a link list that has the provision for the storage of the above data. Whenever a new client is joining the firm, he should be allotted a new customer id and added in the link list. Whatever the transaction he is performing that should also be linked to the client id. At any point of time, user should be able to view his portfolio that includes the number of share he holds, purchase price, total value of the inventory, etc.

Finally, if he quits the broker firm, his records need to be deleted from the link list irrespective of his position in the link list (first, middle, or the last). All the deleted record should be stored in the deleted link list. This will enable the firm to track all those customer who had the account with him but not operating now. This will enable the firm:

- To know the total number of account deleted
- Reason why clients are closing the account.
- To identify the gap in the services offered and to fill those gaps
- To meet the regulatory compliances needed for maintaining the client details.

Beyond, the above details, implementer can assume any other information that is not described above pertaining to the variety of information.

Exercise

A. **Short answer type question**

1. What is the need of a link list?

2. What are the various overhead of a link list?

3. Describe the advantage of array over link list.

4. Describe the link list advantages over the array.

5. What are the advantages of having two pointers first and end in the list?

6. How inserting at the beginning is different from inserting at any other position in a link list?

7. Is inserting in between the link list is same as inserting at the end? How it can be managed in the insertion logic?

8. Write a program to swap the first node with the second node, third node with the forth node and so on.

9. Write a program to swap the first node with the last node, second node with the penultimate node and so on.

10. Write a program to add two list using the + operator (operator overloading).

11. Write a program to traverse the next node by overloading

the ++ operator (operator overloading).

12. Write a program to overload the following operator in link list

    a) = (that checks whether number of nodes are same in two list).

    b) - (that traverse to one node back in a link list).

    c) > to check whether the link list one is of more size than the second one.

13. Why deleting the first node is different from deleting the any other node?

14. What are the precautions to be taken while deleting the first node?

15. How deleting the in between node is different from deleting the last node?

16. What are the points that need to be borne in mind during the creation of an orderly list?

17. What are the major limitations of a link list?

18. Prove the advantage of self-organizing list over normal link list? Relate the self-organization method discussed with their computer usage.

19. Why circular link list is used over linear link list?

20. How circular link list is different from the linear link list?

21. What are the drawbacks of circular link list over linear link list?

22. How the display function of circular link list is different from the linear link list?

23. How to delete the last node of the circular link list? Discuss in detail the pointer adjustment.

24. Describe the necessary changes you will incorporate, while inserting the node at the first position of circular link list.

25. Consider two link list, list1 and list2. Delete the node of list1 from the position given in list2. For instance, if the list1=(m, n, o, p, q, r, s), list2=(1, 3, 4) then the resultant list will be {n, q, r, s}

26. Write a function that compares whether two given list (list1 and list2) are same or not, while comparing consider the content of the link list.

27. Write down the function to count the number of nodes using recursion.

28. Write a function to create the link list using recursion.

29. Write a function to reverse the link list by using

a) Iterative method

b) With recursion

30. Write a function that moves any given node of the link list to the first position. For instance, if user is giving the node 4, then the 4th node should result as first node.

31. In the given link list, consider one more data member count. Initially, it is 0 for the node that is created. Once this node is accessed (if the given node to be searched or to be displayed etc.) the count should incremented by 1. Adjust the position of the nodes based on the count. For instance, node with the maximum count should be placed at the first position. Node with the second highest count should be placed at the second position. If the count is same then place them as per the following algorithms.

    a) First come first serve technique to be used, means the node available at the position should not be changed.
    b) Consider the value (data part), if it is less then place the node before the node having greater value.

B. Multiple choices Question

In the given questions one or more option may have the right answer. Select the one that best describe the answer.

1. In the list program, the new operator returns which of the following data types:

a) Int type c) void type

b) Node type d) None of these

2. Size of node used in the link list is

a) 02 bytes c) 04 bytes

b) 06 byes d) None of these

3. New is same as its counterpart malloc function of 'c' language

a) True

b) False

4. Circular link list

a) Allows traversal in both the direction

b) Allows traversal only in one direction.

c) No movement is possible.

d) None of these

5. In orderly link list

a) Elements are arranged in ascending order.

b) Elements can be arranged in descending order.

c) Both 'a' or 'b'

d) None of these

6. Complexity of linear link list in the worst case is:

   a) O(1) c) O(n^2)

   b) O(n) c) None of these

7. Worst case complexity of linear link list and the orderly link list is same:

   a) True b) False

8. If in the link list, the searching method is based on binary search technique, then there is:

   a) No effect on the performance.

   b) Performance will be improved.

   c) None of these

Chapter 4
Doubly link list

Chapter Objective

- Defining the limitation of link list
- Defining the doubly link list and structure of a doubly link list.
- Creation of a doubly link list.
- Traversal in a doubly link list.
- Insertion in a doubly link list.
- Deletion the node in a doubly link list.
- Circular doubly link list
- Display of circular doubly link list
- Inserting into a circular doubly link list
- Deletion from a circular doubly link list

4 Doubly Link List

Doubly link list is a special case of a link list in which each node will have two pointers instead of one pointer as the case with the link list. Among these two pointers, one point to the address of previous node, while other points to the address of next node. Doubly link list was needed due to the various limitations of link list.

4.1 Limitations of Link List

Although the link list is offering better results but is suffering from the major limitations related to non-traversal in backward side. This is attributed to the fact that link list is maintaining only one pointer that holds the address of next node. Consequently, traversal was possible only in one direction i.e. from start node towards the end node (last node). Once end node is reached there is no way to traverse towards the first node.

Limitation discussed above has been addressed by the doubly link list. It maintains two pointers instead of one pointer. Node of doubly link list consists of three parts that include

- Data portion
- Two pointer (one for the next and one for the previous)

Figure of the node structure has been illustrated in the following figure 4-1. The data part of the link list may be primitive data type or complex or user defined data type. It can also contain the combination of built-in data type or the user defined data type.

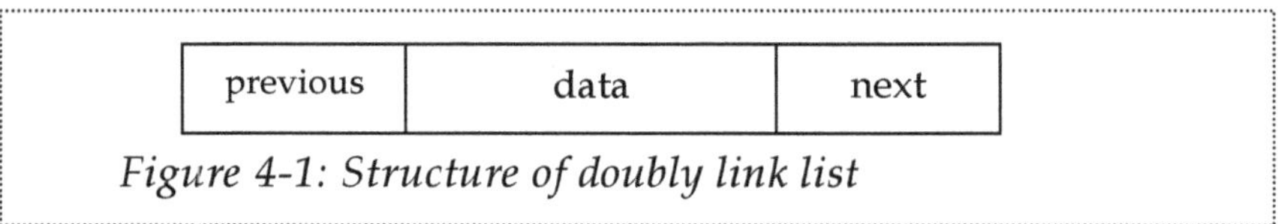

Figure 4-1: Structure of doubly link list

Both the pointers will hold the address of another node. One pointing to the previous and the other to the next as illustrated in the figure 4.1.

4.2 Creation of a Doubly Link List

During creation of a doubly link list, structure of the doubly link list(DLL) node need to be defined. During creation of the DLL, once the node is created, the needed space will be allotted. It will be followed by connecting both pointers (previous and next) to the NULL, whereas the data part will be filled with the needed data. Class and other functions needed for the above objectives have been depicted as follows:

```
// structure of the doubly link list
class dnode
 {
public:
int info;
dnode *prev,*next;
};
// class of doubly link list
class dlist
```

```
{
dnode *first, *end;
public:
dlist()
{
first=NULL;
}
};
```

During the creation of a doubly link list, we create it node by node. To create the node, we allocated the needed space. Allocation of memory to a newnode, connecting the previous and next pointer along with the node data has been given as follows:

```
dnode *newnode;
newnode=new dnode;
newnode->prev=NULL;
newnode->next=NULL;
newnode->data=5;
```

Complete operation of a creating a node of a doubly link list, its data and allocation assignment has been illustrated in the following figure.

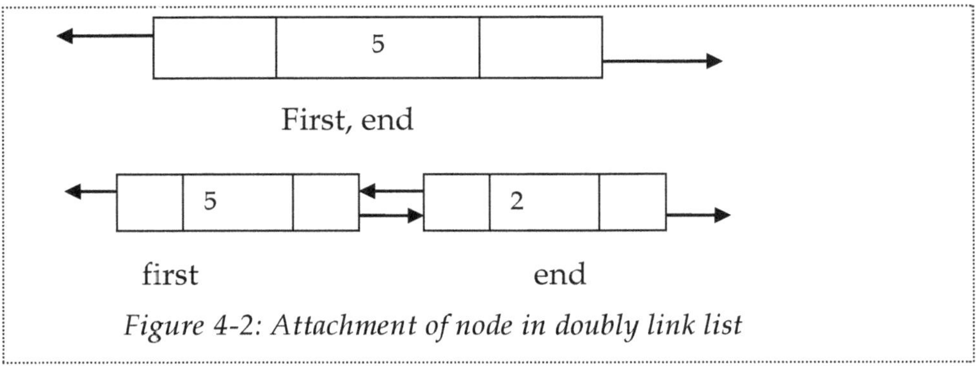

Figure 4-2: Attachment of node in doubly link list

4.3 Displaying items of a Doubly Link List

In doubly link list, traversal is possible in both the direction. We can start from the first node and using the next pointer can reach up-to the last node. Similarly, from the last node, we can reach to the first node by using the previous node. We have employed both the method to traverse the doubly link list. Each of them has been enumerated in the following programs.

```
Program: To display the item of a doubly link list
//traversing from first to the last node using next pointer
void doubly_display()
{
dnode *current;
current=first;
while(current!=NULL)
{
cout<<current->data;
current=current->next;
}        // end of while loop
```

```
}       // end of function display
```

Similarly, traversal from the last node to the first node can be accomplished by using previous node as depicted in the following program:

```
Program: To display the content of the doubly link list
//traversing from last node to the first node using previous pointer
void display_end()
{
dnode *current;
current=end;
while(current!=NULL)
{
cout<<current->data;
current=current->previous;
}       // end of while
}       // end of function
```

```
//class for the node of a doubly link list
class dnode
{
public:
    int data;
    dnode *prev,*next;
};
```

```
class  dlist
{
    int n;
    dnode *first,*last;

    public:
        //constructor to initialized the data member
        dlist();
        //To create the node in doubly link list
        void create(int);
        //To count the number of node
        int count();
        //To search element in doubly link list
        int search(int);
        //To insert the element at particular position
        void insert(int, int);
        //To reverse the doubly link list
        void reverse();
        //To concatenate the doubly link list
        dlist operator+(dlist);
        //To display content of node
        void display();
        //To display content from last to first
        void display1();
};
```

Definition of the functions declared in the above class has been given in the following program.

```
// defining constructor for the doubly link list
dlist::dlist()
{
  first=NULL;
  last=NULL;
}

          //function to create the node of a doubly link list
          void dlist::create(int item) // creation of link list, front to end
          {
                dnode *current,*temp;
                if(first==NULL) // if no node create the first node
                {
                first=new dnode;
                first->data=item;
                first->next=NULL;
                first->prev=NULL;
                last=first;
                }
                else
                {
                temp=new dnode;
                temp->data=item;
                temp->next=NULL;
                temp->prev=last;
                last->next=temp;
                last=temp;
                }
             }
          //function to display the element of doubly link list
```

```
        //Display from front to last using next pointer.
void dlist::display()
   {
         dnode *current;
         current=first;
         cout<<"Data in doubly linked list(front to last):\n";
         while(current!=NULL)
         {
               cout<<current->data<<" <-> ";
               current=current->next;
         }
         cout<<endl;
   }
 // function to display the node element from last to first
void dlist::display1()
   {
         dnode *current;
         current=last;
         cout<<"Data in doubly linked list from end to first:\n";
         while(current!=NULL)
         {
               cout<<current->data<<" <-> ";
               current=current->prev;
         }
         cout<<endl;
   }
```

4.4 Inserting item (node) in a Doubly Link List

In a doubly link list, a new node can be inserted at any position including first, middle and the last position. In doubly link list insertion of the node is less cumbersome in comparison to the singly link list. Complexity is reduced due to the availability of both way traversal that exist in the doubly link list. During insertion of the node/ element following steps can be followed:

- Traverse to the position where user is intending to insert the node.
- Intending position should be less than or equal to length of the doubly link list, if it is more than total number of node in that case node cannot be inserted.
- If the above is met, then traverse the node before which the node is to be inserted.
- Find out the next pointer of the current node.
- Connect the new node with the forward node and the node lies before this current node.
- If the node is the first node change the pointer of the first node to this new node.
- Similarly, if the node to be inserted is the last node, change the pointer of the last node to this new node.

All the above cases have been discussed in the following sub-sections.

A. **Insertion at the beginning**

In a doubly link list, node can be inserted at the beginning of the link list but in that case the first pointer will be shifted to this new node that is attached at the first position. Complete process has been defined as follows:

- Create the new node.
- Connect its next pointer to the already existing first pointer.

Once it is connected to the first node, then correspondingly first pointer is moved to the newnode as this node has become the first node. Same has been illustrated with the help of an example. In the given example, node having value 3 is to be attached at the first position. After the attachment of this new node, it will become the first node.

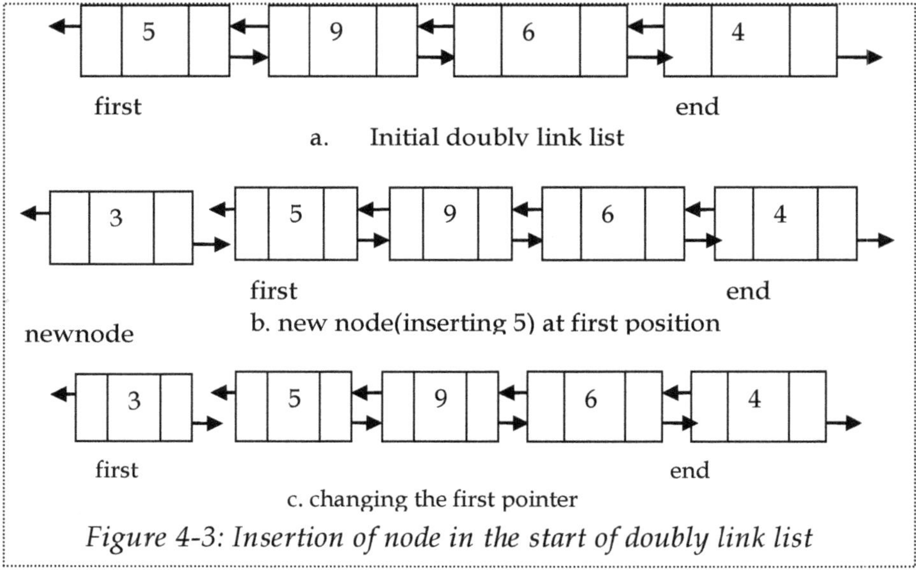

Figure 4-3: Insertion of node in the start of doubly link list

B. **Insertion other than the first position**

In this case, we have considered that node to be inserted is at any position in the doubly link list excluding the first position that has been managed in the above case. Whenever, we will insert it to any other position i.e. in the middle position or at the last position, we will follow the following steps:

i. Create a new node.
ii. Traverse to the position, where the node is to be inserted.
iii. Connect the next pointer of the newnode node to the next node of the node reached.
iv. Connect the previous pointer of the newnode to the node reached.
v. Finally, connect the next pointer of the reached node to this newnode.

The entire procedure has been illustrated in the following figure in a step by step method.

By carefully implementation of the logic, second and third conditions (insertion in between and last) can be merged into one. We have implemented the program considering all the insertion position. Complete implementation has been depicted in the following program:

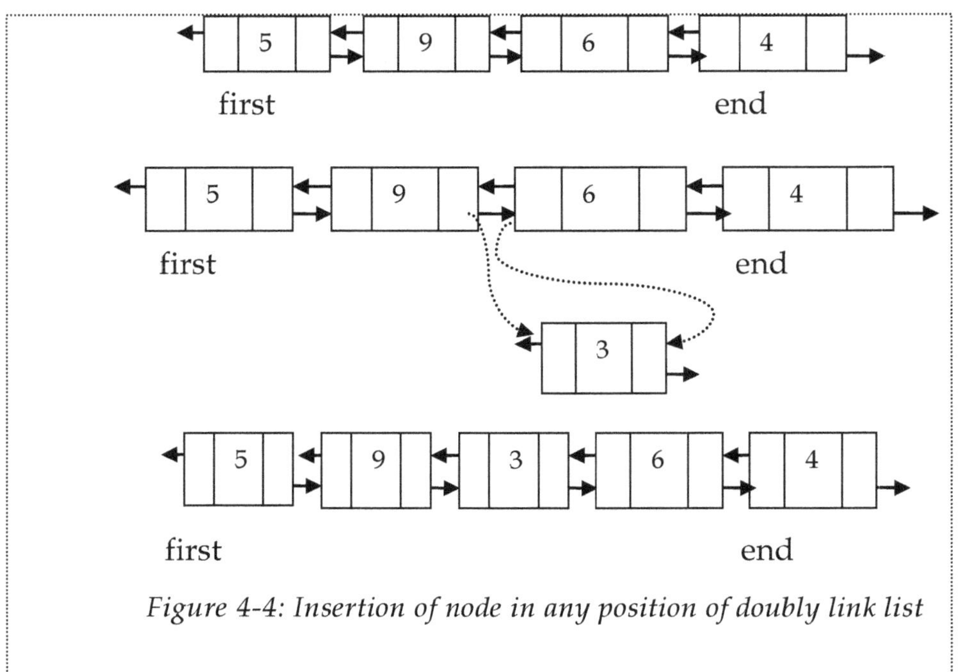

Figure 4-4: Insertion of node in any position of doubly link list

```
// function to insert the node at specific location. Takes two
//arguments, one is the position where the node is to be inserted and the
//second is the elements value that need to be inserted.
void dlist::insert(int pos, int el)
     {
     int b=count(); //finding out the number of nodes
     cout<<"Length of list :"<<b<<endl;
     if(pos<=b+1) //checking insert location is less than length+1
      {
       cout<<"Inserting "<<el<<"  at position"<<pos<<endl;
       node *current,*forward,*temp; //pointer for first and next node
```

```
current=first;
temp=new dnode;
temp->data=el;
temp->next=temp->prev=NULL;
        if(pos==1)       //checking the first position
         {
         //temp->prev=NULL;
          temp->next=first;
        first->prev=temp;
           first=temp;
           }
 else if(pos<=b)
 {
 for(int i=1;i<pos-1;i++)
 current=current->next;
 forward=current->next;
 temp->next=forward;
 temp->prev=current;
 current->next=temp;
 forward->prev=temp;
// forward->prev=temp;
 }
 else
 {
 last->next=temp;
 temp->prev=last;
 temp->next=NULL;
 last=temp;
 }
 cout<<"Node inserted at position "<<pos<<endl;
```

```
        }
        else
        cout<<"Can't be inserted\n";
          }
```

4.5 Deleting the item (node) from Doubly Link List

To delete a node from a doubly link list, we have considered the cases given below and will be manipulated accordingly. Various cases of deleting the node from the doubly link list includes the following:

- Deletion from the first position
- Deletion in any other location (other than the first)

4.5.1 Deleting the first node

To delete the first node, procedure to be employed is different from that of any other node. Due to the deletion of the first node, the pointer holding the first node address will be lost. Consequently, first position needs to be shifted to the new first position before deletion. Required changes need to be reflected in the existing doubly link list. Deleting the node from the doubly link list can be carried out by adhering to the steps mentioned below:

- Find out the node location where the node to be deleted. It should be less than or equal to the size of the link list (number of node in a doubly link list).
- If the node to be deleted is the first node, save the first node

in the temp pointer. Move the first node pointer to the second node of a doubly link list.

- Delete the first node that is stored in the temp node.

Since the node to be deleted is the first node, in this case, the first node is to be stored in the temp node. Move the first node to the second node of the existing list. Previous node is still pointing to the first node. To remove this node from the list, store NULL to the previous of the new first node. Finally, remove the original first node of the link list.

To determine if the node is first node, we examine the previous pointer of the node. If this pointer is NULL then it denotes the first node, therefore it is to be handled accordingly.

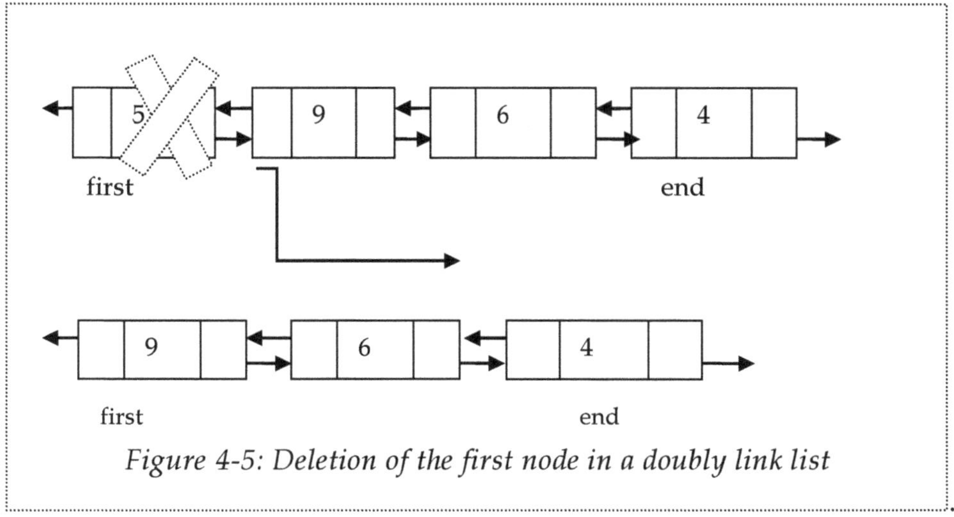

Figure 4-5: Deletion of the first node in a doubly link list

Deletion of the cases, deletion of first node and any other node has been given in the function deletenode depicted in section 4.5.2.

4.5.2 Deleting the node other than the first node

If the node to be deleted is other than the first node (including the last node), in that case the node to be deleted is to be stored in the temp node. Connect the previous node to the next of the current node. Finally, delete the temp node. Complete function to accomplish this task has been depicted in the following program.

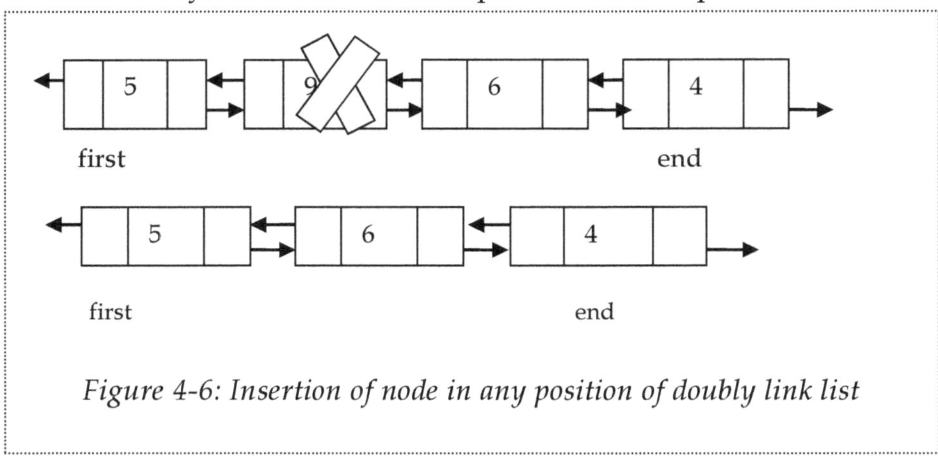

Figure 4-6: Insertion of node in any position of doubly link list

```
//function to delete node from doubly link list
void dlist::deletenode(int el)
{
//int found=0;
dnode *current,*temp;
current=first;
while(current!=NULL)
  {
  if(current->data==el)
    {
    //Node to be deleted is the last node
```

```
  if(current->next==NULL)
  {
  last=current->prev;
  current->prev->next=current->next;
  delete current;
  break;
  }
  else if(current->prev==NULL)// node is first node
   {
   current->next->prev=current->prev;
   first=current->next;
   delete current;
   break;
   }
   else
   {
   // any other node to be deleted
  current->prev->next=current->next;
  current->next->prev=current->prev;
  delete current;
  break;
  }
  }
 current=current->next;// otherwise continue to move to the next node
 }
```

4.6 Searching element in a doubly link list

Doubly link facilitates the traversal in both the direction. For instance, we can traverse from front to end as well as from end to first. A node consisting of an element may be searched during the traversal. Due care is to be taken to ensure that traversal should be limited only to the number of nodes existing in the list. As soon as node consisting of the element encountered, searching should terminates. The whole procedure is depicted in the following program.

```
//function to search an element from a doubly link list
int dlist::search(int element)
        {
                int flag=0;
                dnode *current;
                int b=count();
                current=first;
                for(int i=1;i<=b;i++)
                {
                        if(current->data==element)
                        {
                        flag=1;
                        break;
                        }
                        current=current->next;
                }
               return flag;
        }
```

In the program depicted above, we have declared a variable flag to represent the status of item to be searched. We have initialized it to '0' to represent that item is not present in the list. If item to be searched is found in the doubly link list, loop is terminated with the help of break statement, and status of flag is set to the new value of 1 to represent that item searched in the list. Finally, the status of the flag is returned to the caller.

4.7 Counting number of nodes in a doubly link list

Counting the number of node in a doubly link is needed on many occasion. Counting the number of node is the significant function in a doubly link list. Counting all the node of a doubly link list does not involve much complexity. Here the user has to start from the first node and go up-to the last node. Counting the node is needed during traversal of nodes. Since, doubly link list facilitates traversal in both the direction; therefore we can also count the number of node by starting traversal from the end. During this traversal, we can use the previous pointer to reach up-to first node, at the same time we can count the number of nodes in the doubly link list. However, in out example we have considered traversal from the beginning to the end node. Same has been depicted in the following program.

```
//Program to count the number of node in doubly link list
int count( )
{
dnode *current=first;
int cnt=0;
while(current!=NULL) // till the double link list is not exhausted
{
cnt++;          //count the node
current=current->next;        // move to the next node
```

```
}
return cnt;
}
```

4.8 Circular doubly link list

Even though doubly link list permits the traversal in both the direction yet sometime we need to connect the last node to the first node. Such type of doubly link list is known as circular doubly link list. Doubly link list has the following advantages.

a) Does not have any null pointer.

b) Improves the efficiency, specifically if required to be traversed from the last towards the first node.

c) Improves the performance, if required to be traversed from first node towards the last node side.

Circular doubly link list has been illustrated in the figure 4-7.

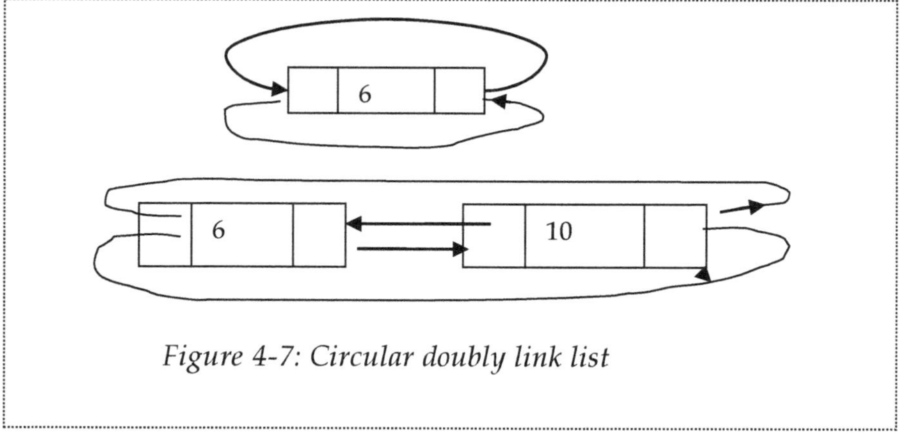

Figure 4-7: Circular doubly link list

4.8.1 Creation of circular Link list

Creation of circular doubly link list is different from its counterpart (doubly link list). Once the first node is created, unlike the doubly link list we do not point to the previous and next pointer to the NULL. Instead, we connect them to the node itself. Same has been illustrated in the figure 4-7 (a). When the second node is created, it previous node is connected to the first node. A pointer of the first node is also to be adjusted, because the next pointer of the existing node will point to this newnode and the next pointer of this new node to be pointed to the first node.

Class to perform various activities (function) in doubly link list has been depicted in the following program.

```
#include<iostream.h>
#include<conio.h>
// class to define the structure of a node in a doubly link list
class dnode
{
public:
int data;
dnode *prev;
dnode *next;
};
// Class for the doubly link list
class dblyList
{
dnode *first;
dnode *end;
```

```
public:
dblyList()
{
first=NULL;
end=NULL;
}
void create(int);
void display();
void insert(int,int);
int count();
void deletenode(int);
};
```

4.8.2 Function to create circular doubly link list

In the creation of the circular doubly link list, we have considered two pointers namely first and end. These two pointer represent the first and the last node of the doubly link list. By using the last next, we can traverse to the first node of the circular doubly link list. Correspondingly, we can also reach to last node we using the first previous. When the first node is created and the doubly link list is having only one node in that case both the first and the last node will point to the same node. To insert the other node, pointer of last node and the previous pointer of the first node need to be connected to the newly created newnode. Complete program has been given as follows.

```
// To create the first node
void create(int element)
```

```
{
if(first==NULL)
 {
 first=new dnode;
 first->data=element;
 first->next=first;
first->prev=first;
end=first;
return;
}
//to create any other node
dnode *newnode;
newnode=new dnode;
newnode->data=element;
newnode->next=end->next;
newnode->prev=end;
end->next=newnode;
first->prev=newnode;
end=newnode;
}
```

After inserting the node into the circular doubly link list, we need to view the data of the node available. This objective can be accomplished with the help of display function. In the display function, due care need to be observed to avoid the infinite looping. Since, in the circular doubly link list last node is connected to the first node, therefore, loop must terminate at the 'end' node, and failure to terminate the loop will lead to the infinite loop. Program to display of all the data of a circular link list has been given in the display function.

```
void dblyList::display()
 {
 dnode *current=first;
 while(current->next!=first)
  {
  cout<<current->data<<"->";
  current=current->next;
  }
  //to display the data of last node
  cout<<current->data<<"->";
  }
```

4.8.3 To count the number of nodes in circular doubly link list

To count the number of nodes in a circular doubly link list, we can traverse from the front or from the back. Since, doubly link list is circular, due care is to be observed to prevent the condition of cycling, otherwise doubly link list will not terminate. In our case, we have used the condition by comparing it to the first node itself. Function has been given as follows:

```
// To count the number of node in a doubly link list
  int dblyList::count()
  {
// initialize the count to 0
 int c=0;
// store the address of first to the current node
```

```
dnode *current=first;
// Run the loop till we are not reaching to the first node
while(current->next!=first)
 {
 c++;  // increment the count
// move the list to the next node.
 current=current->next;
}
 //One node was left due to current->next;
 c=c+1;
 return c;
}
```

Initially, the variable 'c' represents the number of count has been initialized with the zero. In each traversal, we increment this variable by one. Since, we have terminated at the last node, therefore this node has not been counted. To count this node we have incremented the current value of c by 1. Finally, value of c has been returned to the caller.

4.8.4 To insert a node at a given position

During all the operations that are needed to be carried out in a circular doubly link list, due care need to be observed to avoid the cycling. Inserting the node in any position is not at all exceptional. Correspondingly, to insert the node in a circular doubly link list, the precaution that needs to be observed cannot be undermined. When the node to be inserted is in between, then there is no difference between the circular doubly link list and the doubly link list.

However, there is substantial difference while inserting the node at the first and last position. Complete procedure of inserting the node in a circular link list has been depicted as follows:

- The given position where the node to be inserted should be valid (must lie between first and last node).
- If the position where node to be inserted at first position, connect the previous node of the newnode to the previous node of the existing first node. Connect the next pointer to the first node. Name this newnode as first node by shifting the first pointer to this newnode. Similarly change the next pointer of the last node to this newnode (first node).
- To insert the node in-between (other than the first and the last node). Replace the next pointer of current node (Node after which the newnode is to be inserted) newnode to the next pointer of the existing node. Connect the previous not of the forward node to this newnode. Connect the next pointer of the current node to the newnode and finally, previous pointer of the newnode to be connected to the current node.
- To insert at the end position, replace the next pointer of this newnode with the existing next pointer of the end node (it is pointing to the first node). Connect the next pointer of the existing end node to the newnode (this will act as last node), connect the previous node of newnode to the existing last node. Finally, move the end node to this newnode.

```
// To insert the node at given position
void dblyList:: insert(int element, int pos)
 {
 int n=count();
  dnode *current,*temp;
 temp=new dnode;
 temp->data=element;
 if(pos<=(n+1))
 {
    if(pos==(n+1))
  {
  // insert at the end
      temp->prev=end;
  temp->next=end->next;
 end->next=temp;
 first->prev=temp;
 end=temp;
 }
 else
   {
    current=first;
   int i=1;
   while(i<pos)
   {
   current=current->next;
        i++;
   }
   temp->next=current;
   temp->prev=current->prev;
   current->prev->next=temp;
```

```
    current->prev=temp;
    //if the position is 1, change the first pointer
    if(pos==1)
    first=temp;
   }
  }
  else
  cout<<"Cannot be inserted, Position is more than length"<<endl;
  }
```

4.8.5 To Delete the node from a circular doubly link list

Deletion of a node from a circular doubly link list is substantially different from the doubly link list. Due care needs to be observed while deleting the first or the last node of the circular doubly link list. If the first node is to be deleted, in that case, first is to be moved to the next of the existing first node. The new first has to be made circular; therefore, this new first has to be connected to the end node. Correspondingly, the last node of the circular doubly link list need to be adjusted. The End node, need to be connected to the first node of the doubly link list. Same has been depicted in the following program.

```
//To delete the node based on a  user supplied value
  void dblyList:: deletenode(int element)
   {
   dnode *current,*prev1=NULL,*temp;
   current=first;
   do{
```

```
    if( current->data==element)
    {
    break;
    }
    prev1=current;
   current=current->next;
   }while(current!=first);


// if node to be deleted is first node
 if(prev1==NULL)
     {
     temp=first;
     current=first->next;
     //connecting the new first to the last node
      first->next->prev=first->prev;
     end->next=current;
     first=current;
    }
// if node to be deleted is the last node
else if(current==end)
    {
    temp=current;
//Connecting the first node to the last node
   first->prev=prev1;
   // connecting the last node to the first node
   prev1->next=first;
    end=prev1;
    }
// if the node to be deleted is the in-between node
```

```
    else
    {
    temp=current;
    prev1->next=current->next;
    current->next->prev=prev1;
    }
   delete temp;
   }
```

4.8.6 Doubly Link list using template

Doubly link that has been discussed has considered the integer type of data. If we need to implement it for any other data type then program need to be modified accordingly. To address this situations we suggest implementation of template doubly link list. This template link list will get modified according to the type needed. List can be implemented similar to link list implementation using pointers. Changes are needed to be made only due to the template formation only. Complete code has been given as follows for the convenient of the readers.

```
//operations on double ended linked list
#include<iostream.h>
#include<conio.h>

 template<class t>
class dnode
{
```

```
        public:
    t data;
    dnode *prev,*next;
};
template<class t>
class  dlist
{
        dnode<t> *first,*last;

    public:
            //constructor to initialized the data member
            dlist();
            //to create the doubly link list
            void create(t);
            //to count the number of node
            int count();
            //to search element in doubly link list
            int search(t);
            //to insert the element at particular position
            void insert(int, t);
            //to reverse the doubly link list
            void reverse();
            //to concatenate the doubly link list
            dlist operator+(dlist);
            //to display content of node
            void display();
            //to display content last to first
            void display1();
            void deletenode(t);
};
```

```
//constructor to initialized the data member
template<class t>
dlist<t>::dlist()
{
   first=null;
   last=null;
}
//function to delete node from doubly link list
 template<class t>
void dlist<t>::deletenode(t t1)
{
//int found=0;
dnode<t> *current,*temp;
current=first;
while(current!=null)
  {
  if(current->data==t1)
   {
   //node to be deleted is the last node
   if(current->next==null)
   {
   last=current->prev;
   current->prev->next=current->next;
   delete current;
   break;
   }
   else if(current->prev==null)// node is first node
    {
    current->next->prev=current->prev;
    first=current->next;
```

```
    delete current;
    break;
    }
    else
    {
    // any other node to be deleted
   current->prev->next=current->next;
   current->next->prev=current->prev;
   delete current;
   break;
   }
   }
  current=current->next;
  }

}

          //function to create the doubly link list
          template<class t>
          void dlist<t>::create(t item)
          {
                dnode<t> *current,*temp;
                if(first==null)
                {
                first=new dnode<t>;
                first->data=item;
                first->next=null;
                first->prev=null;
                last=first;
                }
```

```
            else
            {
            temp=new dnode<t>;
            temp->data=item;
            temp->next=null;
            temp->prev=last;
            last->next=temp;
            last=temp;
            }
        }
//function to display the element of doubly link list
template<class t>
void dlist<t>::display()
{
        dnode<t> *current;
        current=first;
        cout<<"data in doubly linked list(front to last):\n";
        while(current!=null)
        {
                cout<<current->data<<" <-> ";
                current=current->next;
        }
        cout<<endl;
}
template<class t>
void dlist<t>::display1()
{
        dnode<t> *current;
        current=last;
        cout<<"data in doubly linked list from end to first:\n";
```

```
        while(current!=null)
        {
                cout<<current->data<<" <-> ";
                current=current->prev;
        }
        cout<<endl;
}

//reverse function
template<class t>
void dlist<t>::reverse()
{
int n;
        n=count();
        dnode<t> *current;
        current=last;
        cout<<"the data after reversing the linked list:\n";
        for(int i=1;i<=n;i++)
        {
                cout<<current->data<<" -> ";
                current=current->prev;
        }
}

//count function
template<class t>
int dlist<t>::count()
{
        int c=0;
        dnode<t> *current;
```

```
            current=first;
            while(current!=null)
            {
                    c++;
                    current=current->next;
            }
            return c;
    }


    //to insert el at particular position
    template<class t>
    void dlist<t>::insert(int pos, t el)
    {
            int b=count();
            cout<<"length of list :"<<b<<endl;
            if(pos<=b+1)
            {
            cout<<"inserting "<<el<<"  at position"<<pos<<endl;
                    dnode<t> *current,*forward,*temp;
                    current=first;
                    temp=new dnode<t>;
                    temp->data=el;
                    temp->next=temp->prev=null;
                    if(pos==1)
                    {
                            //temp->prev=null;
                            temp->next=first;
                            first->prev=temp;
                            first=temp;
```

```
                }
                else if(pos<=b)
                {
                        for(int i=1;i<pos-1;i++)
                        current=current->next;
                        forward=current->next;
                        temp->next=forward;
                        temp->prev=current;
                        current->next=temp;
                        forward->prev=temp;
                        // forward->prev=temp;
                }
                else
                {
                        last->next=temp;
                        temp->prev=last;
                        temp->next=null;
                        last=temp;
                }
                cout<<"node inserted at position "<<pos<<endl;
        }
        else
        cout<<"can't be inserted\n";
}

//search function
template<class t>
int dlist<t>::search(t element)
{
        int flag=0;
```

```
                dnode<t> *current;
                int b=count();
                current=first;
                cout<<"searching element "<<element<<endl;
                for(int i=1;i<=b;i++)
                {
                        if(current->data==element)
                        {
                        flag=1;
                        break;
                        }
                        current=current->next;
                }
               return flag;
          }

          //overloading + operator
          template<class t>
          dlist<t> dlist<t>::operator +(dlist<t> l)
          {
                dlist l6;
                l6.first=first;
                l6.last=last;
                l6.last->next=l.first;
                l.first->prev=l6.last;
                return l6;
          }

int main()
{
```

```
int n,el;
dlist<int> l1,l3,l2;// creating the doubly list for integer type
clrscr();
l1.create(34);
l1.create(7);
l1.create(153);
l1.create(40);
l1.display();
//l1.insert(4,112);
l1.display();
if(l1.search(40))
cout<<"element found"<<endl;
else
cout<<"element not in doubly link list"<<endl;
cout<<"enter element to be deleted"<<endl;
cin>>el;
l1.deletenode(el);
l1.display();
getch();
return 0;
}
```

4.9 Case Study based on doubly link list

Implement the case given in the link list chapter and implement the same using doubly link list. If the same program is implemented using doubly link list, then what will be the effect on performance.

Extend the doubly link program enumerated in the link list

example by including more data members. These members should be relevant to the student details. These members have been given as follows:

Table 4.1: Student description

S.No	Data members	Description
1.	*Stud_id*	*Unique id of all the students.*
2.	*Student_name*	*Name of a student*
3.	*Subject*	*Name of the subject(each student will have 5 subjects)*
4.	*Marks*	*Marks of the subject (for all the above 05 subjects, there will be there corresponding marks).*
5.	*Total*	*Total of marks in all the above subjects*

a. Each node should contain the above information. Consider the case that total numbers of students are 20. Keep the data in the doubly link list itself. Write a function that should organize the records (nodes) of the doubly link list based on total marks. For instance, student secured the maximum marks to be put at first position, then the second highest, etc.

b. write a function, to search the node (record) in the given doubly link list.

c. Modify the above program by extending on more data member in the doubly link list count. Based on the number of time the record (node) is searched, the value of count should increment by 1.Re-arrange the nodes based on the count. For instance, if the 4th node has the maximum count then it is to be positioned at the first position.

Exercise

4.10 Descriptive questions

1. Write a function that creates the doubly link without traversing the doubly link list.
2. Modify the above function, so that there is no need to check whether the first node is NULL or not.
3. Write a function that insert a new node in the doubly link list. Function should manage the following:
    a) Whether the list is existing or not.
    b) Whether the position given is within the permissible range or not. For instance, if the total numbers of nodes are 5 and the given position where node to be inserted is 8 then it should not be allowed.
4. Write a function that delete a node in the doubly link based on the following factors:
    a. Based on existing list.
    b. Consider the position given is within the permissible range or not. For instance, if the total numbers of nodes are 5 and the given position where node to be deleted is 8 then it should not be allowed.
    c. Delete the node based on the value received from the user.
5. Write a function to delete a node from a doubly link list.

a) To delete the first node of doubly link list.
b) To delete the node that is in between (other than first and last).
c) To delete the node existing at the end.

Once the node is deleted adjust the pointers accordingly. For instance, if the last node is deleted in that case the previous node has to be pointed to the NULL as now it is acting as last node.

4.11 Multiply choice questions

1. What will be the size of the class used to define the structure of the doubly link list.

a. 02 bytes c. 40 bytes.
b. 06 bytes d. 12 bytes.

2. Can we modify the create function by including the pointer as an argument?

a. Yes
b. No.

(Write down the points in support and against of your statement and get it verified from your faculty).

3. If the current is pointing to the current node of a doubly link list. To access the two nodes ahead of current, following statement can be used.

a. Current->next c. current->next->next
b. Current->next->prev d. None of these

4. If the current is pointing to the current node and forward is pointing to one node ahead of current. Then the code current->next=forward->prev points to the
    a. Current node.
    b. One node ahead of the forward node.
    c. One node previous to the current node.
    d. None of these

5. In the above question, to delete the node that is in between in a doubly link list the code given current->next=forward->next, delete forward node is:
    a. Correct
    b. Wrong

Chapter 5
Stack

Chapter Objective

- Defining stack
- Defining various operations permitted on the stack
- Describing the push and pop function
- Describing the nop and returning the top of the stack.
- Displaying the items in a stack.
- Describing the application of stack.
- Creating the dynamic stack.
- Creating the stack using template

5 Stack

In our daily life, we witness many usage of stack data structure. For instance, when we visit the party/functions, there we pick the plates from the top. Whenever caterers need to place more plates, he is placing the new plates on the top of the existing plates. Same is the case with our new data structure and it is popularly known as stack. It is widely used data structure in plenty of applications that include tree traversal, balancing of the tree, etc.

5.1 Stack Definition

In line with the above example, we can consider that stack is a data structure that is considered to be opened from one end. This open end is known as top, insertion and deletion operations are permitted from the top end only. Since, items are arranged one after other, where new elements are inserted at the top of the existing elements. Consequently, the item inserted at last is removed first. Process in which we insert the item last is removed first is known as Last in First out (LIFO) order. Correspondingly, it can be concluded that stack works on LIFO order.

The complete process of insertion of items has been illustrated in the figure 5-1.

Initially, we have considered that the stack is empty; top of the stack is initialized with -1 to represent this condition. First element 'A' is inserted, correspondingly, the top moves to the 0th index as illustrated in the figure 5-1 (a). Similarly, other items 'B' and 'C' are also inserted, correspondingly, top also moves upwards, refer figure 5-1 (b, c). Irrespective of operation (push or pop) performed on the stack, top will always pointing to the last element of the stack.

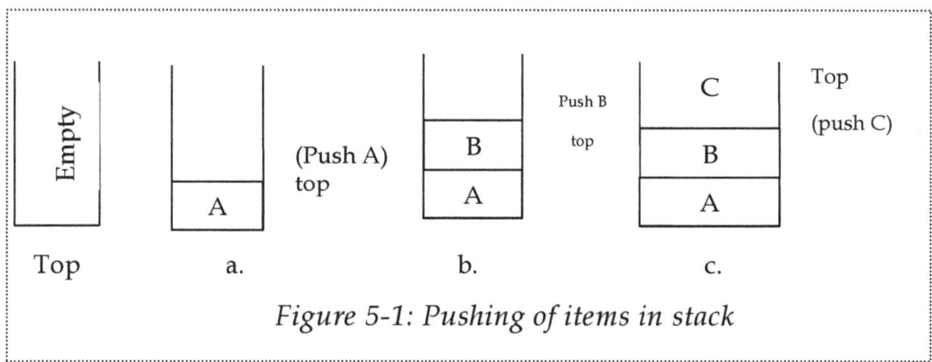

Figure 5-1: Pushing of items in stack

5.2 Operations on stack

In a stack, two major operations are carried out and related to the insertion and removal of the items from the stack.

Push: Inserting the element(s) into the stack is known as push. Once the items are pushed into the stack, top is incremented by one, therefore top moves towards the capacity of the stack. Once the capacity is full and still we intend to insert more item(s) on the stack then this event is known as overflow. Since, it will result in data loss, therefore provision to avoid the overflow is extremely desirable. Push operation has been illustrated in the figure 5-1.

Pop: Removing the items from the stack is known as pop operation.

In the pop operation, items are removed from the top, correspondingly, top moves towards the base of the stack. Once the stack is empty, still we remove the elements from the stack, it is known as underflow. Pop has been illustrated in the figure 5-2.

Consider the case where we have already three elements in the stack, therefore stack will point to the top position. In the figure 5-2, the top element of the stack is 'C', therefore, top is at index 2. Once the one item is popped then top will get decremented by one index and will point to 'B' (refer figure 5-2 b)

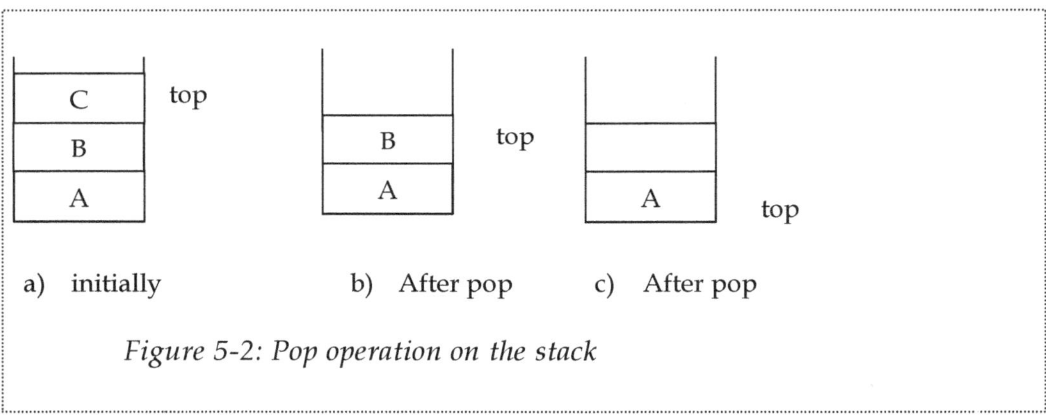

Figure 5-2: Pop operation on the stack

Nop: Beyond the push and pop operation there is another possible operation that can be carried out on the stack, it is known as NoOperation (Nop). In the Nop, there is no operation takes place. In other terms, there is no movement of the top; instead, activities are carried out without the movement of the top. For instance, displaying the elements of the stack falls under this category, since it does not involve any movement of the top of the stack. The other example related to the Nop is top of the stack element, in which top element is to be returned without moving the top pointer.

5.3 Implementations of Stack

Stack is a widely used data structure in computer science, usage of stack improves the overall performance and simplifies the code. In stack, many times we know the number of elements that need to be inserted. However, many times predicting the number of items to be inserted cannot be predicted accurately. Correspondingly, to cater these needs, stacks are categorized into:

- Static stack
- Dynamic stack

In stack, if total number of items that are needed to be inserted is known/ predicted in advance, then such type of stack can be implemented with the help of **static stack**. Such stacks give better performance in comparison to the dynamic stack.

In cases, if the total number of items to be inserted is not known or variation of minimum number of items to be inserted to the maximum number of items to be inserted is huge, in such cases, we use another type of stack known as **dynamic stack**. But this stack involves the performance overhead related to memory allocation and de-allocation.

5.3.1 Static Stack

Static stack is implemented with the help of an array. Before creating the stack, its structure for the type of information that will be stored in the stack is to be defined. The other constraint is related to the top pointer that will point to the top of the stack. Class denoting the data member and the operations that can be accomplished on the data member has been given as follows:

5.1 Program for the push, pop and display function of the static stack.

```
// Program that depicts that push and pop operation on the stack
const int size=5;          // size of the stack
// Defining the structure of the stack
class stk
{
int stack[size];
int top;
public:
// constructor to initialize the value of top
stk()
{
top=-1;
}
// To push the element in the stack
int push(int);
//To pop the element from the stack and return the top/pop element
int pop();
// To display the items in the stack.
void display();
// To display the number of element in the stack.
void count_elements();
// To examine whether the stack is empty or not
```

```
int isEmpty();

};
```

Initially, the stack is empty and it is denoted by assigning the value of -1 to top. Whenever an item is inserted into the stack, it is examined for its capacity (represented by size) to avoid overflow. If the stack is not full then only item(s) are allowed to be inserted into the stack. Correspondingly, top pointer is incremented by +1 to denote the new position of the top.

Push function returns the integer value. This value is utilize to determine whether the push operation was successful or unsuccessful. If it is successful, push function returns 1, whereas, in case of failure, it returns the value 0.

```
// function to implement the push operation of stack.
int stacks::push(int element)
        {
         if(top==(size-1))
         {
        cout<<"overflow, more elements cannot be inserted \n";
        return 0;
         }
         else
         {
         stack[++top]=element;
         }
        return 1;
        }
```

To pop the element from the stack, first we would check for the empty condition. If the stack is empty then underflow message will be flashed to the user. To check the empty condition, we check the value associated to the top variable.

If(top==-1)

Value of -1 is represents the empty condition.

If there are one or more elements in the stack, then pop operation can be performed. Before pop operation, the top element of the stack is stored in the temp variable. Afterwards, the top moves one pointer below and finally the value of the top stored in the temp variable is returned to the caller (was stored at the top of the stack) function, for the later usage, if any.

```
//function to pop the element from the stack
int stacks::pop()
            {
                  int a=0;
                  if(top==-1)
                  {
                              cout<<"underflow:\n";
                }
                  else
                  {
                     a=stack[top--];
                  }
                 return a;
```

```
            }
```

We have also designed the function isEmpty() to determine, whether the stack is empty or not. This function can be utilized before the pop operation is called. If the stack is empty then pop should not be permitted, instead suitable message need to be flashed to the user. It returns 1/true, if the stack is empty otherwise returns 0/false. Same has been illustrated in following program.

```
// To examine whether the stack is empty.
int stacks::isEmpty()
            {
                        if(top==-1)
                        return 1;
                        else
                        return 0;
            }
```

Despite of executing the push and pop operation, we have not aware of the elements that are available in the stack. To accomplish this objective, the function display () has been created. This function displays all the elements in the stack. It starts from the top and goes up-to the bottom of the stack. To ensure that top is not moving from its position, a new variable't' has been used and the value of top is assigned to this variable.

```
// Program to display the element(s) of the stack.
void stacks::display()
            {
                        for(int i=top;i>=0;i--)
```

```
            cout<<stack[i]<<" ";
            cout<<endl;
    }
```

On various occasions, we would need to determine the number of elements in the stack at any particular point of time. To accomplish this objective, we have created the count_elements() function.

5.3.1.1 Counting the number of elements

To count the number of elements in the stack, we have started from the top and continued up-to the base. During this looping, variable cnt is incremented by 1. Finally, count is returned to the caller function.

```
//function to count the number of element(s) in the stack;
int stacks::count_elements()
  {
//initialize the t with top and cnt with 0.
int cnt=0,t=top;
  while(t>=0)
  {
  cnt++;          // increment the cnt
  t--;            // move towards the base
  }
  return cnt;
 }
```

All the functions discussed above can be called from the main function. This function act as a single point of execution of all the function declared and defined. Once this function is also written, we can make usage of all the functions already defined.

```
// Calling the function from the main function
int main()
{
int n,n1;
stacks s1;
clrscr();
if(s1.isEmpty())
cout<<"Stack is empty"<<endl;
else
cout<<"Stack is not empty";
s1.push(10);
s1.push(5);
//s1.push(7);
s1.push(14);
cout<<"Total number of elements in stack are:
"<<s1.count_elements()<<endl;
s1.push(90);
//s1.push(299);
cout<<" Element(s) in the stack are:"<<endl;
s1.display();
n=s1.pop();
cout<<" Element pop is "<<n<<endl;
getch();
return 0;
}
```

5.3.2 Dynamic stack

Although, stack is widely used data structure on various occasions specifically, we need to work in the LIFO order. However, static stack suffers with the following limitations:

I. Number of elements to be inserted should be known before creation of stack.

II. If the size requested is too less than many elements will not be inserted in the stack. At the same time, if the space allocation requested for the stack is more than huge space of the array cannot be utilized by the stack.

To address the above issues, dynamic stack can be used. Dynamic stack is implemented with the help of a node that is dynamically provisioned when the need for data storage is realized. (Users who are not familiar with link list are requested to please refer the link list chapter before reading this section for better clarity)

Dynamic stack consist of two parts.

- Data part (Consist of data)
- Next pointer (Reflects the address of next pointer from the top).

Data part consists of the data that need to be inserted in the stack. Top points to the current position of the stack and facilitates insertion of the elements inside the stack.

Working of the dynamic stack is depicted in the following program:

```
// Class to define the node of the stack
```

```
class stacknode
 {
 public:
 int data;
 stacknode*next;
 };
//Class stack to perform various operation
class stack
{
//int data;
stacknode *top;
public:
stack();
void push(int);
int pop();
void display();
};
```

Initially, the dynamic stack will be empty. To highlight this condition, we have initialized the top with the NULL. Since, all the stacks will be created from the empty condition, Therefore; we have initialized it with the help of constructor.

Once the items are inserted (push) into the stack, top will move to the new position. Insertion of the stack is illustrated in the following figure 5-3.

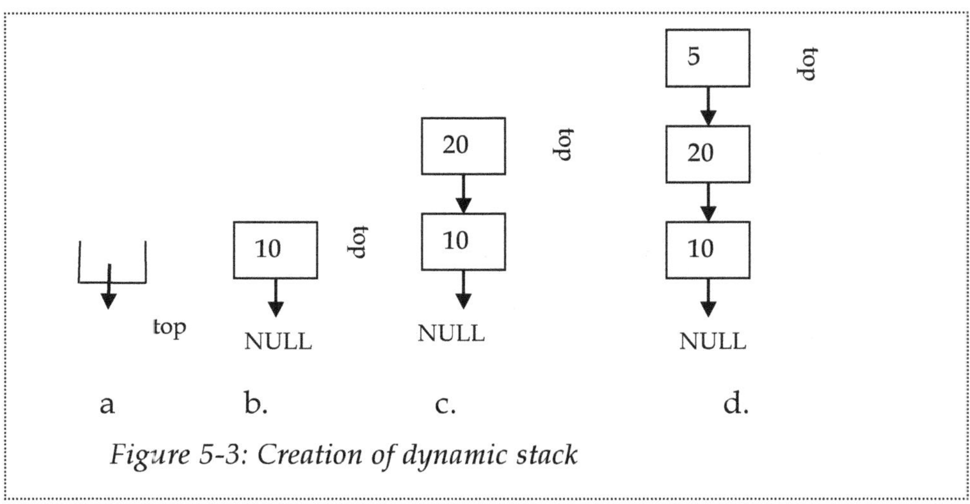

Figure 5-3: Creation of dynamic stack

Initially, the stack is empty; therefore top will be pointing to the NULL. When 10 is inserted, top will point to the new position. Similarly, when 20 is inserted the new position of top is demonstrated in the figure 5-3 (c).

```
stack::stack()
{
top=NULL;
}
void stack::push(int element)
 {
  if(top==NULL)
   {
   top=new stacknode;
   top->data=element;
   top->next=NULL;
   }
```

```
  else
  {
  stacknode *temp;
  temp=new stacknode;
  temp->data=element;
  temp->next=top;
  top=temp;
  }
}
```

To display the items of dynamic stack, we use the current pointer, which accepts the address of the top and facilitates it in retaining the value of top. In our program, temporary variable has been represented with the name current. To traverse the entire element, while loop is used that executes till all the elements are not traversed.

```
void stack::display()
  {
  stacknode *current;
  current=top; // storing the address of top to the current
  cout<<" Elements in the stack are: "<<endl;
  while(current!=NULL)
   {
   cout<<current->data<<"   "; //display the data
   current=current->next;      // move to the next node, towards the base
   }
   cout<<endl;
 }
```

To pop the items from the function, we have used the function pop. Before taking out (pop) any element, it is first examined for the availability of any item in the stack. In case of no items in the stack, message for the stack empty is displayed and the failure status is returned from the function. In case, if one or more item are available in the stack, the item that is removed is returned.

```
// function to pop the element of the dynamic stack
int stack::pop()
  {
  if(top==NULL)
  {
  cout<<"Stack is empty "<<endl;
  return 0;
  }
  stacknode* temp=top;
  int el=temp->data;
  top=top->next;
  delete temp;
  return el;
}
```

Similarly, we can create the size () function for the dynamic stack that count the number of element in the stack. To accomplish this task, we have started from the top and reached up-to the base. During this traversal, variable representing the count is incremented by one. Function to represent the size of the dynamic stack is depicted below:

```
// function to determine the size (number of count) of the dynamic stack
int stack::size()
  {
int count=0;
if(top==NULL)
  {
  cout<<"No element in the stack "<<endl;
  return count;
  }
  stacknode *current;
  current=top; // storing the address of top to the current
   while(current!=NULL)
    {
    count++;
    }
 return count;
 }
```

Sequence of calling the stack function is ascertained by the main function. It is depicted in the following program.

```
// program to call the function from the main
int main()
 {
 stack s1;
 clrscr();
 s1.push(90);
  s1.push(5);
 s1.push(32);
cout<<"Element before pop"<<endl;
```

```
 s1.display();
cout<<"pop element "<<s1.pop()<<endl;
 cout<<"pop element "<<s1.pop()<<endl;
 s1.display();
 getch();
 return 0;
 }
```

5.4 Stack Implementation using template

In the above given examples, we have implemented the stack for the integer type. Now if the requirement changes, where we need to implement it for the complex data type or any other type, in that case program need to be modified/re-written and tested. To avoid such situation, a stack for generic type may be created; such stacks are capable to implement the various types of data. Since, implementation will change for the dynamic and static stack. Therefore, we have separately implemented for each of them. Same has been depicted in the upcoming sub-section.

5.4.1 Static stack using template

```
#include<iostream.h>
#include<conio.h>
const int size=5;
template <class t>
```

```
class stacks
{
    t stack[size];
    int top;
    public:
            stacks()
            {
                top=-1;
            }
        int push(t);
        t pop();
        int isEmpty();
        void display();
        int count_elements();
};
template<class t>
 int stacks<t>::count_elements()
  {
  int cnt=0,t1=top;
  while(t1>=0)
  {
  cnt++;
  t1--;
  }
  return cnt;
 }

            template<class t>
            int stacks<t>::push(int element)
            {
```

```
            if(top==(size-1))
            {
                    cout<<"overflow element not entered\n";
                    return 0;
            }
            else
            {
               stack[++top]=element;
            }
           return 1;
    }
template<class t>
   t stacks<t>::pop()
    {
            t a=stack[top];
            if(top==-1)
            {
                    cout<<"underflow:\n";
            }
            else
            {
               a=stack[top--];
            }
           return a;
    }
           template<class t>
    void stacks<t>::display()
    {
            for(int i=top;i>=0;i--)
            cout<<stack[i]<<" ";
```

```
            cout<<endl;
      }
            template<class t>
      int stacks<t>::isEmpty()
      {
            if(top==-1)
            return 1;
            else
            return 0;
      }
int main()
{
int n,n1;
stacks<int> s1;
clrscr();
if(s1.isEmpty())
cout<<"Stack is empty"<<endl;
else
cout<<"Stack is not empty";
s1.push(10);
s1.push(5);
//s1.push(7);
s1.push(14);
cout<<"Total number of elements in stack are:
"<<s1.count_elements()<<endl;
s1.push(90);
//s1.push(299);
cout<<" Element(s) in the stack are:"<<endl;
s1.display();
n=s1.pop();
```

```
cout<<" Element pop is "<<n<<endl;
getch();
return 0;
}
```

5.4.2 Dynamic stack using template

```
#include<iostream.h>
#include<conio.h>
//using namespace std;

const int size=5;
template <class t>
class stacks
{
    t stack[size];
    int top;
    public:
            stacks()
            {
                    top=-1;
            }
        int push(t);
        t pop();
        int isempty();
        void display();
        int count_elements();
};
```

```
template<class t>
 int stacks<t>::count_elements()
  {
  int cnt=0,t1=top;
  while(t1>=0)
  {
  cnt++;
  t1--;
  }
  return cnt;
 }



            template<class t>
            int stacks<t>::push(int element)
            {
                   if(top==(size-1))
                   {
                          cout<<"overflow element not entered\n";
                          return 0;
                   }
                   else
                   {
                      stack[++top]=element;
                   }
                 return 1;
            }
         template<class t>
            t stacks<t>::pop()
            {
```

```
            t a=stack[top];
            if(top==-1)
            {
            cout<<"underflow:\n";
            }
            else
            {
               a=stack[top--];

            }
           return a;
      }
          template<class t>
      void stacks<t>::display()
      {
            for(int i=top;i>=0;i--)
            cout<<stack[i]<<" ";
            cout<<endl;
      }
          template<class t>
      int stacks<t>::isempty()
      {
            if(top==-1)
            return 1;
            else
            return 0;
      }
int main()
{
int n,n1;
```

```
stacks<int> s1;
clrscr();
if(s1.isempty())
cout<<"stack is empty"<<endl;
else
cout<<"stack is not empty";
s1.push(10);
s1.push(5);
//s1.push(7);
//s1.push(14);
cout<<"total number of elements in stack are: "<<s1.count_elements()<<endl;
s1.push(90);
//s1.push(299);
cout<<" element(s) in the stack are:"<<endl;
s1.display();
n=s1.pop();
cout<<" element pop is "<<n<<endl;
n=s1.pop();
cout<<" element pop is "<<n<<endl;
n=s1.pop();
cout<<" element pop is "<<n<<endl;
if(s1.isempty())
cout<<"stack under flow"<<endl;
else
{
n=s1.pop();
cout<<" element pop is "<<n<<endl;
}
getch();
```

```
return 0;
}
```

5.5 Application of stack

Stack is one of the data structures that are widely utilized in various applications. Users are using this data structure explicitly or implicitly. For instance, in non-recursive traversal of the tree this data structure is explicitly used. In the recursion, it is implicitly used by the user. In addition, stack is utilized in the application such as parenthesis matching, infix to postfix conversion, evaluation of complex expression. These applications of the stack have been discussed in the following sub-section in detail.

5.5.1 Parenthesis matching

Parenthesis matching has much significance in the evaluation of mathematical expression. Stack is widely used in the parenthesis matching. We have already learned in mathematics that the order of closing the bracket is depended on the order they have opened. The bracket that is opened first is closed in the last. It is illustrated with the help of following example.

2+ [4-9+1-{23*5-(54+12) +90/15} +98]

In the given example '('is opened at the end, accordingly it has to be closed first. Similarly, it is to be applied on the other brackets. It is equally significant that the bracket opened is also closed.

Otherwise, this will also leads to the parenthesis mismatch. In brief, the followings are to be examined for correctness of parenthesis:

i. Brackets are opened and closed in the correct sequence.

ii. Numbers of open brackets have the correspondingly closing brackets.

iii. Closing bracket should not be more that the brackets opened.

To accomplish the above objectives, stack can be extremely useful. To evaluate any expression, we consider it made of operator and operand. '+', '-', '*', etc. are known as operator whereas bracket is known as operand. We scan the given expression, character by character; stack pushes the brackets that are having the openings. Once it encounters the closing bracket, it pops from the stack. The bracket that is received should have the similarity with the closing bracket. If it is the matching opening of the closing brackets then it checks the other element. In case of non-match program terminates at this point itself and flashes the suitable message related to mismatch

We have discussed two functions based on brackets.

i. Bracket checking.
ii. Expression evaluation

In the bracket checking program, each brackets are given priority. In the program, it is examined that brackets with the higher priority is not replacing the bracket of lower priority. In other terms '('should not come before '['or '{'. Various possibilities that may take place with the parenthesis mismatching have been illustrated in the figure 5-4.

In our program, we would scan from the beginning of the expression, character by character. Once the opening bracket is encountered, we will push it into the stack. Once the closing bracket is encountered, the top element of the stack will be pop (). This item will be checked with the closing brackets, if it is correct matching then we will proceed further otherwise we terminate here itself and the error message will be shown the user.

To meet the case of extra opening bracket, stack is checked, if no item in the expression, whoever, if the stack is not empty then it is the case of extra opening bracket. Similarly, if the closing bracket is encountered and the stack is empty, it is the case of extra closing brackets. All these cases have been considered in the following figure 5-4.

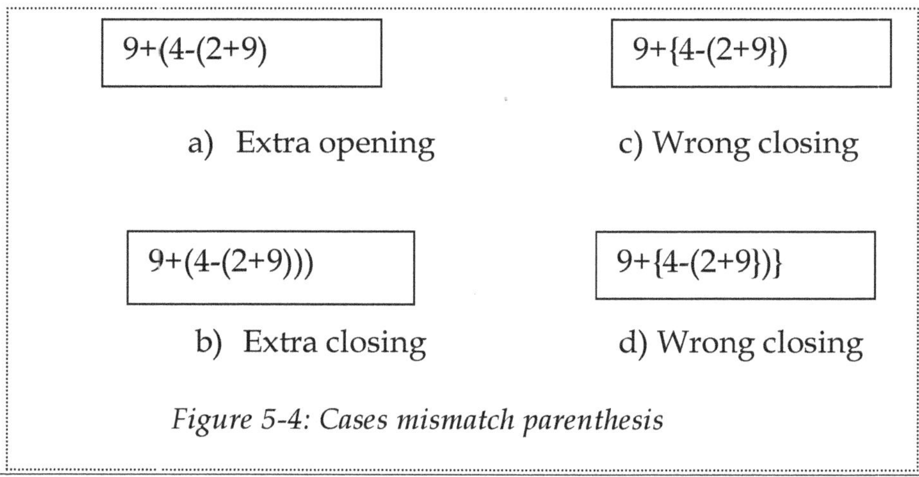

Figure 5-4: Cases mismatch parenthesis

To evaluate the expression considering the various cases discussed above, we have used the dynamic stack (linked stack) that was previously created by us. Program is discussed in the following example.

```
#include<dyn.h>
class appl
{
public:
void parenth(char*); // function to match the parenthesis
int open_brack(char); // To determine whether the opening of a bracket
int close_brack(char); // To determine whether the closing of a bracket

int matching(char,char); // To examine that opening bracket has the ......
                        // corresponding closing brackets
};
int appl::matching(char sym, char expr)
 {
 int ans=0;      // initially, mismatch
 if((sym=='(' && expr==')')||(sym=='{' && expr=='}')||(sym=='[' &&
expr==']'))
 ans=1;          // Matching exist
 return ans;
 }
 int appl::open_brack(char b)
  {
  int flag=0;
  if(b=='(' || b=='{'||b=='[')
  flag=1;
  return flag;
```

```
}
int appl::close_brack(char b)
{
int flag=0;
if(b==')' || b=='}' ||b==']')
flag=1;
return flag;
}
void appl::parenth(char expr[])
{
int i=0;
stacks<char> s1;
while(expr[i])
{
if(open_brack(expr[i]))
s1.push(expr[i]);
else
{
if(close_brack(expr[i]))
{
if(!s1.empty())
{
char symbol=s1.pop();
 if(!matching(symbol,expr[i]))
   {
   cout<<" Not a matching parenthesis"<<endl;
   return;
   // break;
   }
   // symbol='$';
```

```
}// empty
else
{
cout<<"Extra closing"<<endl;
return;
}// else of empty
} // close brack
} //else
 i++;
}      // while
if(s1.empty())
 cout<<" Brackets are matching"<<endl;
 else
 cout<<" Non Mathcing Brackets"<<endl;
}
int main()
{
clrscr();
appl a1;
char x[]="[(3+(9-4)+]";
a1.parenth(x);
getch();
return 0;
}
```

5.5.2 Conversion of infix to postfix

We evaluate the expression to know the value of any mathematical expression. For human being the widely used notation is known as infix notation in which operator is arranged in the middle. We as a human being are much comfortable with the infix notation. However, computing the infix notation in computer poses tremendous challenge. Computer can use other notations for instance, pre-fix or postfix notations. However, human being is comfortable in writing the infix expressions. Consequently, there is a need to change the expression written in infix notation into prefix or postfix notation. Stack is widely used to convert the infix notation into prefix or postfix notation.

To evaluate the expression, wide varieties of notations are existing and widely used. It is worth to understand that any expression is consist of two components namely operator and operand. Consider the following expressions

3+6*5-56/28

We can classify them as

Operator: +, *, -, /

Operand: 3, 6, 5, 56, 28

To evaluate these expressions, various types of notations exist and their usage is decided based on the appropriateness of computation.

5.5.3 Case Study Based on stack

An airbase has the automatic parking system for the airplane that is used by the airplanes after the daylong flying. These aircrafts are parked one behind the other and the lane where the aircraft is taxing is sufficient to accommodate only one aircraft at a time for moving and parking (Refer the figure 5-5). Consequently, the aircraft that is parked at the last will go for the flying first. In each lane, only fixed number of aircraft can be parked. There are total 3 lanes (lane1, lane2 and lane3) and each of them is having the capacity of 4, 5, 4 respectively. Diagram of parking area has been illustrated in the following figure 5-4.

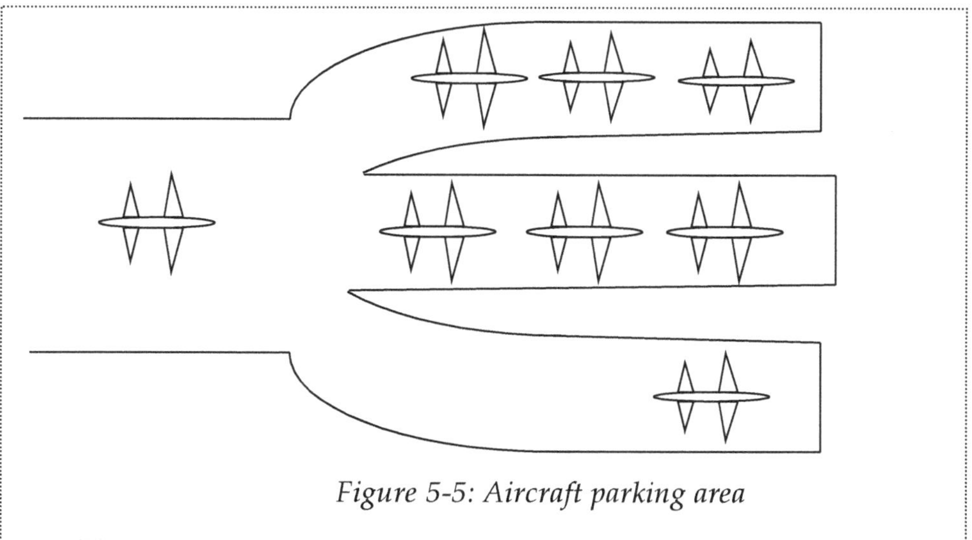

Figure 5-5: Aircraft parking area

Initially, airplanes parking start with one lane, if the lane is full then they are parked in the second lane. Aircraft are parked first in lane1 once it is full to its capacity then the aircraft are parked in lane2; so on and so forth. You have to design a program to accomplish the following objective.

1. To park the aircraft in the respective lanes.
2. Determine the number of aircraft parked in a particular lane.
3. Change the lane of the new aircraft arriving, if the previous lane is full to its capacity.
4. Determine the total number of aircrafts in all the lanes.
5. Generate the suitable message, if the parking lane are full to their capacities and more aircraft (s) are requesting the filled lane for parking.

Exercise

A. **Descriptive answers**

1. Write a stack program, in which top is initialize with 0 and finally, write down the other function such as push and pop.
2. Discuss the drawback, if any, of initializing the stack top from 0.
3. Can we modify the static stack, so that the value of its size is supplied by the user at run time. Explain your answer.
4. Reverse the content of the stack by using
   a) One Stack
   b) By using two stack
5. Write a program to find out whether the string is palindrome or not (Use stack).
6. How we can implement the stack using the queue based approach (If the concept pertaining to queue is not known, refer the next chapter and its implementation).
7. Is it possible to remove the in-between element(s) from the stack? Write your views/comments along with the method, if you feel that elements can be removed from in-between in stack.
8. Write down a large number and store it in the stack, digit by digit. For instance, if number to be stored is 95487245 then it should be pushed in the stack in the following sequence 9, 5, 4, 8, 7, 2, 4, 5.

9. In the above program, find out the sum of all the digits that are pushed inside the stack.
10. Write a program that stores two large numbers. Sum these two numbers using stack.
11. Accept the string; push this string character by character in the stack. Sequence to push the character should be the reverse order of their arrival. For instance, if "Push" is to be inserted then insertion sequence should be h, s, u, P.
12. Extend the above program by finding out the substring from the string pushed into the stack. Substring is the partial string that consists of the part of the string and may be located at the starting, in between or at the last of the string. For instance, if the word inserted is 'Ramayana' then word such as 'Rama' ; 'maya' are its various substring, existing at various position within the given string.
13. Write a function of the stack that will be utilized by us to determine the total number of element(s) in the stack. To accomplish this task, define the:
    a) Count variable as member of the stack class.
    b) Without including the count as data member.
14. How will you define the size of the dynamic stack? Discuss various constraints associated with the size of the stack.
15. How the underflow condition is dealt in dynamic stack? Briefly, discuss various conditions associated with it.

B. **Correct/Modify the given code**

(Assume that variable are declared, and necessary variable(s) are in place)

1. In the given stack top is initialized with 0. To push the element in the stack the following code is written:

```
int push(int element)
{
if(top==size)
cout<<"stack is full";
return;
else
stack[++top]=element;
}
```

2. To pop the element from the stack the following code is written;

```
int pop()
{
int x=stack[top];
if(top<0)
{
cout<<"stack underflow";
}
return x;
}
```

3. To pop the element from the stack the following code is written;

```
int pop()
{
```

```
int x=stack[top--];
if(top>size)
{
cout<<"stack underflow";
}
return x;
}
```

4. In the display function, following code has been written:

```
void display()
{
int beg=0;
while(beg<=top)
cout<<stack[beg++]<<endl;
}
```

```
void display()
{
int t=top;
while(t>=0)
cout<<stack[t++]<<endl;
}
```

After correcting both the functions (if any), which version of them will be preferred by you. Justify.

5. In the dynamic stack, the code written is:

```
void push(int element)
{
snode * temp;
```

```
temp=new snode;   // creation of a new node
snode->data=element;       // assigning the numeric value
snode->next=NULL;          // pointing the next to the NUL
top=temp;   // assigning the top to this new position
}
```

6. In the dynamic stack, to pop the element from the stack the following code is written

```
int pop()
{
int x=top->data;
if(top==NULL)
cout<<" Stack underflow"<<endl;
return;
delete top;   // Remove the top node
top=top->next;       // move the top to the previous position
}
```

7. In a stack based template, pop function is written; find out the possible problem that may occur in this code.

```
t pop()
{
t x=top->data;
if(top==NULL)
cout<<" Stack underflow"<<endl;
delete top;      // Remove the top node
top=top->next;          // move the top to the previous position
}
```

Chapter 6
Queue

Chapter Objective

- Defining queue and various operations permitted on a queue.
- Creation of a static and dynamic queue.
- Traversal of a queue.
- Insertion and removal of items from a queue
- Circular queue.
- Creating the queue using template
- Application of a queue

6 Queue

In the stack, insertion and removal of the item was permitted only from one end, that end was known as top. Consequently, item inserted at the last was coming out first. To ensure that the items are removed in the order they were inserted, this can be achieved with the help of queue.

Queue is a data structure that can be considered as open from both the ends. Insertion is accomplished from the rear end, whereas removal of the item is taking place on the other end known as front. Same is illustrated in the following figure.

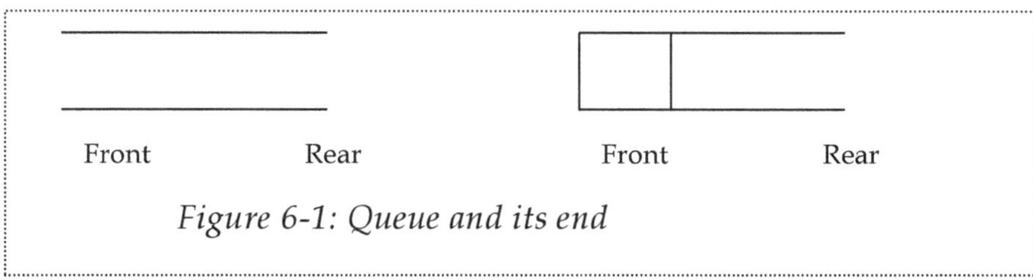

Figure 6-1: Queue and its end

6.1 Static and dynamic Queues

Static and dynamic queue are two types of categorization of the queue that is based on the method of creation. Dynamic queue is having the advantage of unlimited size however, suffers from the performance issues during the creation time. We have discussed both the types of queue in the following sub-section.

6.1.1 Static Queue

In queue, elements are inserted from the end known as rear, once the items are inserted, corresponding to that rear pointer moves from the front towards the rear end. Once the rear has reached to the extreme end (capacity of the queue) then more items cannot be inserted. If we try to insert more items in a queue then it is known as overflow.

Insertion of the item inside the queue is also known as enqueue.

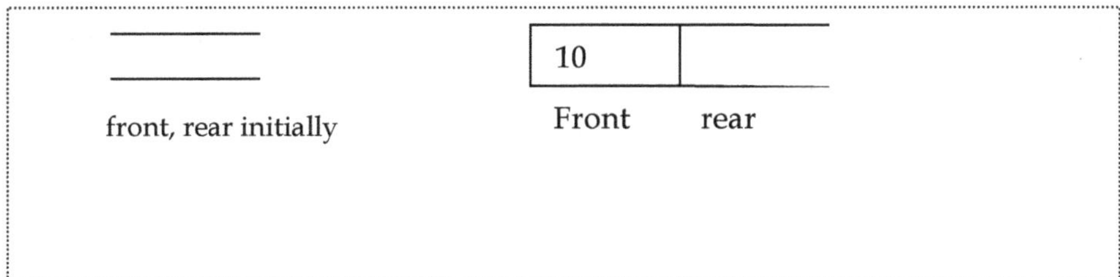

Figure 6-2: insertion into a queue

Initially, front and rear has been initialized with -1. Therefore, they are not pointing to any of the index of queue. Once the first item is inserted than first is initialize with 0, correspondingly, rear is also incremented. Enqueue of items governs the position/movement of rear index of a queue. During insertion, rear can move maximum up-to its set limit of the size. Once rear is reached to the last position, insertion of any further elements will leads in overflow.

Complete working of inserting the elements in the queue has been illustrated in the following figure.

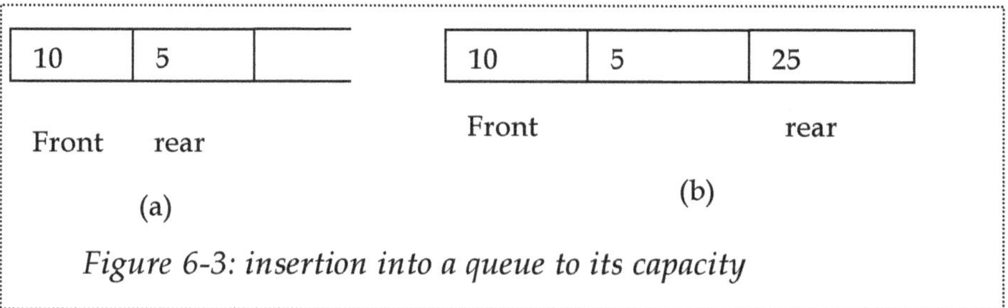

Figure 6-3: insertion into a queue to its capacity

In the static queue, first and foremost requirement is to define the size of the queue so that the size needed for the queue can be allocated at the compile time itself. During insertion of each element, rear is checked to know whether items can be inserted or it is already at its optimum level. If it has not reached the optimum position the item is inserted into the queue, otherwise suitable message (queue is full) is generated.

```
const int size=5;
class Q
{
    int front, rear;
    int queue[size];
    public:
    Q( );
    // To insert the element in the queue
    void enqueue(int);
    // To remove the element from the queue
    int dequeue();
    // To display the elements in the queue
```

```
    void display();
    //To investigate, if queue is empty
    int isEmpty();
    // To count the number of elements in the queue
    int count();
    // To shift the front to the 0th index
    void shiftElements();
.....// function to find out the first element, without changing the first
//order
int FrontElement();
};
Q::Q()
  {
   front=rear=-1;
  }

   void Q::enqueue(int element)
  {
   if(((rear-front)==(size-1))&&(rear==(size-1)))
   {
     cout<<"overflow element cannot be entered\n";
     return;
   }
   else if(front==-1)
   {
   queue[++rear]=element;
   front=0;
   }
    else if(rear<(size-1))
     {
```

```
    queue[++rear]=element;
    }

  }
```

6.1.1.1 Display of queue Elements

To display the queue elements, it's worth making use of front and rear index which denotes the range where data elements are lying. During the display of queue element(s), we have to start from the front and reach up-to rear. During this process, front or rear should not get change. To accomplish this objective, we can use the local variables as depicted in the following example.

```
void Q::display()
        {
        if(front>=0) //if any item in the queue
        for(int i=front;i<=rear;i++)
        cout<<queue[i]<<" ";
        }
```

6.1.1.2 Removing elements from a queue

Queue works on the First in first out order. This implies that element inserted first will be removed first. Since, queue is having two ends (front and rear), it removes the elements from the front, consequently, front will move towards the rear. Before, removing any item from the queue it is ascertained that queue is not empty. Element removed from the queue is stored in the temporary variable and same can be returned. Complete function of dequeue has been shown in the following example.

```
int Q::dequeue()
   {
    int a;
    if((rear==-1)||(front==-1))
        {
          cout<<"underflow:\n";
          return 0;
        }
          else
          {
           a=queue[front];
           front++;
          if(front>rear)//after removal if queue is empty
           {
             front=rear=-1;
           }
          }
          return a;
   }
```

6.1.1.3 Counting number of elements

To count the number of elements in a queue, we have to start from the front. Since front may be at 0th index or may be away from it, if some of the items are removed (dequeue). Counting should continue up-to the rear element as it denotes the position up-to where the element exist in the queue.

```
// Program to count the number of elements in the queue
int Q::count()
{
int c=0;
int f,r;
f=front,r=rear;// initialize f with front and r with rear
while(f++<=r) //execute the loop till last element is not reached
{
c++;    //count the elements
}
return c;        // return the count
}
```

6.1.1.4 To find out the first element of the Queue

This function can determine the first element of the queue without changing the first index. Once the element(s) of the queue are displayed, it will again display all the element(s) including the first element that has been returned by the FirstElement() function. Code of the function is enumerated in the following example:

```
// Program : Write the program to determine the first element of the
queue without changing the first index.
int firstelement()
 {
if(first==0)
{
```

```
cout<<" queue is empty";
return 0;
}
int x=queue[first];      // Store the first element of the stack
return x;       // return the first element
}
```

6.1.1.5 Main function

Functions defined in the preceding sub-section have been performing their objectives. To call them, we can make use of main function, where they will be called as illustrated in the following example.

```
int main()
{
clrscr();
Q q1;
q1.enqueue(90);
q1.enqueue(5);
q1.enqueue(78);
q1.enqueue(35);
q1.enqueue(10);
q1.enqueue(14);
cout<<" Total number of elements "<<q1.count()<<endl;
q1.display();
cout<<"Dequeue item: "<<q1.dequeue()<<endl;
cout<<"Dequeue item: "<<q1.dequeue()<<endl;
cout<<" Total number of elements "<<q1.count()<<endl;
q1.display();
```

```
if(q1.isEmpty())
  cout<<"Queue is empty"<<endl;
 else
 cout<<"Not empty"<<endl;
getch();
return 0;
}
```

6.1.1.6 Limitation of queue

Queue suffers from the major limitation due to dequeue operation that is taking place. In dequeue front is moved towards the rear. Although, space will exist but user will not able to utilize that space, since front is moved ahead. To overcome this limitation, elements can be moved from their middle position to the new position starting from the first index. Consequently, front and rear value needs to be changed.

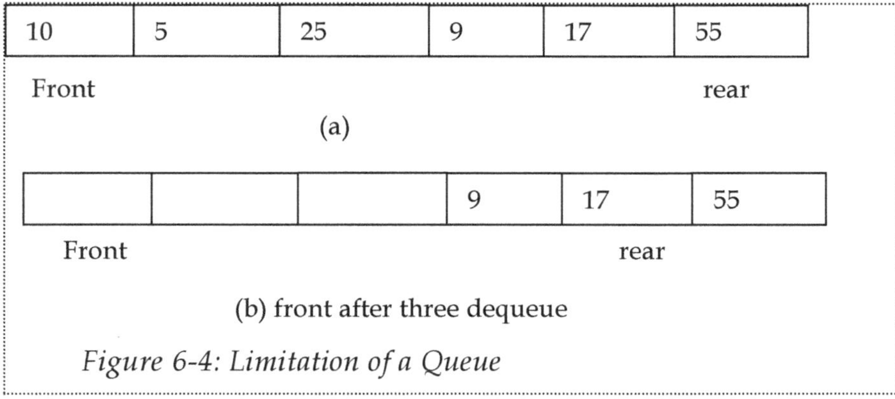

Figure 6-4: Limitation of a Queue

Shifting operation may be preferred for the small size of list;

however for the queue of huge size shifting element will be costly affair and will need huge resources for shifting the elements.

```
// To shift the Element after dequeue
void Q::shiftElements()
{
int f=front,t=-1;
while(f<=rear)
 {
 queue[++t]=queue[f++];       // initialize the front member in the 0th index
 }
 front=0;
 rear=t;
 cout<<endl<<"Items shifted in the Q"<<endl;
```

6.1.2 Dynamic Queue

In the dynamic queue, nodes are created similar to that of link list node. In dynamic queue there is no need for testing the full condition, as it is controlled with the resource in use. However, empty condition need to be tested similar to previous case.

Structure of the dynamic queue has been defined with the help of following class. Various functions along with their objectives have been given in the following program.

```
#include<conio.h>
#include<iostream.h>
//Structure of queue node
class qnode
```

```
{
public:
int info;
qnode *next;
};
//class for queue
class queue
{
//definining the front and rear pointer
qnode *front,*rear;
public:
//constructor for queue
queue();
//function to enqueue in dynamic queue
void enqueue(int);
//function to deque in the queue
int dequeue();
//To display the items in the queue
void display();
```

Initially, there are no elements in the queue; therefore, front and rear have been initialized with NULL. To accomplish the task of initialization, constructor has been used.

To enqueue the element, two cases have been considered:

- No element(s) in the queue.
- There is one or more element(s) in the queue.

Once, there are no element, at that point of time, front and rear both will be NULL. Therefore, while inserting the first element, rear is created and allocated the space. In this case, front and rear will be pointing to the same element.

In the second condition, element will be inserted at the rear. Consider this node as temp, connect the rear to this temp and move the rear to this last position. Same has been depicted in the following function.

```
// Function to enqueue the element in the queue
void queue::enqueue(int x)
{
if(rear==NULL)          // If queue is empty
 {
 rear=new qnode;
 rear->next=NULL;
 rear->info=x;
  front=rear;
 }
else                    // if more than one element are in the queue
 {
  qnode *temp;
temp=new qnode;
temp->info=x;
temp->next=NULL;
rear->next=temp;
rear=temp;      // moving the rear to new last position
}
}
```

To dequeue the elements from the queue, the element first inserted is taken out first. In the given queue, during dequeue the first element is to be removed from the queue. Before dequeue the three cases may occur:

i. Queue is empty.
ii. Queue has only one element
iii. Queue have more than one element

If the queue is empty then no item is removed and unsuccessful flag (0) is returned.

In the second case, item is removed from the front. As a result, the queue will be empty. To reflect this change, first and rear has to point to the NULL.

In the third case, where the queue has more than one element, front has to be moved to the next position whereas the previous front that is stored in the temp has to be deleted to free the space that was earlier occupied by the front pointer.

```
// Function to dequeue the element from the queue
int queue::dequeue()
{
int x=front->info;
if(front==NULL)
 {
 cout<<"Queue is empty"<<endl;
 }
 else
 {
```

```
qnode *temp=front;
if(front==rear)
{
front=NULL;
rear=NULL;
delete temp;
return x;
}
front=front->next;
 }
return x;
}
```

During enqueue items are inserted, whereas in the dequeue items are removed from the queue. At the end there are some items that are left in the queue. To witness the change that is reflected, we can use the function display. This function demonstrates the items currently in the dynamic queue.

To display the items, we start from the front and continue to access the node till we are not reaching up-to the end of the queue. The end of queue is represented by the rear.

```
void queue::display()
{
qnode *current;
if(front==NULL)
{
cout<<"queue is empty"<<endl;
return;
```

```
}
 current=front;
  while(current!=rear)
 {
 cout<<current->info<<endl;
current=current->next;
}
cout<<current->info<<endl;
}
```

The isEmpty () is one of the other functions that has the significant role in this program. It can supports both the enqueue and dequeue. During enqueue, it can be used to check whether the queue is empty or not. Correspondingly, the next course of action can be decided.

This function also plays a significant role while calling the dequeue function. We can include the function in the isEmpty() condition. If the queue is empty then dequeue operation will not occur. isEmpty() function has been defined in the following program.

```
int queue::isEmpty()
 {
 int flag=0;
 if(front==NULL)
  {
  flag=1;
  }
  return flag;
  }
```

All the above discussed function can be called as they are shown in the following main function.

```
// Main function to call the queue function
void main()
 {
 clrscr();
 queue q1;
q1.enqueue(40);
q1.enqueue(27);
if(q1.isEmpty())
 {
 cout<<"Q is empty"<<endl;
 }
//q1.enqueue(12);
//q1.enqueue(64);
q1.display();
int j;
j=q1.dequeue();
cout<<" element deleted "<<j<<endl;
q1.display();
j=q1.dequeue();
cout<<" element deleted "<<j<<endl;
if(q1.isEmpty())
 {
 cout<<"Q is empty"<<endl;
 }
q1.display();
j=q1.dequeue();
cout<<" element deleted "<<j<<endl;
```

```
q1.display();
getch();
}
```

6.2 Queue using template

Dynamic queue has the wide usage in data structure. It can be applied for several data types. The program that has been discussed is using the integer data type. If we have to use the character data type, enumerated program need to be modified. Accordingly, program need to be modified for the various other needs. One of the major uses of queue is in traversal of a tree, particularly for the breadth wise traversal of the tree.

To address such issues, so that the data type can be changed on the fly, we can use the queue template. Program that illustrates the use of template type of queue has been given as follows:

```
#include<conio.h>
#include<iostream.h>
//Structure ofqueue node
template<class t>
class qnode
{
public:
t info;
qnode<t> *next;
};
//class for queue
```

```
template<class t>
class queue
{
//defining the front and rear pointer
qnode<t> *front,*rear;
public:
//constructor for queue
queue();
//function to enqueue in dynamic queue
void enqueue(t);
//function to deque in the queue
t dequeue();
//To display the items in the queue
void display();
//To check for queue empty or not
int isEmpty();
};
template<class t>
queue<t>::queue()
{
front=NULL;
rear=NULL;
}
template<class t>
void queue<t>::enqueue(t x)
{
if(rear==NULL)
 {
 rear=new qnode<t>;
 rear->next=NULL;
```

```
rear->info=x;
 front=rear;
}
else
{
 qnode<t> *temp;
temp=new qnode<t>;
temp->info=x;
temp->next=NULL;
rear->next=temp;
rear=temp;
}
}
template<class t>
void queue<t>::display()
{
qnode<t> *current;
 if(front==NULL)
{
cout<<"queue is empty"<<endl;
return;
}
current=front;
 while(current!=rear)
{
cout<<current->info<<endl;
current=current->next;
}
cout<<current->info<<endl;
}
```

```
template<class t>
t queue<t>::dequeue()
{
t x=front->info;
if(front==NULL)
 {
 cout<<"Queue is empty"<<endl;
 }
 else
 {
 qnode<t> *temp=front;
 front=front->next;
 if(front==NULL)// if no node in the bst
 rear=NULL; // point the rear also to the NULL
 delete temp; // Delete the node
 }
 return x;
 }
 template<class t>
 int queue<t>::isEmpty()
  {
  int flag=0;
  if(front==NULL)
   {
   flag=1;
   }
   return flag;
   }

void main()
```

```
{
clrscr();
queue<int> q1;
q1.enqueue(40);
q1.enqueue(27);
if(q1.isEmpty())
{
cout<<"Q is empty"<<endl;
}
//q1.enqueue(12);
//q1.enqueue(64);
q1.display();
int j;
j=q1.dequeue();
cout<<" element deleted "<<j<<endl;
q1.display();
j=q1.dequeue();
cout<<" element deleted "<<j<<endl;
if(q1.isEmpty())
{
cout<<"Q is empty"<<endl;
}
q1.display();
j=q1.dequeue();
cout<<" element deleted "<<j<<endl;
q1.display();
getch();
}
```

6.3 Circular queue

As previously mentioned, queue suffers from a limitation due to the movement of front towards rear, therefore empty space are not utilized. Even though shifting has been suggested as one of the method to remove the empty space before the front of the queue, however, its overhead cannot be ignored if the data that need to be shifted are huge. To address this issue, circular queue is used.

In circular queue, items can be inserted till front is not encountered. In circular queue, index is re-initialized with zero once it attains the maximum value. This is accomplished with the usage of mod operator. We are aware that mod is widely used in calculating the remainder and this remainder will not go more than the value of its right hand value. For instance, if the size of the queue is 4 then due to the usage of remainder method, the potential values will lie in the range of 0 to 3.

To insert the element in the queue, we have created the function insert. This function accepts one argument as integer type and does not return a value. To insert the values, we increment the rear. Once rear is incremented, it is always examined with the front, so that it should not overlap the value (does not insert the value more than the capacity of the queue). Complete function has been enumerated in the following example.

```
// Program to insert the item in a circular queue.
void insert(int &n)
        {
                if((rear+1)%size!=front)
```

```
            {
             rear=(rear+1)%size;
            queue[rear]=n;
            if(front<0)
             front=0;
            }
            else
            {
              cout<<"Queue overflow, element not inserted:\n";

            }
        }
```

Once the elements are inserted, then the other major task is to remove the items from the queue. Before removing the item from the queue, it is examined that queue is not empty. During removal of the item, it is removed from the front of the queue. Correspondingly, front head towards the rear index. Here, we have considered the two significant cases of queue:

- That queue has only one element (front and rear at the same position).
- There is more than one element in the queue.

Both the cases have been considered in the remove() function discussed as follows:

```
// Program to remove the items from the queue
 int remove()
        {
```

```
int a=0;
if(!empty())
{
 if(front==rear)                    //only one element in the queue
  {
   a=queue[front];
   front=rear=-1;
   }
   else
   {              // More than one element in the queue
    a=queue[front];
    front=(front+1)%size;
   }
}
else
{
  cout<<"Queue underflow:\n";
}
return a;
}
```

The other significant function is empty function. This function ascertains whether the queue is empty or not. If the queue is empty it returns 1 else returns 0.

```
// function to check if any item in the list or empty
 int empty()
        {
                if(front==-1)
                return 1;
```

```
        else
        return 0;
    }
```

Finally, it is worth discussing the display function. Although, it appears to be simple function as we have learned from various other display function. Due to circular queue is involved, where value ranges in fixed limit. A great care need to be observed, to fulfill the cited definition of the circular queue. In the discussed function, we have started from the front position and continued till we have not reached to the tail (last element). Once last element is reached, loop is terminated and the remaining item is displayed. Before, displaying the element(s), it is ascertained whether the queue is empty or not. If the queue is empty, no more items are displayed, instead message of this regard is displayed (that the queue is empty).

```
void display()
    {
        if(empty())
        {
         cout<<"Empty queue:\n";
        }
        else
        {
          int r,f;
          r=rear;
          f=front;
          while(f!=r)
```

```
                {
                        cout<<queue[f]<<endl;
                        f=(f+1)%size;
                }
                cout<<queue[f]<<endl;
            }
        }
```

Function discussed above can be included in the class as shown in the following program. These class members can be called by the class instance from the main function. Calling of various members has been illustrated in the following program.

```
#include<iostream.h>
#include<conio.h>

const int size=4;          // Size of the queue
class CQ
{
    int queue[size];
    int front,rear;
    public:
            CQ()
            {
                    front=-1;
                    rear=-1;
            }
        void insert(const int &);
void display();
void remove();
```

```
int empty();
};
int main()
{
 CQ q1;           // Creating instance of the queue
clrscr();
q1.insert(10);  //inserting the element in the queue
q1.insert(45);
q1.insert(90);
q1.insert(21);
cout<<"Elements in the queue are "<<endl;
q1.display();   // display of the queue
q1.remove();
q1.remove();
q1.remove();
cout<<"Elements after removal"<<endl;
q1.display();
q1.insert(17);
q1.insert(56);
q1.insert(34);
cout<<"Elements in the queue are "<<endl;
q1.display();
q1.remove();
q1.remove();
cout<<"Elements after removal"<<endl;
q1.display();
getch();
return 0;
}
```

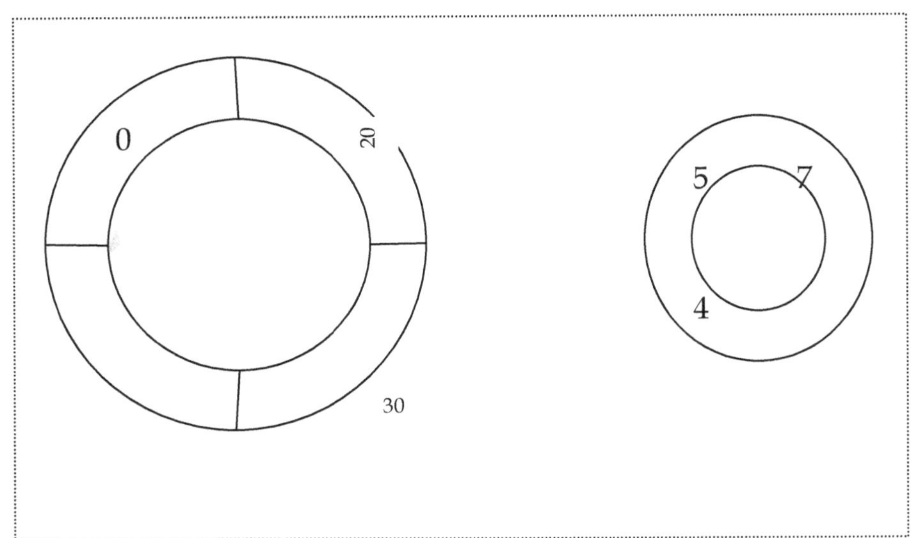

6.4 Priority queue

In our daily life, we do not follow the first come first serve sequence always. Instead, we have to assigned priority to one service over the other. For instance, at the toll booth, police vehicle, ambulance, etc. do not need to pay the taxes, at the same time they are given more priority over others. Similarly, there are many more instances where one task is getting more priority over others.

To resolve the tasks, where the priority of one task is more over other cannot be addressed by normal queue. Instead, in such cases we use priority queue. In the priority queue, elements having higher priority are moved to front instead of the time of their arrival. This arrangement ensures that the elements with higher priority are served first. To achieve this objective, all the elements are also having their priority. Before they are served, if any element with the higher priority arrives displaces them at the back. Such queue where the elements are arranged in the order of priority instead of arrival time, such type of queue is known priority queue.

Priority queue can be implemented with the help of heap. Complete implementation has been enumerated in section............

6.5 Case Study based on Queue

In a hospital there are a number of department exist which are offering the specialized treatment of their department. The major department that are existing are dermatology, cardiology, Gynecology, Pathology, etc. To get the treatment patient visits to the relevant department there he is allotted a token number. Allotment of taken number is purely based on the time of arrival. Separate queue is maintained for the particular department.

Hospital maintains the following information about the patient.

S.No	Information	Type of information
1.	Patientid	Stores in alphanumeric
2.	Social_id	Numeric value
3.	Occupation	Character value

4.	Disease_reported	Character value
5.	Treatment prescribed	Character value
6.	Previous treated	Yes/No
7.	Token number	Number
8.	dateOfVisit	Date

Based on the above information, solve the following challenges the hospital has to encounter.

1. Allot the unique token number to the patient.
2. Store all the information related to the above field.
3. Total number of patient in a particular queue.
4. How many patients waiting in the hospital.
5. How many patients arrive in a day (you can take the average of week or month)?
6. Which type of data structure is preferred by you? Explain its advantage of any other data structure which you may consider near appropriate.

EXERCISE

A. **Short answer type questions**

1. How to define the queue? What are the different operations that are possible on queues?
2. How many ends are used to insert and remove the elements from the queue? How this phenomenon is implemented in the queue?
3. What are the major drawbacks of queue? How these drawbacks are addressed?
4. What are the various methods with the help of which we can overcome the drawback of queues?
5. Implement the function that counts the number of element in the queue?
6. How circular queue is different from the normal queue?
7. How the circular feature in a circular queue is ensured in the given program?
8. During the insertion of elements in the circular queue, what are major considerations that need to be addressed?
9. Write a function to search an element from the circular queue?
10. Write a program to reverse the stack elements using queue?
11. Write a program to concatenate the element of two queues using operator (+) overloading.

12. Write a program to compare the two arrays on the basis of element count, by using operator (>) overloading.
13. Write a function to implement the priority while inserting the elements in the queue.
14. In a circular queue, how to ensure that once all the elements are dequeue then it is pointing to the Null condition.

B. **Correct the code, if any**

1. In the given queue, front and rear has been initialized with 0. Insert function of the queue has been given as:

```
void insert(int x)
{
if(rear+1==size)
cout<<"queue overflow"<<endl;
++rear=x;
}
```

2. In the circular queue, front and rear has been initialized with -1. Insert function of the queue has been given as:

```
void insert(int x)
{
if(rear+1==size)
cout<<"queue overflow"<<endl;
rear+1=x;
}
```

3. In the circular queue, front and rear has been initialized with -1. Insert function of the queue has been given as:

```
void insert(int x)
{
if(rear+1==front)
cout<<"queue overflow"<<endl;
rear+1=x;
}
```

4. In dynamic queue, front and rear has been initialized with NULL. Correct the following code for enqueue.

```
void enqueue(int x)
{
if(front==rear)
{
front=new qnode;
front->data=x;
front->next=null;
}
else
{
qnode *temp;
temp=new qnode;
temp->data=x;
temp->next=null;
rear->next=temp;
}
```

5. In dynamic queue, front and rear has been initialized with NULL. Correct the following code for dequeue.

```
qnode* dequeue( )
{
if(front==rear)
{
cout<<"queue is empty";
```

```
}
else
{
qnode *temp;
temp=front;
rear=rear->next;
}
}
```

6. Is it possible to remove the item from the middle of the queue? True/False

7. In queue, inserting the first element and other element is to be considered in the same manner. True/False
8. What is the reason for using a "circular queue" instead of a regular one?

a) the running time of enqueue() is improved
b) reuse empty spaces
c) you can traverse all the elements more efficiently
d) None of the above

9. One difference between a queue and a stack is:

A. Queues require linked lists, but stacks do not.
B. Stacks require linked lists, but queues do not.
C. Queues use two ends of the structure; stacks use only one.
D. Stacks use two ends of the structure, queues use only one.

10. If the characters 'D', 'C', 'B', 'A' are placed in a queue (in that order), and then removed one at a time, in what order will

they be removed?

A. ABCD

B. ABDC

C. DCAB

D. DCBA

11. Suppose we have a circular array implementation of the queue class, with ten items in the queue stored at data[2] through data[11]. The current capacity is 42. Where does the insert method place the new entry in the array?

A. data[1]

B. data[2]

C. data[11]

D. data[12]

12. Consider the implementation of the Queue using a circular array. What goes wrong if we try to keep all the items at the front of a partially-filled array (so that data[0] is always the front).

A. The constructor would require linear time.

B. The getFront method would require linear time.

C. The insert method would require linear time.

D. The isEmpty method would require linear time.

13. In the linked list implementation of the queue class, where does the insert method place the new entry on the linked list?

A. At the head
B. At the tail
C. After all other entries those are greater than the new entry.
D. After all other entries those are smaller than the new entry.

14. In the circular array version of the Queue class, which operations require linear time for their worst-case behavior?
A. getFront
B. insert when the capacity has not yet been reached
C. isEmpty
D. None of these operations require linear time.

15. In the linked-list version of the Queue class, which operations require linear time for their worst-case behavior?
A. getFront
B. insert
C. isEmpty
D. None of these operations require linear time.

16. If data is a circular array of CAPACITY elements, and rear is an index into that array, what is the formula for the index after rear?
A. (rear % 1) + CAPACITY
B. rear % (1 + CAPACITY)
C. (rear + 1) % CAPACITY
D. rear + (1 % CAPACITY)

17. I have implemented the queue with a circular array, keeping track of front, rear, and Many Items (the number of items in the array). Suppose front is zero, and rear is one less than the current capacity. What can you tell me about manyItems?

A. manyItems must be zero.

B. manyItems must be equal to the current capacity.

C. count could be zero or the capacity, but no other values could occur.

D. None of the above.

18. I have implemented the queue with a linked list, keeping track of a front node and a rear node with two reference variables. Which of these reference variables will change during an insertion into a NONEMPTY queue?

A. Neither changes

B. Only front changes.

C. Only rear changes.

D. Both change.

19. Priority Queues Suppose getFront is called on a priority queue that has exactly two entries with equal priority. How is the return value of getFront selected?

A. One is chosen at random.

B. The one which was inserted first.

C. The one which was inserted most recently.

D. This can never happen (violates the precondition)

Chapter 7
Tree

Chapter Objective

- Defining tree and its terminology.
- Defining Binary search tree(BST) in particular.
- Creation of the BST using recursive and non-recursive method.
- Traversal in a BST using recursive and non-recursive method.
- Deletion a node from a BST
- Constructing the BST from the given traversal.
- Searching the element in a BST.
- Description of various methods to determine the height of a BST.
- To determine the mirror of a tree.

7 Tree

Broadly data structure can be categorized into two:

- Linear.
- Non-linear.

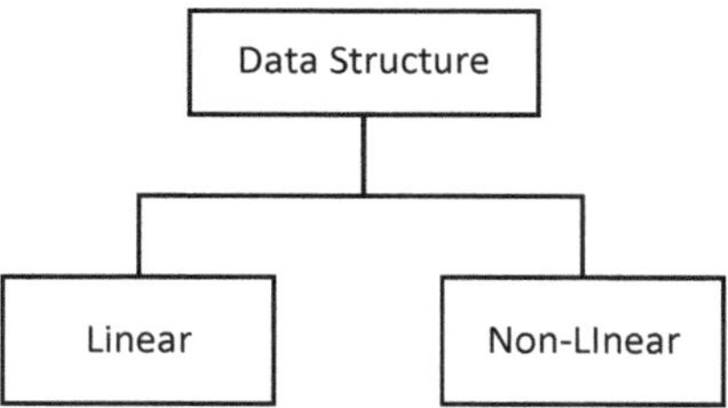

Figure 7-1: Types of data structure

All the topics discussed till now fall under the category of linear data structure. Stacks, Queue, Link list, etc. are the examples of linear data structure. A new data structure known as tree is the example of non-linear data structure. In non-linear data structure, data is arranged in parent-child relationship. Same has been demonstrated in the following figure.

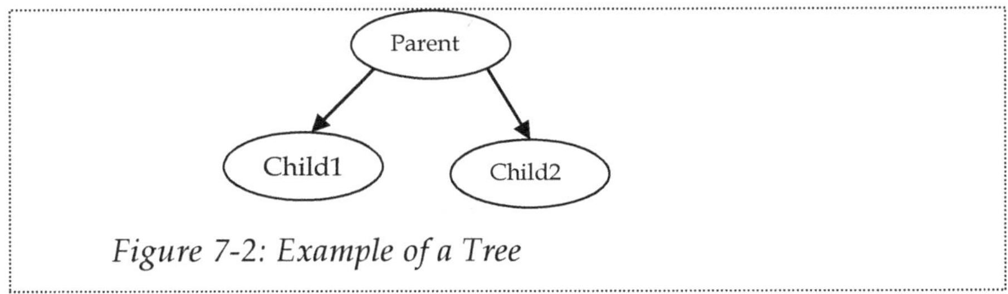

Figure 7-2: Example of a Tree

Trees categorization is determined by the maximum number of child that any parent can accommodate. However, a node may have less node than the maximum number of a node it can accommodate. Trees are termed based on their degree. For instance tree with degree '2' is termed as binary, tree of degree '3' is termed ternary, ...tree of degree 'n' is termed as n-ary tree. For this chapter, we have considered the binary tree only.

7.1 Basic terminology

Tree consist of various nodes, these nodes are arranged in parent and child relationship. The node from where other nodes originate that node is known as root. Node after the root node, if any node is derived then it is known as parent. Each node is acting as child of other node (except the root node). Therefore, tree can be defined as non linear data structure, organized in parent child relationship. Each child are again acting as a tree.

Before discussing the tree, it is worth discussing some of the terms that will be frequently used throughout our discussion.

Sibling: Children of same parent are known as siblings. In the tree, illustrated in the figure 7-3, the two nodes having the values 5 and 40 are siblings, since both of them are children of the same parent i.e. node 20.

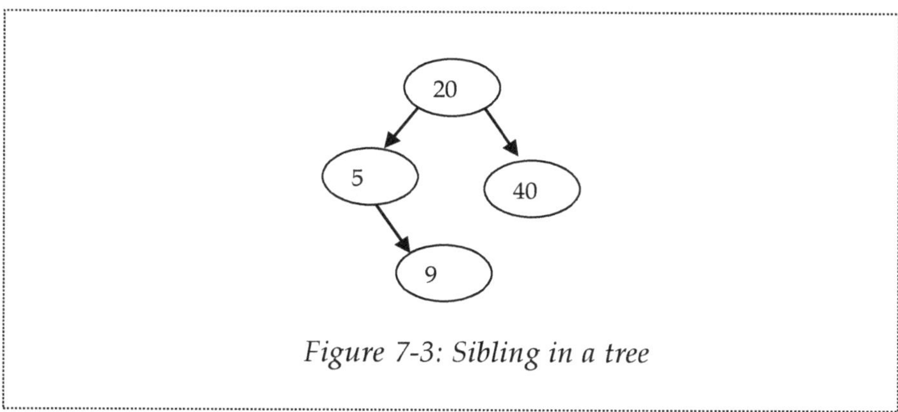

Figure 7-3: Sibling in a tree

Leaf Node: Leaf nodes are the nodes in the tree that don't have any child node. Leaf nodes are also termed as terminal node. In figure 7-3, node having value 9 and 40 are examples of terminal nodes, since they don't have any child node.

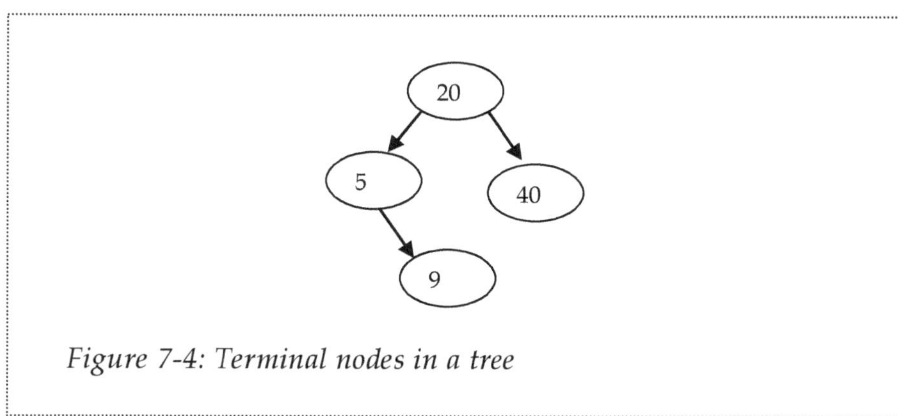

Figure 7-4: Terminal nodes in a tree

Degree of a tree

In a tree the maximum number of child nodes that a particular node can have is known as degree of a tree. If a node can have maximum two children then it is known as binary node. Examples of a degree is given in the following figure.

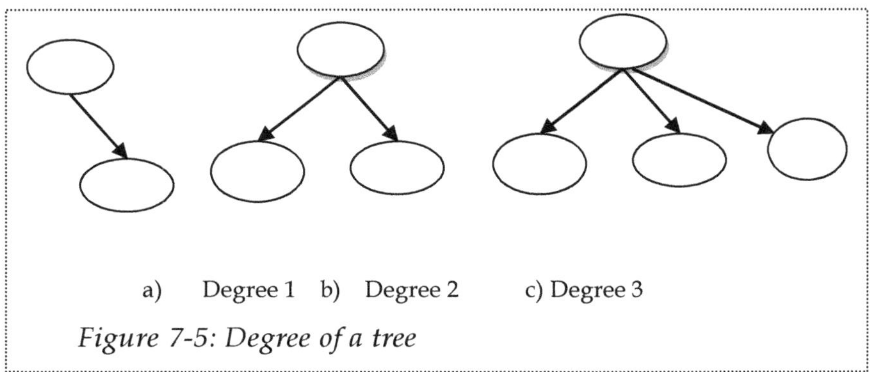

a) Degree 1 b) Degree 2 c) Degree 3

Figure 7-5: Degree of a tree

Non-terminal node: Nodes in a tree having at least one child are known as non-terminal node. It can also be defined as all the nodes other than the terminal nodes are termed as non-terminal node. In figure 7-4, nodes having value 20, 5, 40 are the example of non-terminal node.

Strictly Balanced Binary tree: Trees in which all the children have at-least two nodes or no node (in case of leaf node). Such a tree is known as strictly binary tree. In the following figure strictly tree has been illustrated. Strictly balance tree is also known as almost balanced tree.

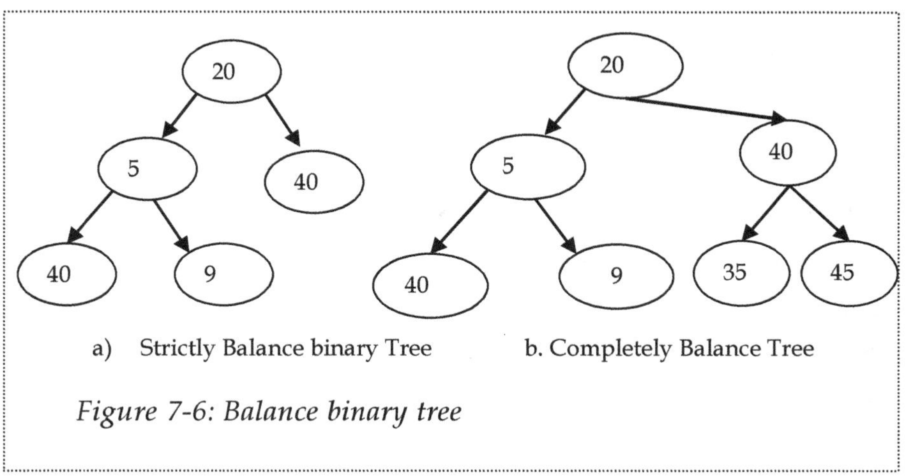

a) Strictly Balance binary Tree b. Completely Balance Tree

Figure 7-6: Balance binary tree

Completely Balanced Binary tree: A binary tree can be termed as completely balance binary tree, if all its nodes are having both the nodes, other than leaf node. In addition, all the leaf nodes must be at the same level. This property makes the completely balanced tree different from the almost balanced binary tree.

7.2 Binary Search Tree

Binary search tree (BST) is the special case of a binary tree in which nodes are inserted depending upon their values. BST has to follow additional restrictions that are applicable to the binary tree:

a) All the right nodes are more than the parent node.
b) All the left nodes are less than the parent node.

c) Comparison starts from the root, and continues up-to the NULL.

Therefore, while creating the BST special attention is to be paid, as explained in the upcoming section.

7.3 Creation of Binary search tree

Consider that the list of items are required to be inserted into the BST. The first item of the list is assigned to the root node of the BST, rest are compared with the root element to route them left or right. The whole procedure has been demonstrated in the following figures.

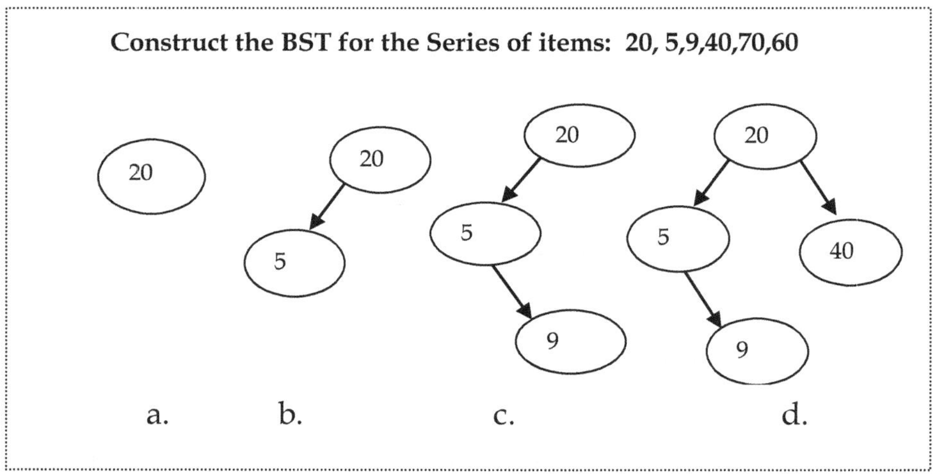

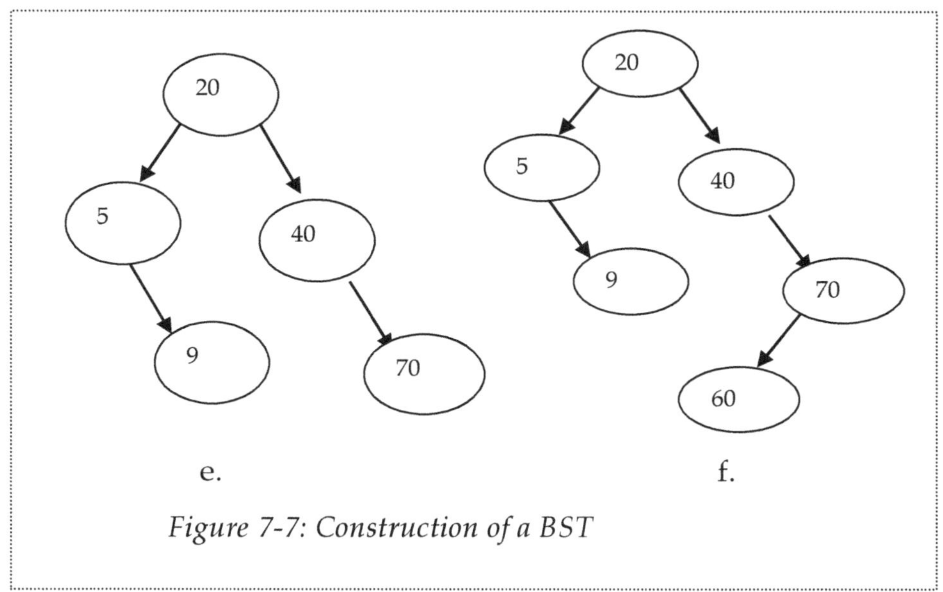

Figure 7-7: Construction of a BST

As illustrated in the figure 7-4. First the root node is created and it is having the value of 20, the other element are compared with this node if it is more than this node it will be attached to the right, otherwise it will be attached to the left. Consequently, the next item i.e. 5 on arrival will be checked with root node (20), since it is less therefore, it will leads towards the left side. Since, no left node is existing so this node will be attached to the left hand side. The next number is 9. Again the comparison starts from the root node(20), since 9 is less than the 20 so it will be move towards the left, After heading one level left, node having the value of 5 is reached, since, 9 is more than 5 therefore it will head towards the right of 5, since, no node is attached to the right of 5, that's why this node will be attached to the right of 5, refer figure 7.7 b..

The next number in the series is 40, again the comparison will start from the root i.e. 20, since 40 is more than the 20 it will head towards the right of 20, since the tree don't have any node attached to the right of 20, the new node having value of 40 will be attached to the right of 20, it is illustrated in the figure 7.7 'c'. Continuing to create the tree, the next node to be inserted in the tree will have the value of 70. Corresponding to the previous node, comparison will start from the root node(20), since, 70 is more than 20 it will head towards the right hand side, going one level down, it is again compared with the node 40, since still it is more, therefore it will head towards the right of this node also, since its right is NULL, consequently, it will be attached to the right of this node, same has been illustrated in the figure 7.7 'd'.

The next node to be inserted is having value 60. Corresponding to the previous insertion, comparison will restart from the root node(20), since it is more than 20, therefore it will head towards the right of this node, during heading one level down towards the right, 40 is encountered, since 60 is more than the 40, therefore, it will head towards the right of it. Now, 70 will be encountered, since 60 is less than the 70, therefore, it will head towards the left of it. Since, it's left is NULL, consequently, 60 will be attached to this node. Final tree has been illustrated in the figure 7.7 'e'.

A. **Program to create BST (Non-recursive)**

First we would like to define the structure of the BST. It consists of left and right child, and the data part. Therefore, its structure of the class is shown as follows:

```
class tnode
{
public:
int info;
tnode *left, *right;
};
```

It is significant to understand that the member created here must be public, otherwise they will not be accessible outside the class.

Class to create the BST has been shown below:

```
class bst
{
tnode *root;
void create(int);
};
```

Creation of tree need to be started from the root node. This can be accomplished by the following statements.

```
root=new tnode;
root->left=root->right=NULL;
root-data=element;
```

Consequently, structure as illustrated in the following diagram will be created.

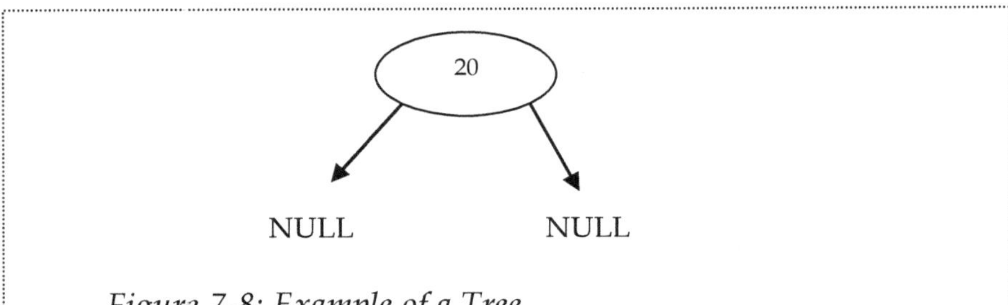

Figure 7-8: Example of a Tree

```
// Program to create a BST
void bst::create(int element)
 {
 //creating the root of bst
 if(root==NULL)
 {
 root=new bnode;
 root->info=element;
 root->left=root->right=NULL;
 return;
 }
  //creating a node to be inserted in a bst(root already exist)
 bnode *temp,*r;
 temp=new bnode;
 temp->info=element;
 temp->left=temp->right=NULL;
 //initializing the r with root
 r=root;
 while(r!=NULL)
 {
 // if element is less than r then move to the left
```

```
if(element < r->info)
  {
  // if left is NULL attach the temp node to the left side.
 if(r->left==NULL)
 {
 r->left=temp;
 break;
 }
 else
   r=r->left;  // Move to the left
}
else if(element > r->info)
  {
  // if element is more than r move toward the right
  if(r->right==NULL)
  {
  //if right is NULL attach temp to the right
   r->right=temp;
  break;
   }
   else
   r=r->right; // go to the right node
  }
}
}
```

B. Recursive BST Creation

In the recursive BST creation, we are creating the BST similar to that of non-recursive function. However, in the recursive function we are making use of recursive call. In our program, we have divided the working of the program as:

i. Creation of root.
ii. Inserting the left or right node in a BST.

To accomplish the first objective, we have created the rec_create(int data) function and same has been depicted in the following program. If the root is not NULL (tree is already existing), in that case rec_create(bnode*,int) has been called.

```
void bst::rec_create(int data)
{

if(root==NULL)        // if no
 {
 root=new bnode;
 root->left=root->right=NULL;
 root->info=data;
 return;
 }
 bnode *r=root;
rec_create(r,data);
}
```

If the tree is existing, then the new value will be compared with the root value, if the new value is less, it will be routed towards the left side. If the left side is NULL, then the new node will be created and it will be attached to the left side.

In the other case, if the new value to be inserted is more than the root node, it will be routed to the right side. If the right side is NULL then a new node with the passed value will be created and attached to the right side of the tree.

Recursive function has been depicted in the following program.

```
void bst::rec_create(bnode *r,int data)
 {
 if( data < r->info)
  {
  if(r->left==NULL)
   {
   bnode *temp;
   temp=new bnode;
   temp->info=data;
   temp->left=temp->right=NULL;
   r->left=temp;
   return;
   }
   rec_create(r->left,data);
 }
 else
  {
  if(data> r->info)
   {
   if(r->right==NULL)
    {
    bnode *temp=new bnode;
    temp->left=temp->right=NULL;
    temp->info=data;
```

```
    r->right=temp;
    return;
    }
    rec_create(r->right,data);
  }
  }
  }
```

7.4 Traversal in a BST

Visiting each node of a tree once is known as traversal of a tree. To display the value of each node, we have to visit each node of a BST. There are different types of traversal methods existing, these methods depends on how we are traversing the information part of the tree. Correspondingly, traversal can be accomplished in the following ways:

- Pre order traversal
- In order traversal
- Post Order traversal

Each of them has been discussed in the following sub-section.

7.4.1 Pre-order Traversal

In the pre-order traversal, we are visiting the information part first then continue heading towards left. Once the extreme left node is reached(next left is NULL), then we try to move to the right. After reaching to the right again, we try to move to its extreme left. If no right is available then we reach to one level up and try to visit its right node. This process continues till all the nodes are not visited.

Sequence of traversal in pre-order is as follows:

- Info
- Left node
- Right node

To execute the above steps, we can follow recursive and non-recursive approach. Recursive approach is extremely simple and needs few line of code, whereas non-recursive approach is lengthy and requires usage of another data structure that include Stacks and queue that are already created. In our discussion, we have considered both the approaches.

A. **Recursive approach for Pre-Order traversal**

In the recursive approach, we continue to traverse towards the left till we do not encountered the NULL. This condition has been given in a base condition. If the NULL is encountered, it traverse the right side once and again continues traversal towards the left as discussed before. The traversal method is illustrated in the following figure.

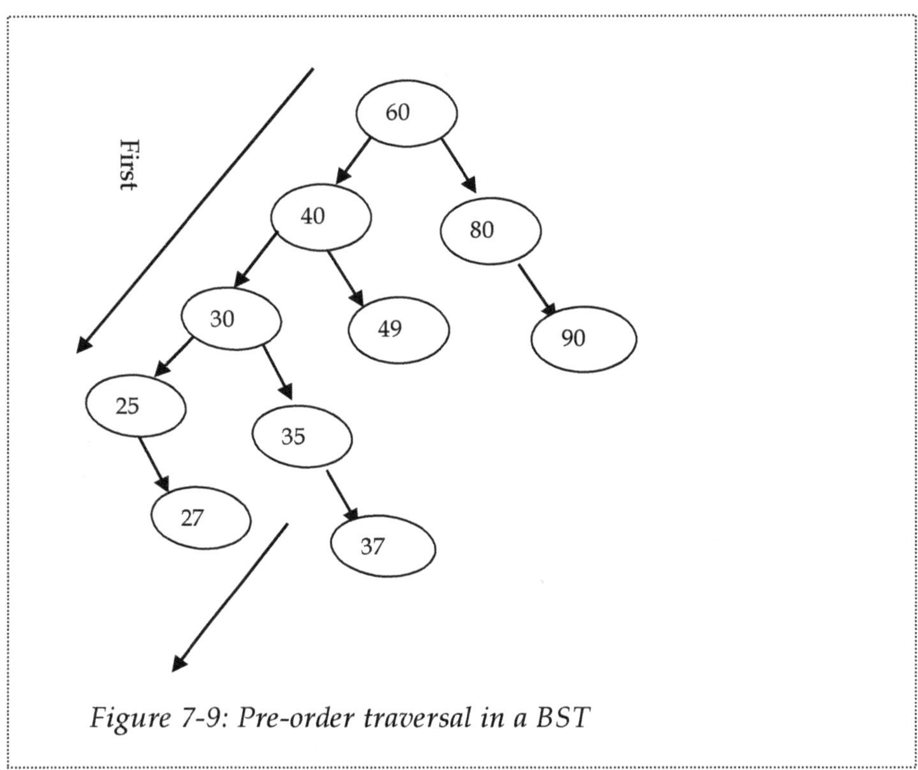

Figure 7-9: Pre-order traversal in a BST

Consider the case of figure 7-9, Here the traversal will commence from the root node. In this case it is 60, data of this node will be displayed and the node will be pushed into the stack. Now, we will be heading towards left since the considered node is not NULL, this new node is 40, again it will be pushed into the stack. Correspondingly, we will continue to move towards the left, if the considered node is not NULL, at the same time node visited is inserted into the stack. Consequently, next traversed nodes are 30, 25. After reaching to 25, as soon as we will be heading towards the left, the node will result in NULL. Then it will try to head towards the right of the node that was inserted in the stack. In this case, it is 25, the right node to this node is 27. This node is visited, and we would like to continue towards the left of this current node, since, there is no left node therefore, condition will result in false. From the stack we will pop the other node here the node is 30. Since its left is already visited. Then it would attempt to traverse to its right. Since it right is not NULL, therefore, the next visited node will be 35. However, its left is NULL, therefore we would not be able to head towards the left. Instead, we would access the right node, in the given tree it is 37. Since, it doesn't have any child node, therefore we would pop the node from the stack. Now, we will get the node having value 40. For this node, we would go one step right and be heading towards the left as before.

In the recursive function, we have to just write three sequence of calling and rest of the actions are implicit. However, in the case of non-recursive method, programmer has to provision for the complete logic. Non-recursive function of the BST has been enumerated in the next sub-section. Traversal in pre-order is enumerated immediately after the following program.

```
void bst::pre_order(const tnode *roote)
        {
                if(roote!=NULL)
                {
                        cout<<roote->data<<endl;
                        pre_order(roote->left);
```

```
                pre_order(roote->right);
        }
    }
```

Pre-order traversal of the BST has been given as follows:

25, 27, 30, 35, 37, 40, 49, 60, 80, 90

B. **Non-recursive traversal**

We can also traversed in pre-order by using non-recursive approach. Traversal method in non-recursive method is not different with the recursive approach. However, it is much more complex relative to the recursive approach defined earlier. In the non-recursive function, we initialize the pointer of root into the new pointer x. To simplify our work, we can import the file that enumerates the dynamic stack defined in the stack chapter.

In the pre-order non-recursive approach, we use the stack to push the stack node explicitly. In this approach, we visit the node and move towards left by inserting the node into the stack. If the NULL is encountered, the node that is pushed at last is pop first. We set the flag as visited to avoid traversing again towards the left side. Node that has been stored with the pop presence of the right node is checked, if the right side is present then it traverse towards the right. After visiting the right, there is possibility that it may have left node, consequently, the visit flag is set to false. Now, traversal will continue towards left. This process will continue till the stack will not become empty. The entire function has been depicted in the following program.

Program: To traverse the tree in pre-order, using non- recursive approach.

```
void bst::pre_orderNR()
{
bnode *x=root;          //initializing the x with the root
int visited=0;          // initializing the visited as false
stacks<bnode *> s;      // declaring the stack as BST node type
s.push(x);              // Push the root into the stack.
do
{
while((x!=NULL)&&(!visited))
{
cout<<"info ="<<x->info<<endl;      // Traverse the node
s.push(x);              // Push the node into the stack
x=x->left;       // continue to move left
}
visited=1;       // Make the visited true, to avoid re-traversal
x=s.pop();       // Pop one node from the stack.
if(x->right!=NULL)    // if right node exists
 {
 x=x->right;     // move towards the right
visited=0;       // set the visited value to false
}
} while(!s.empty());    // Continue till node in the stack exist
}// End of function
```

7.4.2 In-order Traversal

In the in-order traversal, the following sequence is followed for visiting:

- Left node
- Info
- Right node

In the in-order traversal, we head towards the extreme end of the left branch of the tree. During this traversal, nodes are stored in the stack. Once the extreme end of the left is reached then we can access the information. Afterwards, if the right node of the tree is not empty then we traverse towards the right. Again nodes are pushed in the stack till we have not reached the extreme end of this left branch. Once this process is over then we pop the one node and access the information, after that we check for the presence of right node, if it exists then move to the extreme end to its left branch else pop other node stored in the stack.

In-order traversal of a BST illustrated in the figure 7-10 has been given as follows:

In-order Traversal of a BST (figure 7-10)
25, 27, 30, 35, 37, 40, 49, 60, 80, 90

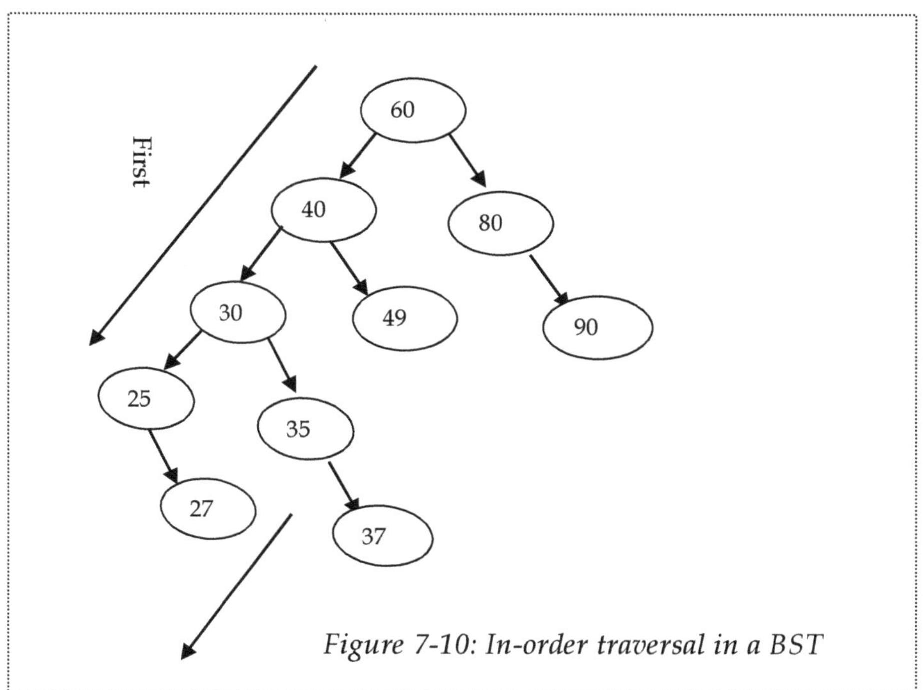

Figure 7-10: In-order traversal in a BST

It is apparent from the above discussion that a we have to follow a repetitive approach for the Traversal. Therefore, we will use the following function to accomplish the in-order traversal:

- Recursive
- Non-recursive

A. **Recursive Approach**

In the recursive approach, we use recursive function to traverse the tree. In the recursive approach, function has the BST node type pointer as an argument. It accepts the root node, following the in-order definition discussed earlier; traversal is taking place in the BST.

The function in-order (root->left) facilitates in heading towards the left side, level by level. Once the extreme end of the left branch is reached, after that we move one step right, if it exist. It is followed by extreme end of the left branch of this new right node. After reaching to the extreme end information is displayed, we move one level up, visit the information part after that check for the presence of right node. Again procedure discussed above is repeated.

In the recursive function, stack is utilized; however usage of stack is implicit to the user, in case of recursive call. Therefore, complexity of managing the stack call is eliminated. Recursive function of the BST has been depicted as follows:

```
Program: Recursive in-order approach to traverse the BST
void inorder(tnode *root)
{
if(root!=NULL)
{
inorder(root->left);     // visit the left node
cout<<"info ="<<root->info; // visit the information
inorder(root->right);  // visit the right node
}
}
```

In-order Traversal of a BST (figure 7-10)
25, 27, 30, 35, 37, 40, 49, 60, 80, 90

B. **Non-Recursive approach**

In the non-recursive approach, programmer has to manage the various sequence of operation needed for the traversal that include creating the stack, push and pop of BST node required for insertion and deletion respectively. Traversal will take place as already explained in the recursive approach. Managing the stack has been depicted in the following program.

```
// Program: Non-recursive approach for the in-order traversal of a BST
#include<stack.h>      //include the stack header file defined earlier
void bst:: inorderNR()
{
//initializing the root with r
bnode *x, *r=root;
//initializing the variable visited with 0
int visited=0;
//creating the stack for the BST node type
stacks<bnode*> s1;
x=r;
//pushing the first element into the stack
s1.push(x);
while(!s1.empty())
 {
 //x=s1.pop();
 //Go to the left if not already visited and
 //Traversed at the extreme end of left branch
 while((x->left!=NULL)&& (!visited))
 {
```

```
// Move to the left
x=x->left;
// Push the node in the stack
s1.push(x);
}
// Make the visit true as left side is visited
visited=1;
// pop the last node from the stack
x=s1.pop();
// visit the extreme left node popped
cout<<x->info<<endl;
// check for the presence of right node
if(x->right!=NULL)
 {
 x=x->right;
 s1.push(x);
 //if right node present, make the visit false
 visited=0;
 }
}
```

7.4.3 Post order Traversal

In the post order traversal, sequence of visiting various nodes and information has been given as follows:

- Left node
- Right node
- Info

From the above sequence it is apparent that first we will move to the extreme left node, then right node and again extreme left node. Once no child is available or the child already visited then only the info is traversed. After traversing the extreme left node (leaf node here) the node stored in the stack is popped and same procedure is to be applied. We continue to apply this procedure till all the nodes are not exhausted.

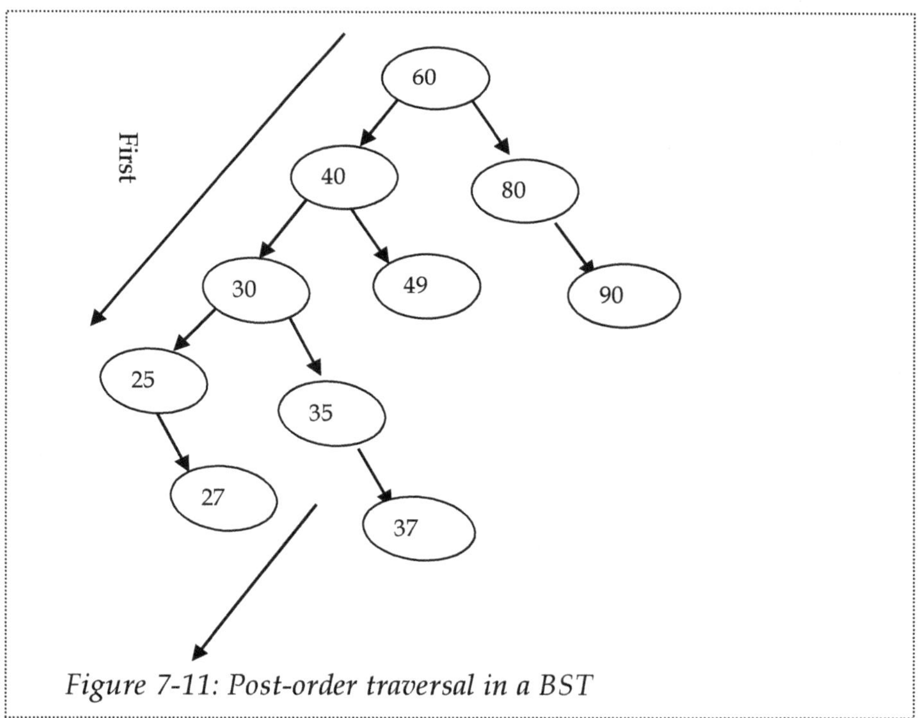

Figure 7-11: Post-order traversal in a BST

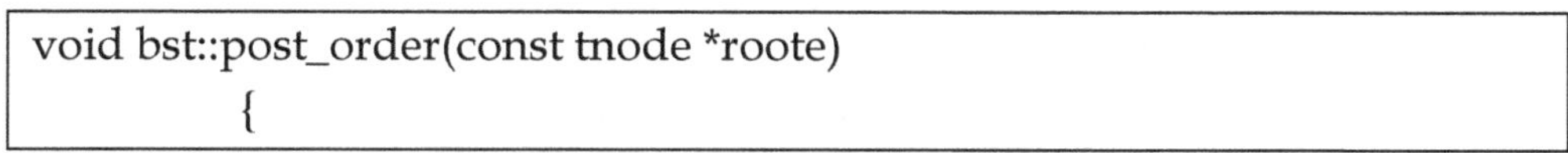

```
void bst::post_order(const tnode *roote)
            {
```

```
        if(roote!=NULL)
        {
        post_order(roote->left);
        post_order(roote->right);
        cout<<roote->data<<endl;
        }
}
```

Traversal of the nodes has been given as follows:

```
25, 27, 30, 35, 37, 40, 49, 60, 80, 90
```

7.4.4 Constructing the tree from the given traversal

We can construct the tree, if we have given the traversal such as in-order and pre-order, or in-order and post-order. Consider a case that the pre-order and in-order traversal has been given as follows:

Pre-order traversal of a tree is: 60, 30, 20, 10, 25, 27, 60, 70, 65, 68, 80

In-order traversal of a tree is: 10, 20, 25, 27, 30, 60, 65, 68, 70, 80

It is possible to construct the BST for the given traversals. To construct the BST, if the two traversal has been given, one is in-order the other is pre-order or the post-order in such case, BST can be easily created. We know from the various traversal enumerated earlier in the chapter that during pre-order traversal, first node that is traversed is the root node. Locate this value in the in-order traversal and divide the given traversal in left and right half. In the in-order traversal, values that are less than the value of pre-order is to be placed in left half whereas, values more than the first node of the pre-order value are placed in the right half. Same has been depicted in the following figures.

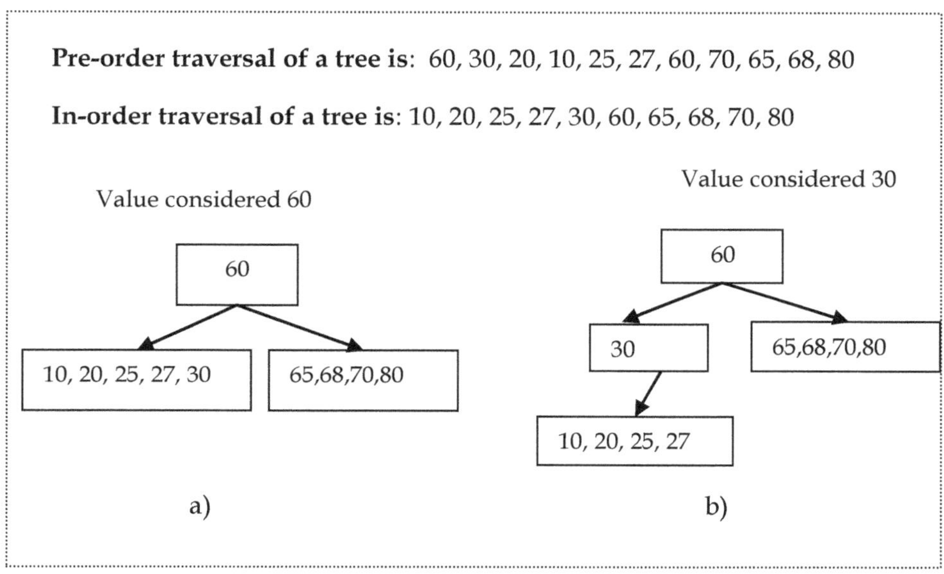

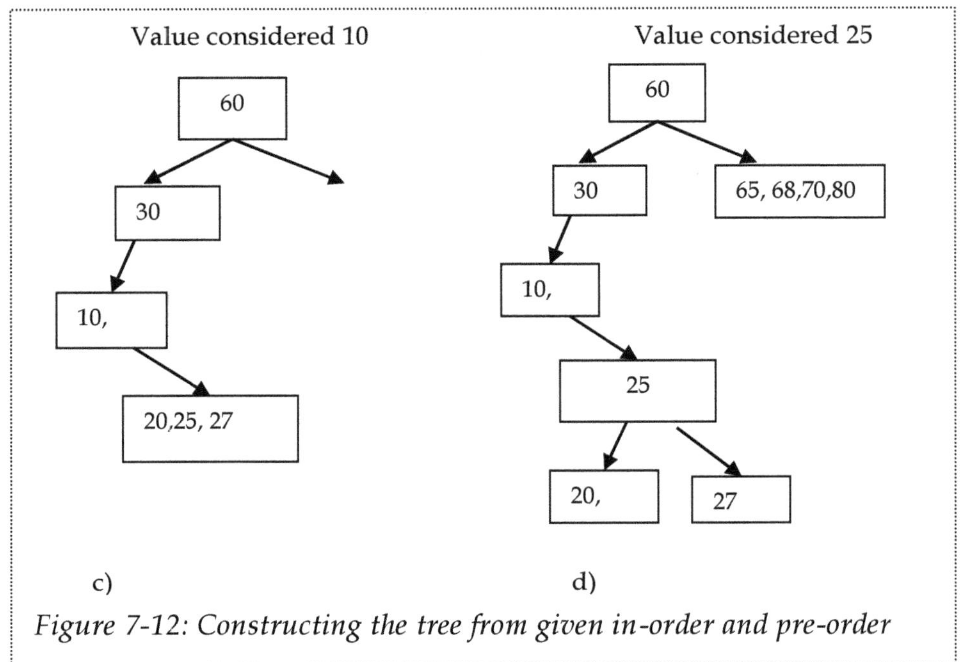

Figure 7-12: Constructing the tree from given in-order and pre-order

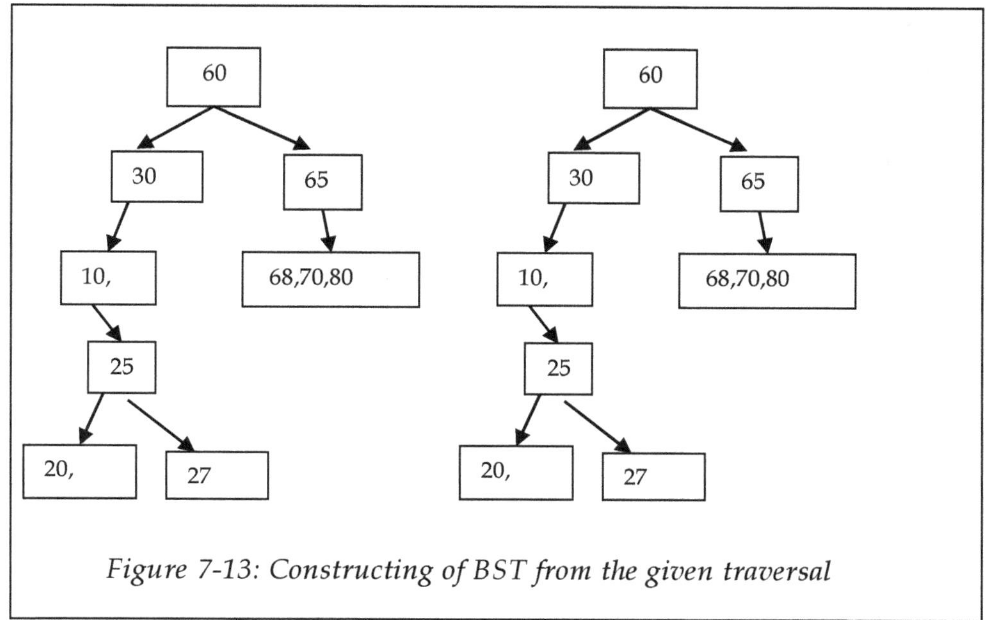

Figure 7-13: Constructing of BST from the given traversal

7.5 Deletion of a node

Data inserted in the BST is required to be deleted in the event when they are no longer needed. Deletion of a node in a BST is more cumbersome in comparison to the insertion of the node. During deletion of a node the following cases need to be considered:

a) Node does not have any child node (leaf node).
b) Node have only one child (may be left or right).
c) Node have both the children.

Deletion of a node for all the above cases has been discussed as follows:

Case a): To delete a node that does not have any child, we need to determine its parent. Once the parent is known, simply make the child pointer of this parent node as NULL, since it will not have any more node.

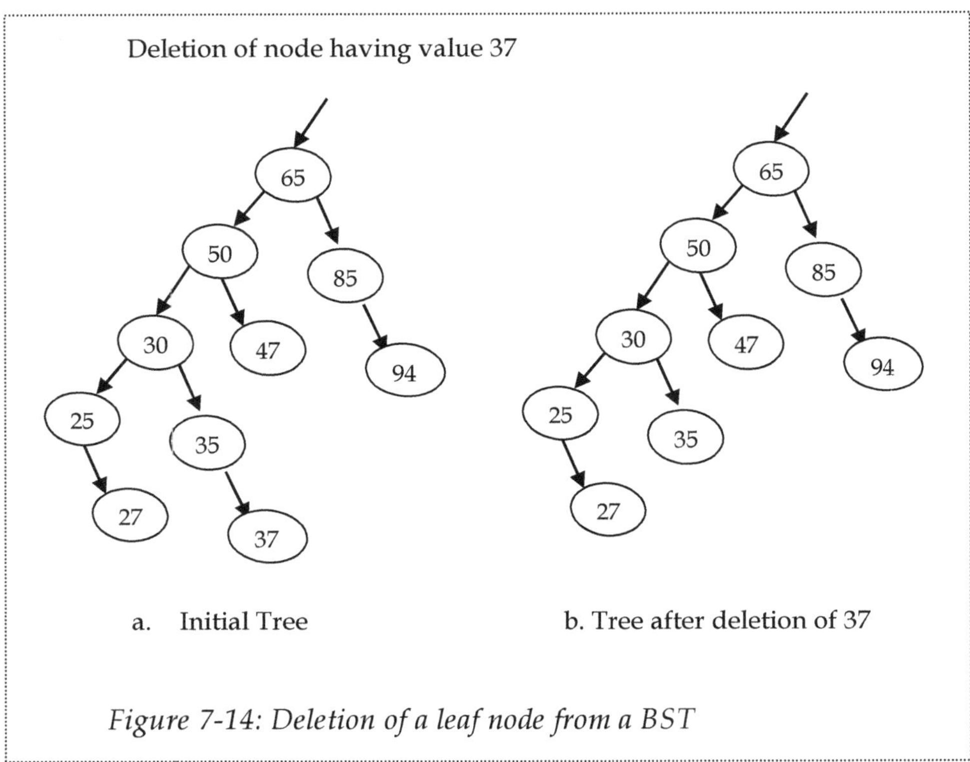

Figure 7-14: Deletion of a leaf node from a BST

Case b): In this case, we have considered that the node to be deleted has only child. This child node may be at the left or the right branch of the tree. In this case, we need to determine the parent node of the node to be deleted. Once, the parent node is determined, we have to find out whether the node to be deleted is left of the parent or the right node. Connect the parent node of the target node(node to be deleted) to the child node of the node to be deleted. Same has been illustrated in the figure 7-15 (a). Resultant tree has been illustrated in the figure 7-15 (b).

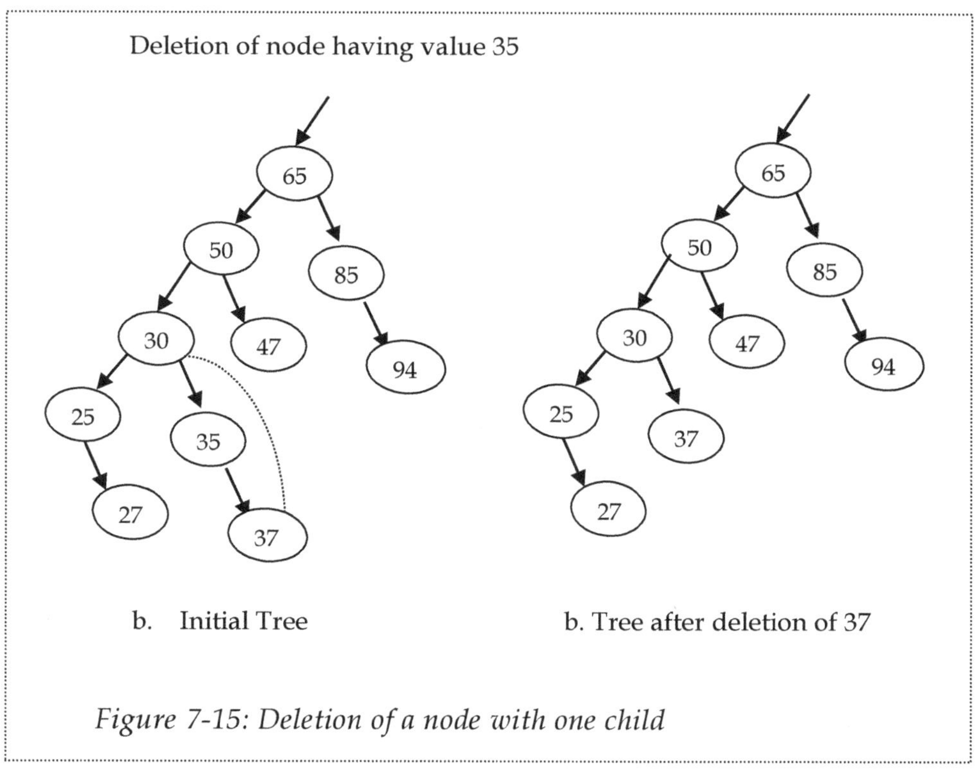

Figure 7-15: Deletion of a node with one child

Case c): In the third case, we have considered the case that the target node (node to be deleted) has both the children (left and right child). In this case also we need to determine the parent of the target node. Since, the node to be deleted has two children. Then both the children cannot be attached to the parent node of the node to be deleted (target node). Since, the parent may already have one child. To delete such node, we can follow any one of the following method.

- Delete by copy
- Delete by merging

7.5.1 Delete by Copying

To delete the node by copying, we do not delete the node physically. Instead, we find out the in-order predecessor or the in-order successor as well as their parent. Value of the node to be deleted is copied with the node of in-order predecessor or in-order successor find out previously. Replace the value of in-order successor node to the value of the node to be deleted and set this node as NULL. Complete program to delete the node using copying method is given in the following program.

[In our approach, to delete the target node, we will find out the in-order successor (instead of in-order predecessor) approach. This node is the left most node of the right child of the target node. Function to determine the in-order successor has been depicted in the following program].

```
// function to determine the in-order successor
bnode *bst::inSuccessor(bnode *current)
 {
 bnode *prev=NULL;
```

```
bnode *insucc;
 current=current->right;
while(current->left!=NULL)  // Go to the extreme left of the BST
 {
 prev=current;
 current=current->left;
 }
 insucc=current;
 if(prev) // if prev is not NULL (prev exist)
  {
  prev->left=NULL;  //set the left child of the prev as NULL
  }
  return insucc;
}
```

Consider the BST given in the following figure 7-16. Node to be deleted(Target node) is 50, if we need to determine the in-order successor then we have to go to the right from where we have to head towards the extreme left end. In the given figure 32 is in-order successor.

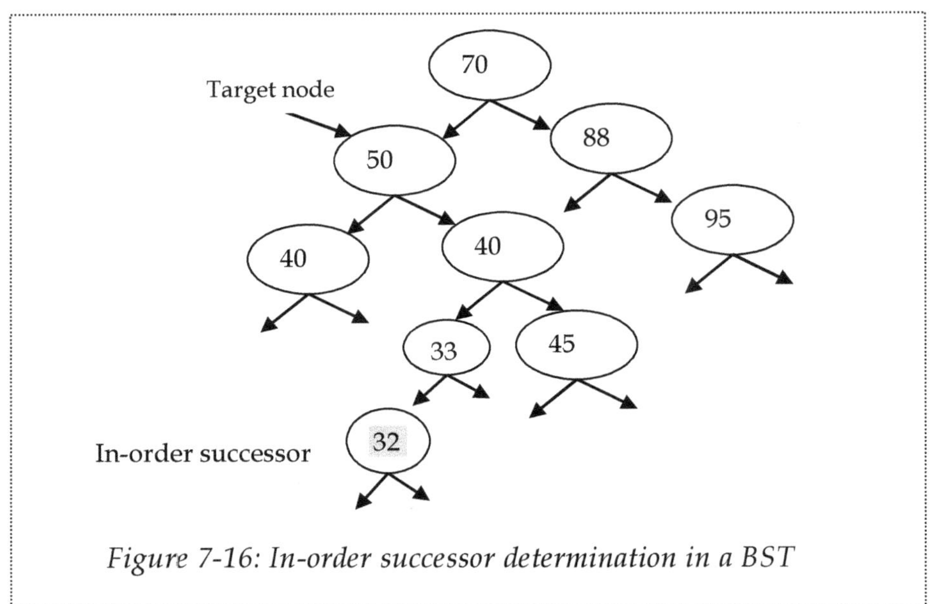

Figure 7-16: In-order successor determination in a BST

Correspondingly, consider the node to be deleted is 30, since it is having two children therefore, case 'c' will be applicable. First we have to determine the in-order successor. In the considered tree it will be 35, since the node 35 does not have any left child. Consequently, the node 35 itself will act as an in-order successor.

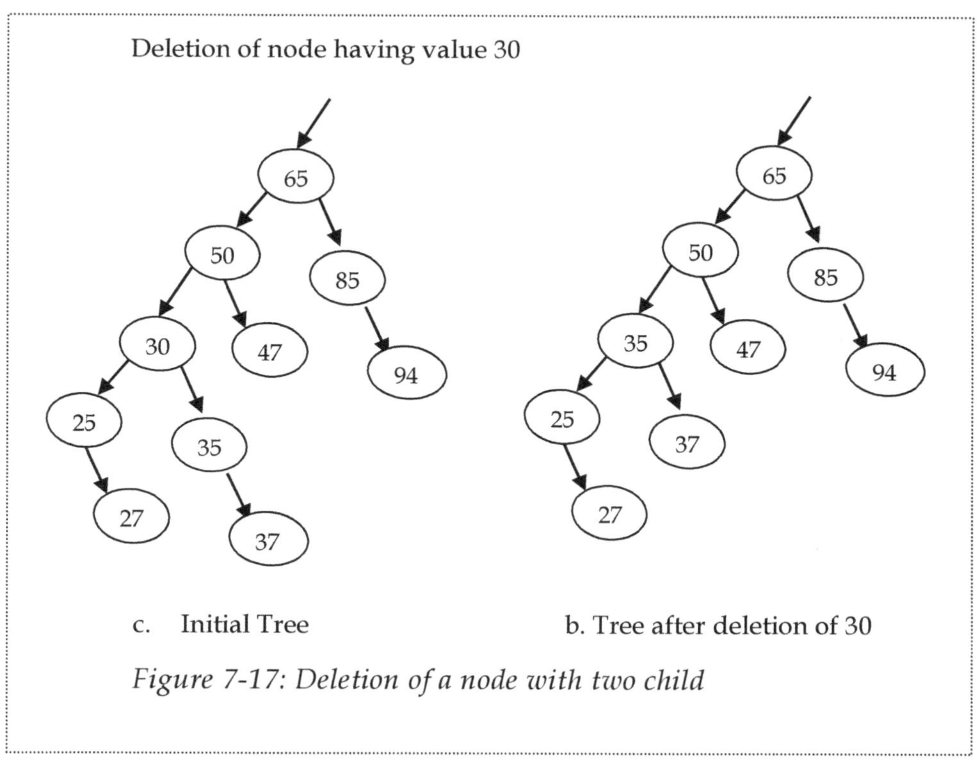

Figure 7-17: Deletion of a node with two child

Once we determine the in-order successor, it is obvious that it will not have any left node. Therefore, we will connect the left node of the target node to the left of in-order successor. Whereas right node will be connected to the in-order successor of this node.

7.5.2 Delete by merging

To delete the node by merging, target node is deleted physically. Since, node to be deleted will have the two children and if its parent is already contains one node then attaching these nodes to the parent is not possible. To address this condition, we have to find out the in-order predecessor or the in-order successor. Consider a case that we have are aiming to determine the in-order successor, in this case we attach in-order successor node in place of the node to be deleted. Since we have reached to the left most node then we are sure that it will not have any left node. Connect the right node of the node to be deleted to the left side of the in-order successor that we have just attached. The above case has been depicted in the following program.

```
void bst::deletenode(int node_data)
{
bnode*r,*parent=NULL,*temp;
r=root;
while(r!=NULL)
 {
 if(r->info==node_data)
 break;
 parent=r;
 if(node_data < r->info)
 r=r->left;
 else
 r=r->right;
 }// end of while
 if(r==NULL)
 {
 cout<<" Data is not in the BST"<<endl;
 cout<<"Press any key to continue...."<<endl;
 getch();
 return;
```

```
 }
 else if((r->left!=NULL)&& (r->right!=NULL))
         {
          bnode *insucc=inSuccessor(r);
          cout<<" we are evaluating Inorder successor= ......."<<insucc-
>info<<endl;
         getch();
         deleteMerge(parent,r,insucc);
         }
else if(parent->info < r->info) // if target(r) node is to the towards right
 {
  if((r->right==NULL)&& (r->left!=NULL)) // if r has only left child
   {
   temp=r;
   parent->right=r->left;
   delete temp;
   }
   else if((r->right!=NULL)&& (r->left==NULL)) // if r has only right
child
   {
   temp=r;
   parent->right=r->right;
   delete temp;
   }
   else if((r->left==NULL) &&(r->right==NULL)) // if r is leaf node
         {
         temp=r;
         parent->right=NULL;
         delete temp;
         }
```

```
 }
 else if(parent->info > r->info) // if target(r) node is to the towards left
 {
 if((r->right==NULL)&& (r->left!=NULL)) // if r has only left child
  {
  temp=r;
  parent->left=r->left;
  delete temp;
  }
  else if((r->right!=NULL)&& (r->left==NULL)) // if r has only right
child
  {
  temp=r;
  parent->left=r->right;
  delete temp;
  }
  else if((r->left==NULL) &&(r->right==NULL)) // if r is leaf node
        {
        temp=r;
        parent->left=NULL;
        delete temp;
        }


 }
```

```
void bst::deleteMerge(bnode* parent, bnode *r,bnode *insucc)
{
bnode *temp=r;
insucc->left=r->left;
if(insucc==r->right)// if insucc is right child itself
insucc->right=NULL;
else
insucc->right=r->right;
if(parent->info < insucc->info)
parent->right=insucc;
else
parent->left=insucc;
delete temp;

}
```

7.6 Searching an item in a BST

Searching in a BST is used to determine the existence of a node(data) in the considered BST. To accomplish the searching, we will follow the technique of in-order traversal. As soon as the node to be deleted is determine, further searching will be terminated and the node consisting of the needed value is returned.

During the searching process if no node is remaining then we can conclude that the target node is not existing in the given tree. In this case NULL will be returned to the caller.

Program to depict the searching in a BST has been given as follows:

Program: Write a program to search a node that consist of a value passed by the user.

```
tnode* bst::search(int el)
            {
            tnode*rt;
            rt=root;       //initialize it with root
            while(rt!=NULL)    // continue search till node is not null
            {
            if(rt->data==el)
            {
            break;
            }
            if(el < rt->data)
            rt=rt->left;
            else
            rt=rt->right;
            }
            return rt;
            }
```

7.7 Counting number of nodes in a BST

There are many instances in which we need to count the number of nodes in a BST. Total nodes of a BST consist is the sum of left half and right half of a tree. Method to count the number of nodes has been depicted in the upcoming sub-section.

7.7.1 Counting the left half nodes

To count the node attached at left side of a BST, we can make use of Queue. Whenever any node is encountered(should not be NULL), it is enqueue into the queue. Afterwards, we dequeue the node and check for the left node, if the left node exist, count is incremented by one. When the queue underflow occurs, we terminate counting and return the total left count to the caller. In this program, we will use the dynamic queue that has already been created by us in the queue section. Complete program is depicted as follows:

```
int bst:: leftCount()
{
int count=0;   // initializing the count to 0
bnode *x=root;          // initializing the x with the root
queue<bnode*> q1;  //defining the queue of bnode type
q1.enqueue(x); // inserting the node into queue
while(!q1.isEmpty()) // Till queue is not empty
 {
 x=q1.dequeue();        // insert the node into the queue
 if(x->left!=NULL) // if left node exist
 {
  q1.enqueue(x->left); // insert the left node in q
  count++;        // increase the count
  }
  if(x->right!=NULL) // if right node exist
  q1.enqueue(x->right);  // insert the right node in q
  }
 return count;
}
```

7.7.2 Counting the right half nodes

Corresponding to the left side node, we can compute the total number of nodes attached to the right side of a BST. We can make use of Queue as shown in the above example. Whenever any node is encountered(should not be NULL), it is enqueue into the queue. Afterwards, we dequeue the node and check for the right node or the left node exist, count is incremented by one. When the queue underflow occurs, we terminate counting and return the total number of right count to the caller. Complete code to accomplish this task has been depicted as follows:

```
// Function to count the right hand side node in a BST
int bst:: rightCount()
 {
 int count=0;
 bnode *x=root;
 queue<bnode*> q1;
 q1.enqueue(x); // inserting the node into queue
 while(!q1.isEmpty()) // Till queue is not empty
  {
  x=q1.dequeue();
  if(x->left!=NULL) // if left node exist
  {
   q1.enqueue(x->left); // insert the left node in q
 }
   if(x->right!=NULL) // if right node exist
{
```

```
q1.enqueue(x->right); // insert the right node in q
count++; // count the right node
}
  }
 return count;
 }
```

7.7.3 Counting all the nodes in a BST

To count the total number of nodes in a BST, we can compute the left half node as well as right half node of a BST. Afterwards, we can compute the total number of nodes by performing the sum of left half and right half. However, we have not counted the root node. Therefore, total node in a BST can be computed by

Total number of node=total number of left node +total number of right node +root node

Consequently, we can use the functions written above, to compute the total number of nodes.

```
leftTotal= int bst:: leftCount();
rightTotal=int bst:: rightCount();
Total no. of nodes=leftTotal + rightTotal +1;
```

7.8 Determining the height of a Tree

Height of a BST is the longest path existing in the left or the right side. For instance, the maximum path may be available towards the right side of the left node. Height of a BST has been explained with the help of following examples.

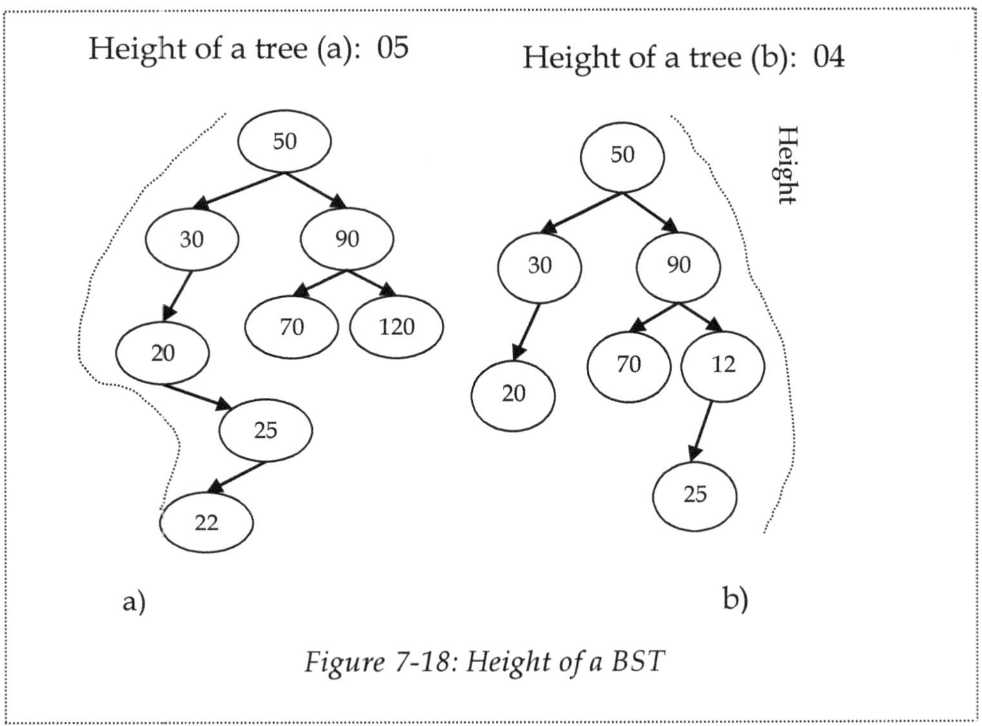

Figure 7-18: Height of a BST

A. **Non-recursive method**

In the non-recursive approach of determining the height of a tree, we are visiting the tree level by level. Once new level is reached, height is incremented. To traverse the level by level, we can utilize the dynamic queue already created in the previous chapter. In this method, if the tree exist the root node is inserted into the queue. This is followed counting the number of nodes in the queue. We can figure out the total number of nodes at a particular level with the help of queue function size that determine the number of nodes in a queue. Initially, number of nodes are 1 (only the root node). We cam dequeue the root and check its left or right node, if they are available they are inserted in the queue. Now the total number of nodes in a queue will be the nodes that are not null and available in the queue. We also increase the height once we access all the node of a tree. This entire process continues till all the nodes of a tree are not accessed. Finally, we return the height of a tree to the caller function. Complete program has been given as follows:

Program: Determine the height of tree (non recursive method)

```
// Non recursive function to determine the height of a tree
int bst::height_NR()
{
int ht=0;          // initially height is 0
queue<bnode*> q1; // create the queue of tree node type
int count=0;   //total number of  node in a queue
bnode *temp; // temporary variable to store bnode
if(root!=NULL)         // if tree  exist
q1.enqueue(root);      // insert the root in the queue
while(!q1.isEmpty()) // Till queue is not empty
{
 ht++; // increase the height
count=q1.size();         // count number of node in a queue
while(count>0)           // while count is not zero ( all the node at
 {                       //particular level are taken out
 temp=q1.dequeue(); // remove the bst node from the queue
 if(temp->left!=NULL)
 q1.enqueue(temp->left);
 if(temp->right!=NULL)
 q1.enqueue(temp->right);
```

```
 count--;          // reduce the count
 }
}
return ht;         // finally return the height to the caller
}
```

B. **Recursive method for height**

In the recursive method of determining the height, we will compute the left height and the right height individually. Once both the heights of a tree are known we can compare them and return the maximum of left and right node to the caller. Following are the functions given using the object oriented approach.

```
Program: Program to determine the height of a tree recursively
// function called from the main function
int bst::height()
{
bnode*r=root;
int h=height1(r);
return h;
}
// function called by the height without the knowledge of main function
int bst::height1(bnode * r)
{
  if (r==NULL)          // if root is null
     return 0;
  else
  {
     /* compute the depth of each subtree */
```

```
    cout<<" Before left and right"<<endl;
    int lheight = height1(r->left);
    cout<<" after left call"<<lheight<<endl;
    int rheight = height1(r->right);
    cout<<" after right call"<<rheight<<endl;

    /* use the larger one */
    if (rheight > lheight)
        return(rheight +1);
    else return(lheight+1);
  }
}
```

7.9 Mirror of a Tree

Once we stand in front of the mirror, we observe that our left hand appears to be as right hand and vice versa. Correspondingly, in the mirror of a tree, the given BST gets transposed. The left node will appears as the right node and the right node appears as left node.

Consider the BST of figure 7-19 (a) it represent the original tree. Mirror of the tree has been illustrated in the figure 7-19 (b). Mirroring can be achieved by connecting the right node to the left node and left node to the right side. To accomplish mirroring we can adopt the top to bottom approach or we can start from the bottom. Mirroring can be accomplished with the help of recursive or non-recursive function. We have commenced our discussion with non-recursive approach.

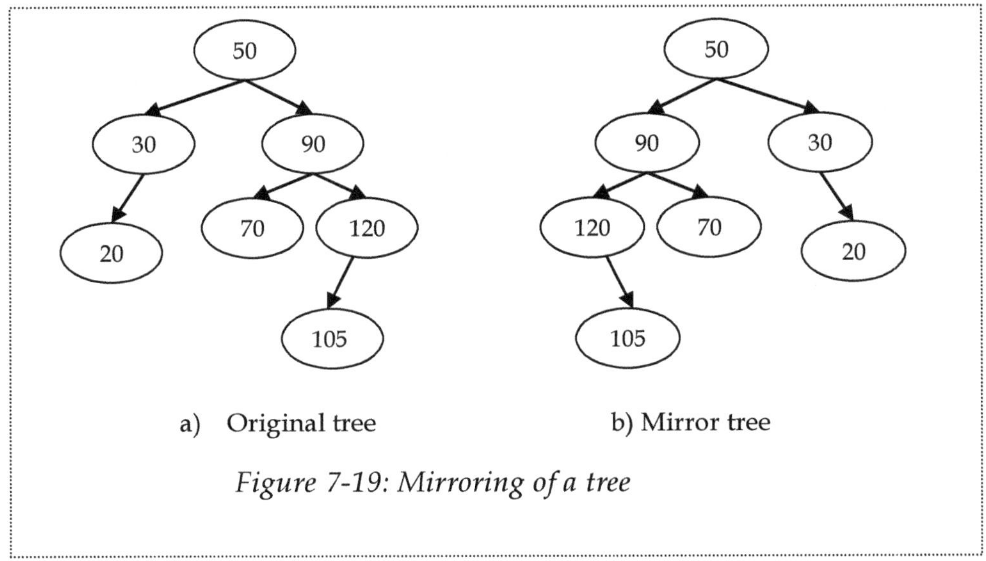

Figure 7-19: Mirroring of a tree

A. **Non-recursive method**

In the non-recursive method of mirroring, we will traverse level by level and transpose the child attached to right and left side. In our approach, we have inserted the node into the queue, we are examining the queue in each iteration whether it is exhausted or not. If all the queue is empty then it signifies that all the nodes has been traversed and the considered tree is transposed.

From the queue, we remove the node one by one which is followed by the exchange of its left and right child. After that we have to examine the availability of left and right node if any one of them is available it is inserted into the queue. In our discussed approach, we have followed the top down approach, which means the mirroring has been started from the top and continued up-to the bottom. Step by step method has been illustrated in the figure 7-18.

```
// function to find out the mirror of a BST
void bst::mirror()
 {
 bnode *current,*temp, *x=root;
queue<bnode*> q1;
q1.enqueue(x); // inserting the node into queue
while(!q1.isEmpty()) // Till queue is not empty
 {
 current=q1.dequeue();        // take out one node from a queue
 temp=current->left;          // swap left and right node
  current->left=current->right;
  current->right=temp;
 if(current->left!=NULL)// if left is not NULL insert in queue
 q1.enqueue(current->left); //insert left node in a queue
 if(current->right!=NULL)    // if right is not NULL
 q1.enqueue(current->right);  // insert right node in a queue
 }// end of while statement
 }       // end of function
```

B. Recursive Approach for Mirroring

In the recursive method, we follow the bottom up approach thereby nodes at the highest level (bottommost) is transposed first. This is followed by the nodes above it. Complete program to demonstrate the mirroring has been depicted below:

```
Problem: Recursive function for the mirroring
void bst:: mirror(bnode *root)
```

```
{
if(root==NULL)
return;
else
{
bnode *temp;
mirror(root->left);
mirror(root->right);
temp=root->left;
root->left=root->right;
root->right=temp;
}
}
```

7.10 Exercises

1. Create a class for a BST. Modify the constructor so that at the time of object initialization node is also created.
2. Create a function to visit each and every node depth wise.
3. Modify the function breadth first traversal. In the modified function, traverse level by level from bottom to top.
4. Write a program, where the display also appears as level by level. (Hint use two queue)
5. Write a program for the pre-order traversal in which use queue to insert the element. Once display is complete display them accordingly.
6. Write a function that displays the number of nodes level by level of a BST.

Chapter 8
Threaded tree

Chapter Objective

- Define the limitation of a BST.
- Defining the threaded tree.
- Defining the various types of threaded tree.
- Defining the limitation of BST related to the height
- Defining the AVL tree.
- Inserting the node in an AVL tree.
- Rotating left, right and left-right, right-left
- Adjusting the balancing factor of an AVL tree.

8 Threaded Tree

In the previous chapter of BST tree, we have witnessed that there are number of left and right branches that are NULL. These NULL increase exponentially with the growth of level of a BST. Backward traversal is the other challenge posed by the BST. These issues can be addressed with the help of threaded tree.

8.1 Need of threaded tree

It is obvious from the previous discussion that the number of NULL node increases with the increase of level. Other major drawback in a BST is that we can traverse only in one direction. To address all these issues, threaded tree is used. In the threaded tree, we connect the NULL pointers of the leaf as follows:

i) Left node is connected to the in-order predecessor.

ii) Right node is connected to the in-order successor.

iii) If no predecessor or successor exist in that case NULL pointer is connected to the root node.

Threaded tree is a special case of BST tree, however it requires extra component to represent the thread. Variety of threaded tree are existing that have their own usage. Major types of threaded tree that are existing include:

i) Left- threaded tree

ii) Right threaded tree

iii) In-order threaded

BST in which only left node is acting as a thread such tree is known as Left-in threaded tree. Similarly, BST in which only right NULL is acting as thread, such BST is known as right-in threaded tree. Tree in which both left and right node are acting as thread then it is known as in-threaded tree.

Threads not only eliminates the NULL node, but also facilitates in backward traversal. In the rest of our discussion, we have considered the in-threaded tree. Once the readers can implement the in-threaded tree, implementing the left-in threaded tree or the right-in threaded tree can be implemented easily.

8.2 Creation of a threaded tree

For our discussion, we have considered the in-threaded tree so that the reader can learn to handle the both types of thread. Structure of a threaded tree and the insertion of a node has been discussed in the following sub-section.

A. Representing the in-threaded tree

In the in-order threaded tree, other than the left and right child that have been represented earlier in the BST chapter, left and right thread also need to be provisioned. Complete structure of the in-threaded tree has been shown in the figure 8-1.

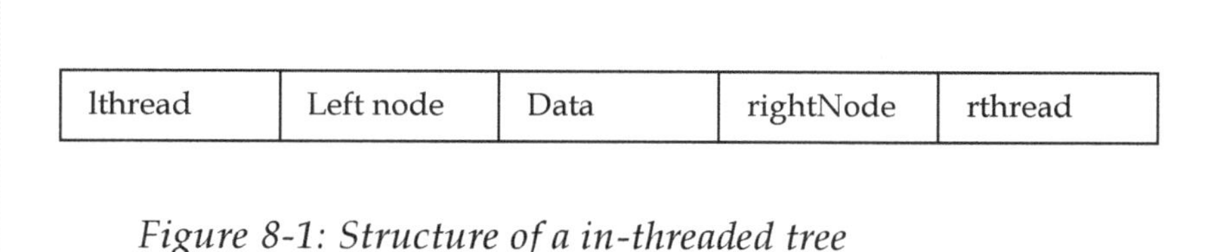

Figure 8-1: Structure of a in-threaded tree

In the above figure, symbols have the following meaning:

lthread: denotes the left thread

leftnode: denotes the left node

data: data part of the tree

rightnode denotes the right node

rthread denotes the right thread

If the rthread=0, it denotes that the node has the right child

If the rthread=1, it denotes that the node has the right thread but does not have right child.

If lthread=0, it denotes that the node does not have the left thread as it is having the left child.

If the lthread=1, it denotes that the node does not have the left child consequently, it is having the left child.

Class to represent the threaded tree node has been depicted as follows:

class threadnode

```
{
public:
int lthread;
int rthread;
int data;
threadnode *left;
threadnode *right;
};
```

In the threaded tree we would be frequently needing to determine the in-order successor and in-order predecessor. In-order successor is the next to be visited during the in-order traversal. Correspondingly, the in-order predecessor in a threaded tree is the node that is traversed just before the newnode during the in-order traversal of the BST. Functions to determine the in-order predecessor and in-order successor have been depicted as follows:

Program: To determine the in-order successor in a threaded tree

```
threadnode* insucc( )
{
if(root->lthread==1)
return root;
else
{
threadnode *succ=root->right;
while(succ->lthread!=1)
 {
succ=succ->left;
}
```

```
}
return succ;
}
```

Pre-order successor in a Threaded tree

```
threadnode * presucc( )
{
if(p->lthread==0)
return p->left;
else
{
threadnode *succ=p->right;
while(p->rthread==1)
p=p->right;
}
return p;
}
```

8.3 Traversal in threaded tree

Traversal in threaded tree is complex procedure. It requires variety of factors to be considered during traversal. Since, thread connects back to the root also therefore, cycling will be formed that will result in infinite looping.

In the normal BST, during traversal we are checking the NULL where we terminate the traversal. Correspondingly, in the threaded tree, we continue to head till thread is not encountered.

```
// Program: Traversal in a Threaded tree
void inorder(threadtree *root)
{
threadtree *r=root;
while(*r!=*root)
 {
cout<<r->info;
r=insucc(r);
}
}
```

8.4 Inserting the node(s) in a threaded tree

Insertion of a node in a threaded tree is a complex procedure and due care need to be observed due to the following reasons:

i) Identifying the location where node to be inserted in a threaded tree.

ii) Adjusting the left and right side pointer of this new node.

iii) Adjusting the pointers and thread of a node acting as a parent node of a new node.

iv) Consider a case that only root node is existing in the in-order threaded tree, in this case the left and right node will not have the node. Consequently, it will have the left and right thread will exist and connect to the NULL.

v) In all other cases left thread is connected to the in-order predecessor and right thread is connected to the in-order successor. In the event if no predecessor or successor exist. In these cases, the thread will be connected to the root node.

Class to defining the various data member and function needed for the threaded tree has been depicted as follows:

```
class threadtree
{
threadnode *root;        // Root of a threaded tree
void insert(int);        // function to insert the node
void inorder();// function for the in-order traversal
};
// inserting the node in a threaded tree
void threatree::insert(int x)
{
if(root==NULL)
{
root=new threadnode;
root->data=x;
root->left=root;
root->right=root;
root->lthread=1;
root->rthread=1;
return;
}
r=root;
threadnode *newnode;
while(1)
{
if(x < r->info)
```

```
{
if(r->lthread!=0)
{
newnode->left=r->left;
r->lthread=0;
newnode->lthread=1;
newnode->right=r;
newnode->rthread=1;
break;
else
r=r->left;
}
else
{
if(r->rthread==1)
 {
newnode->left=r->left;
r->lthread=0;
newnode->lthread=1;
 newnode->right=r->right;
newnode->rthread=1;
r->rthread=0;
break;
}
else
r=r->right;
}         //end of else
}// end of while
```

8.5 AVL Tree

BST gives better performance relative to the linear link list. However, it suffers from many limitations. For instance, consider a case that the list is in the sorted order (items are already arranged in ascending or descending order), in such cases BST performs like the link list. This phenomenon has been illustrated with the help of following figure.

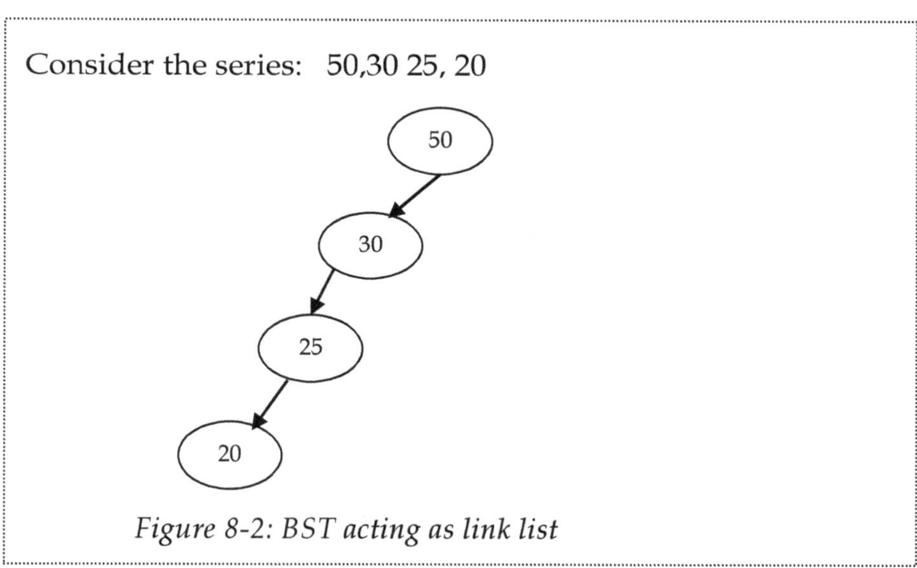

Figure 8-2: BST acting as link list

In the above figure, the series is in descending order, therefore BST is acting as a link list. For the simplicity, we have considered the small series, impact will be higher when the size of the series grows. Consequently, it losses the performance advantages for the creation of the tree.

To address the above issue, modified version of BST known as AVL tree is used. AVL name comes from its developer's namely G. M. Adel'son, Vel'ski and E. M. Landis. It is special type of BST in which a new factor known as balancing factor is also considered. For instance, if the left side of the tree is having one more than the right hand side than balancing factor is increased by +1. If the right side of the tree is having one more level then the left side -1 is added to it. However, if both the left and right side is at the same level, parent will have the 0 balancing factor. In short, the balancing factor is placed as (1,0,-1}, from left to right. AVL tree along with the balancing factor has been shown in the following example. Many authors have also used the symbol {/,0,\} for left heavy, balanced and right heavy respectively. However, in this book we have used the numeric value discussed earlier.

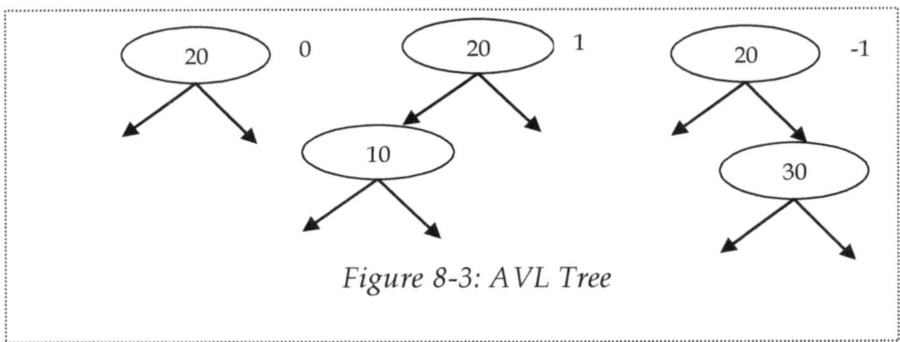

Figure 8-3: AVL Tree

A. **Homogeneous unbalance tree**

In the homogeneous unbalance AVL tree, it is unbalanced due to the unbalancing factor at the same side. For instance, consider the case of figure 8-2 (e & f), both are unbalanced AVL tree. 8-2 (e) is left heavy and the balance factor of the grand parent of node 5 is 2. Similarly, to deter mine the balance factor of the parent of 5 is +1. Therefore, such type of unbalance tree is known as homogeneous unbalanced tree. Correspondingly, it can be defined that the AVL tree shown in figure 8-2 (f) is homogeneous right unbalanced tree.

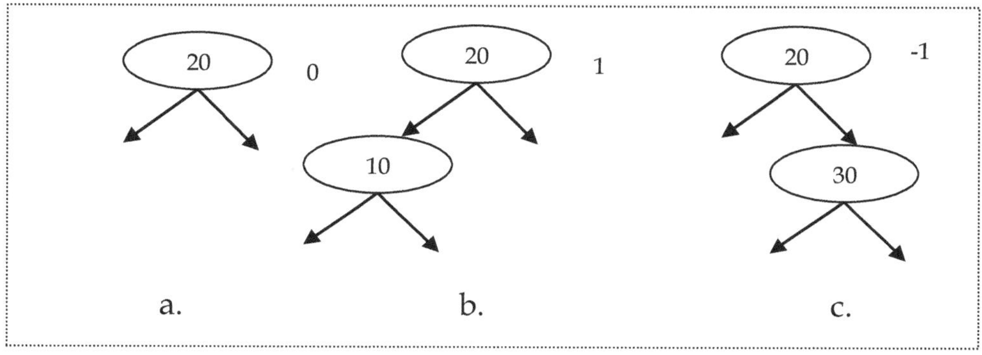

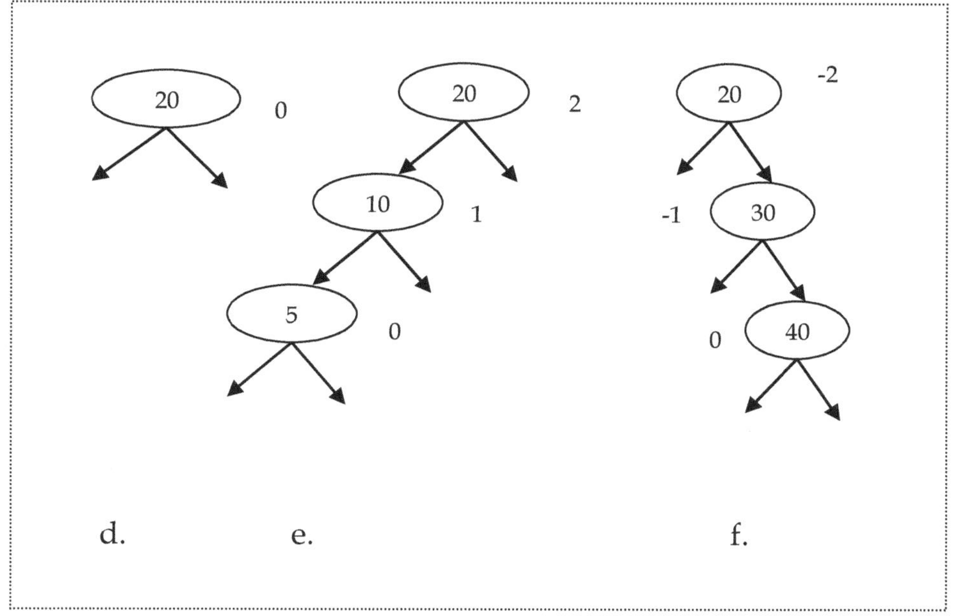

B. **Heterogeneous unbalance tree**

In the heterogeneous unbalance tree, unbalancing effect is

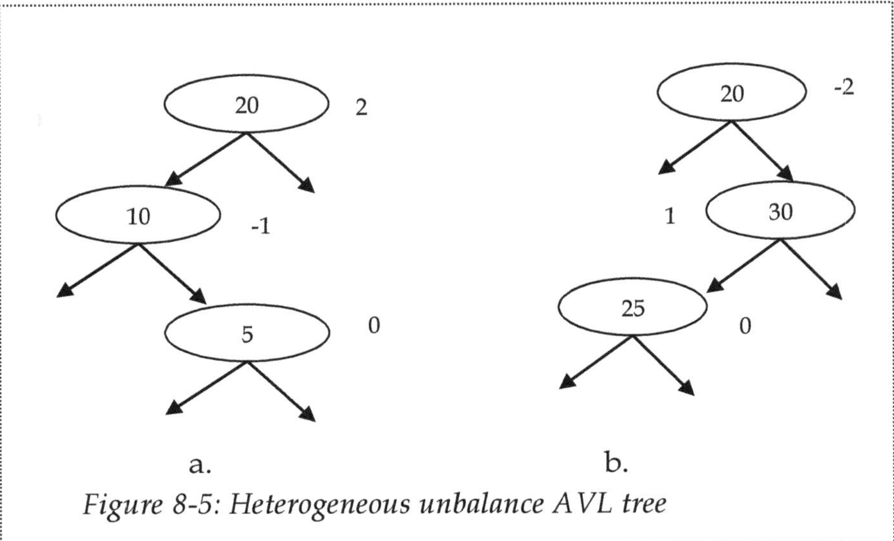

Figure 8-5: Heterogeneous unbalance AVL tree

attributed to the heterogeneous imbalance. For instance, consider the case of figure 8-4 (a) which is having left heavy, however its child is also heavy but it is right heavy. Similarly, 8-4 (b) is right heavy. But when we reaches to its child 30, it's left heavy. The above discussed type of unbalancing is known as heterogeneous unbalancing. To balance such type of AVL tree we have to follow the specific method to balance and the same has been discussed in the rotation section of this chapter.

8.6 Creation of an AVL tree

Although, AVL tree is a special case of BST tree then also necessary changes are to be incorporated in the BST to accommodate the balancing factor which is the key for an AVL tree. This balancing factor will change with the attachment of a node in an AVL tree. Data member of an AVL tree will be as:

```
class AVLnode
{
public:
int info;          // for the data part of the AVL Tree
int bfactor;       // for the balancing factor
AVLnode  *left, *right;          // left and right node of the AVL
};
```

To understand, how the AVL tree will grow, let's understand it with the help of an example. Consider the series, 80,25,66,90, 32, 60,11 while inserting/creating 80 in the AVL tree, there are no node that are existing, therefore, root is to be created and the balance factor of this node will be 0. Consider another number 25, this node will be attached to the left side of the 80 and its balance factor will be 0. Whenever a new node is attached to the AVL, its balance factor is always equal to zero. However, the balance factor of its predecessor need to be changed. This balance factor will propagate upwards up-to the grand parent, if exist. In case the balancing factor of the grandparent is violated, AVL need to be suitably rotated so that it can continue to qualify the definition of AVL tree. Creation of an AVL tree has been illustrated in the following figure 8-5.

Initially, 80 is inserted and its balance factor is changed to 0. Since, it is the root node, consequently balancing cannot propagate upwards.

After 80, another number 25 is being inserted in figure 8-5 (b), since, it is less than 80, it will be directed towards the left hand side and get attached with 80. Balancing factor of this new node will be 0. Balancing factor will be propagate upwards, Since only one node exist above 25, therefore its balancing factor can be determined as

New balancing factor=old balancing factor + 1
New balancing factor=0 +1=1

Therefore, new balancing factor of 80 will be 1.

Take another case (figure c), in which 90 is being inserted. This node will move towards the right side of the root. Balancing factor of this new node (90) will be 0. Balancing factor will propagate to upwards and will be increased by 1. Since, node is attached to the right therefore increment will be -1. New balancing factor can be computed by:

New balancing factor=old balancing factor + (-1)

New balancing factor=1-1

=0

This propagation will not terminate here, instead reach towards the left side of the root. New balancing factor of any node can be computed with the help of formula given above.

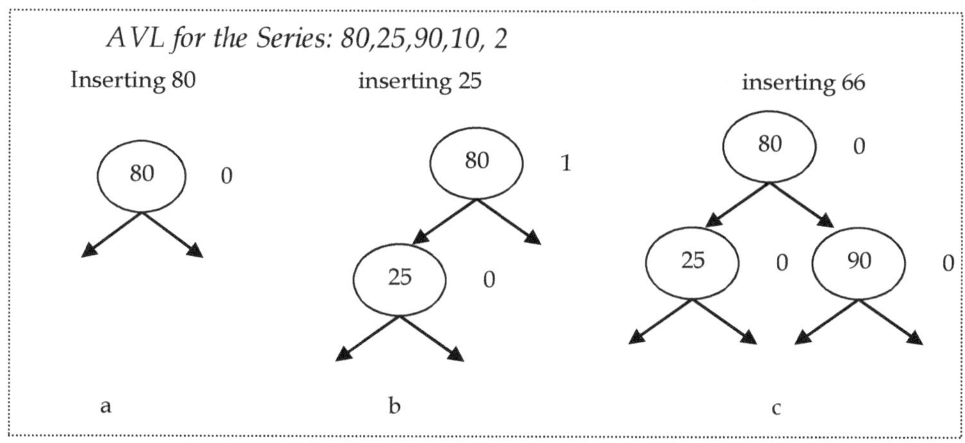

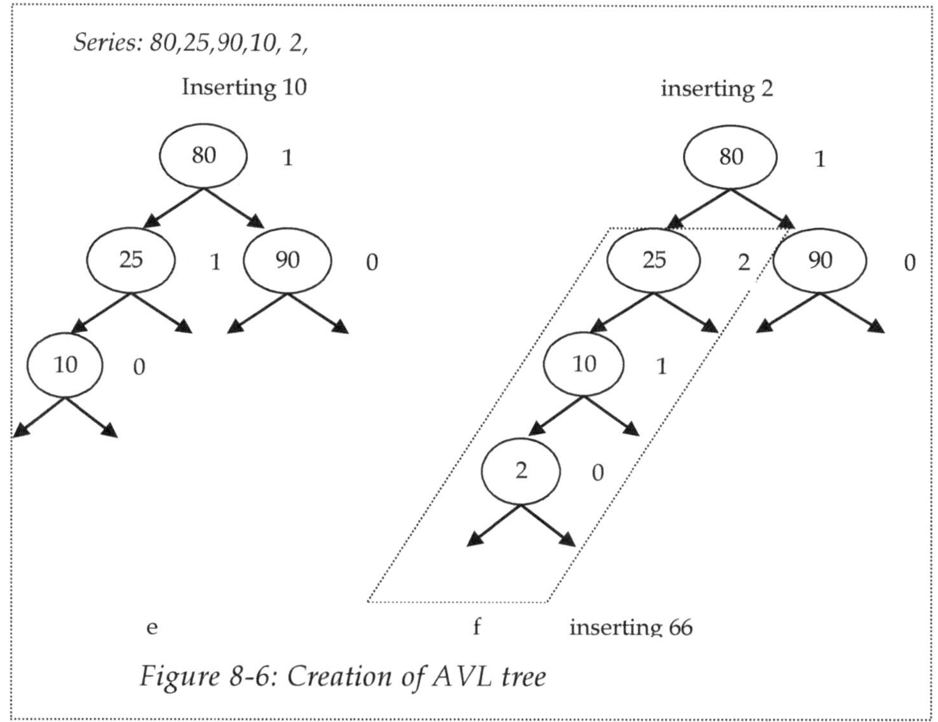

Figure 8-6: Creation of AVL tree

Finally, with the insertion of 10 and subsequently 2, balancing factor of the node 2's grandparent will be changed to 2 and this condition is unacceptable. Therefore, to balance this tree, so that it should qualify the definition of the BST, we rotate the grandparent considering the homogeneous and heterogeneous unbalancing.

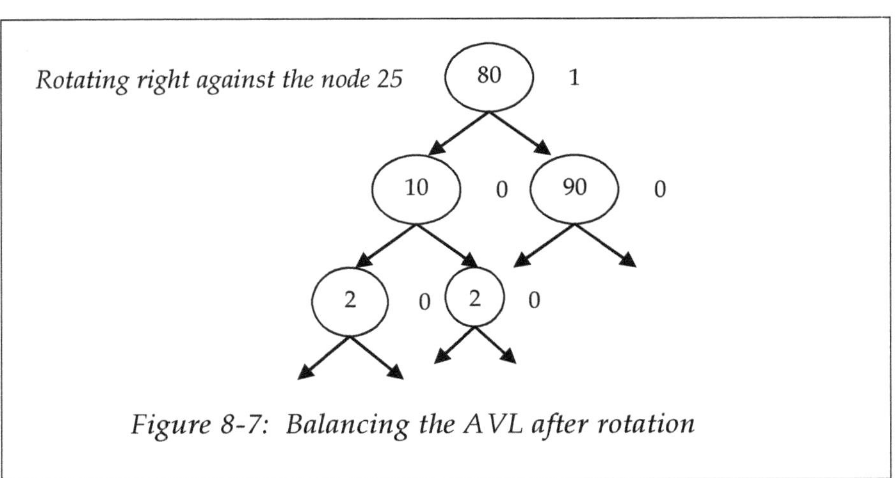

Figure 8-7: Balancing the AVL after rotation

Class for the AVL tree and functions has been given in the following class.

```
class AVLTree// Class to create the AVL Tree
{
AVLnode *root;          // root pointer of the AVL tree
public:
AVLTree();              // Constructor for the AVLTree
void AVCreate(int);              // function to create the AVL Tree
AVLnode *leftRotate(AVLnode *);    // function to left rotate
AVLnode *rightRotate(AVLnode*);  // function to right rotate
AVLnode *LRRotate(AVLnode *);    // function to left right  rotate
AVLnode *RLRotate(AVLnode*);     // function to right left rotate
```

```
void in_traversal(AVLnode*);          // function for the in-order
                                      // traversal in an AVL tree
};
```

8.6.1 Left Rotation

Left rotation is to be given, when the right side of the AVL tree is heavier. Consider the tree illustrated in the following figure.

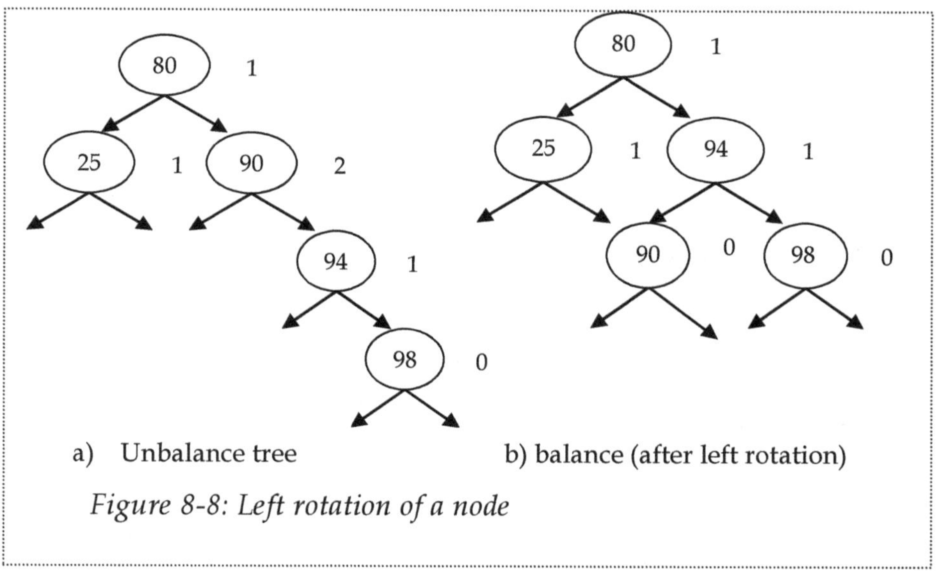

a) Unbalance tree b) balance (after left rotation)

Figure 8-8: Left rotation of a node

In the above tree, once 98 is inserted, as a result this tree becomes unbalanced. Node having the value 90 will have new balancing factor which is equal to 2. Since, this is right heavy, therefore left rotation is to be given against the node 90.

Consider in the figure 8-8 (a), 98 as child, 94 as parent of 98, and 90 as grandparent (gp) of 98. Rotating left against gp node can be accomplished by the following function:

```
void leftRotate(AVLNode *gp)
{
AVLNode *temp;
temp=gp;        // storing gp in temporary storage
if(parent->bf==1)       // if parent is also right heavy
parent=gp->right;
bfadjust(gp);   // adjust the balancing factor of all the nodes after left
                // rotation
parent->left=gp;        // connecting grandparent to the left of parent
temp=parent; // replacing temp with the parent
}
```

8.6.2 Right rotation

After inserting the node if the left node is heavy then it is to be rotated right so that the resultant tree should be balance.

```
void rightRotate(AVLNode *gp)
{
AVLNode *temp;
temp=gp;        // storing gp in temporary storage
if(parent->bf==1)       // if parent is also right heavy
parent=gp->left;
bfadjust(gp);   // adjust the balancing factor of all the nodes after left
                // rotation
parent->right=gp;       // connecting grandparent to the left of parent
temp=parent; // replacing temp with the parent
}
```

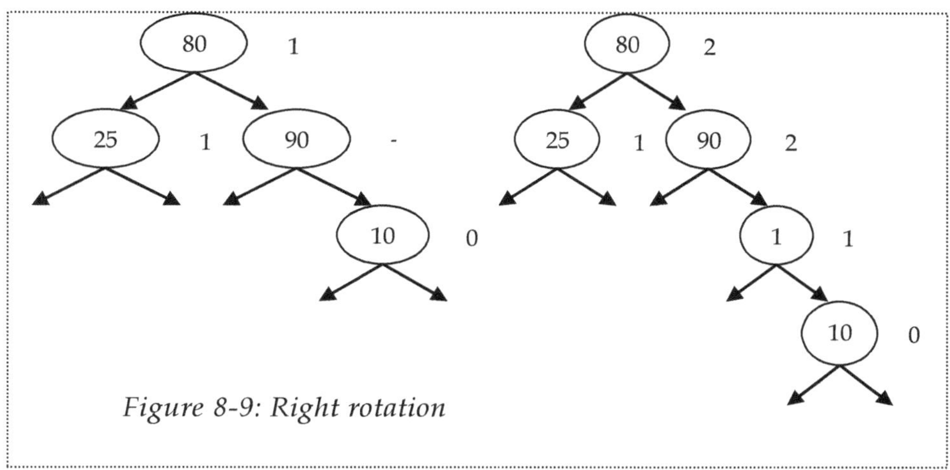

Figure 8-9: Right rotation

8.6.3 Right Left Rotation

In the right left rotation, first BST has to be rotated to the right. Completion of left rotation is followed by left rotation. This type of rotation is to be given in the cases of heterogeneous unbalanced tree. By heterogeneous, we mean if the right is heavy, but traversing downwards it is known that it is resulted due to the left heavy node. BST has already illustrated in the figure 8.5 A and B that is heterogeneously balanced.

8.6.4 Left Right Rotation

In the section 8.7.1, we have considered that both grandparent and parent are right heavy. However, this may be not the case always. It may also happen that grandparent is right heavy but parent may be left heavy. Balancing to the second case is complicated and requires double rotation. Initially, right rotation is given against the parent node. After that left rotation is given against the grandparent node. Same has been illustrated in the following example.

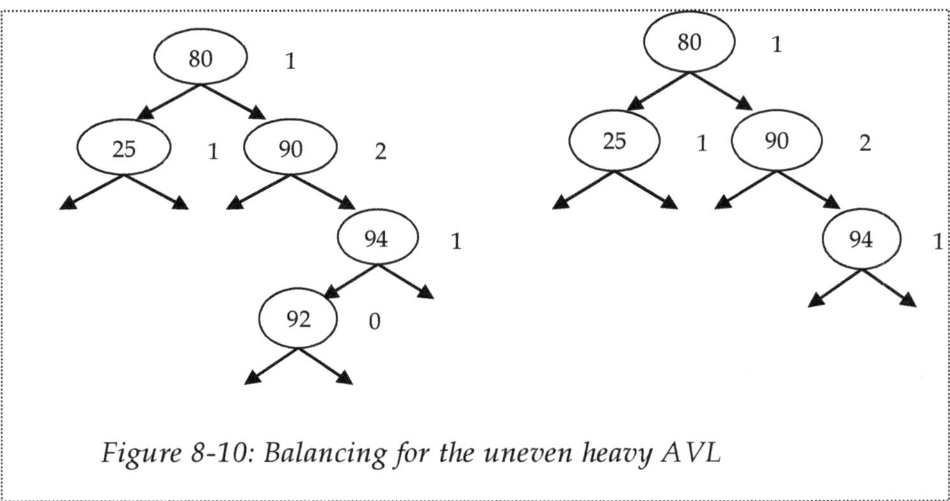

Figure 8-10: Balancing for the uneven heavy AVL

If we consider the AVL tree given in the above figure 8-8, it has been observed that due to insertion of the node having the value 92 to the node 94. Its grandparent 90 has the balancing factor of 2 which is out of the tolerance limit. But when we considered the parent of 92, it has been observed that it is having the balance factor of -1. This indicates that the node is left heavy, so both are differently balanced AVL. In such cases, we have to give double rotation. Initially, the parent has to be given right rotation whereas the grandparent will be given left rotation after the first rotation only.

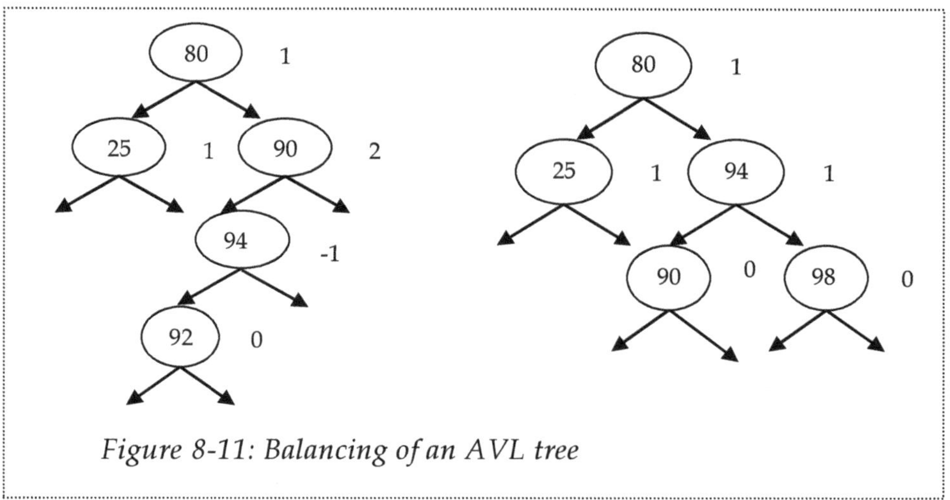

Figure 8-11: Balancing of an AVL tree

8.7 Traversal in an AVL tree

In the AVL tree, traversal is not different from the BST. Indeed, it is more efficient to traverse in the AVL since it is almost balance tree where the depth variation of only 1 is permitted. Popular traversal techniques, for instance, In-order, pre-order, and post-order traversal applicable in the BST are equally applicable in the AVL tree. Readers are requested to please refer the BST portion for this section.

8.8 Inserting the elements in an AVL tree

Inserting the element(s) in the AVL tree is complex work and require a number of considerations. For instance, when the item is inserted in a balance tree, where the balance factor is '0', in such cases the element inserted will not result in the imbalance of the

AVL.

In case if the balance factor is already 1, in that case a number of probability will exist. Consequently, rotation if needed would be govern by the rule of the rotations already specified in the section 8.7

8.9 Deleting the node in an AVL tree

Deleting the node from the AVL tree is equally complex as insertion. Once the node is deleted, AVL need to be checked for the balancing, since deletion of the node may lead to the unbalancing of AVL tree. As soon as it is detected that AVL is unbalanced. We have to rotate the node whose balancing factor has crossed the permissible limit. To balance the node, we can rotate it left or right depending upon the side it has become heavy. Consider few cases as given in the figure 10-9. In case a) and b), after the deletion of the node balancing factor is not crossing the permitted value, consequently no rotation is given. However, in the case c, balancing factor has crossed the permitted value of 1 therefore, we will rotate this node of a tree. Consider the case of 10-9 (a), in the given AVL,

We have to delete the node 2, as a result, AVL has not become unbalanced. Instead, it will become more balance. New balancing factors of various node of an AVL has been illustrated in the said figure.

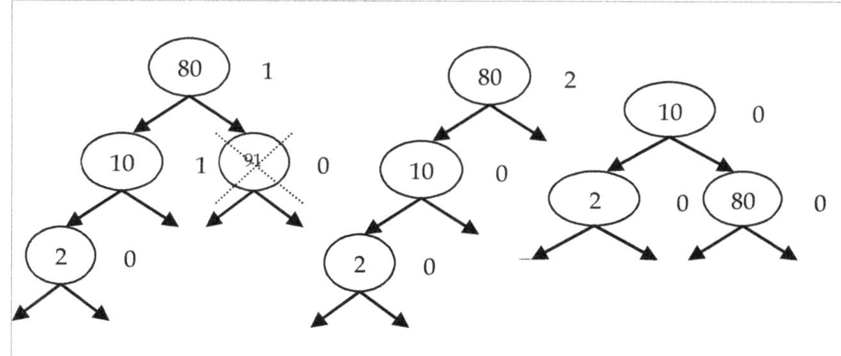

a) Deletion of 91 from the AVL Tree, unbalance AVL, After rotation

Figure 8-12: Balancing the AVL after rotation

In the 8-10 (b), the node 91 has been deleted, as a result, the node 80 will become unbalance and its new balancing factor will be 2. Since, it is left heavy, therefore, right rotation is to be given. Eventually, the node will be balanced after giving the right rotation, as illustrated in the following figure.

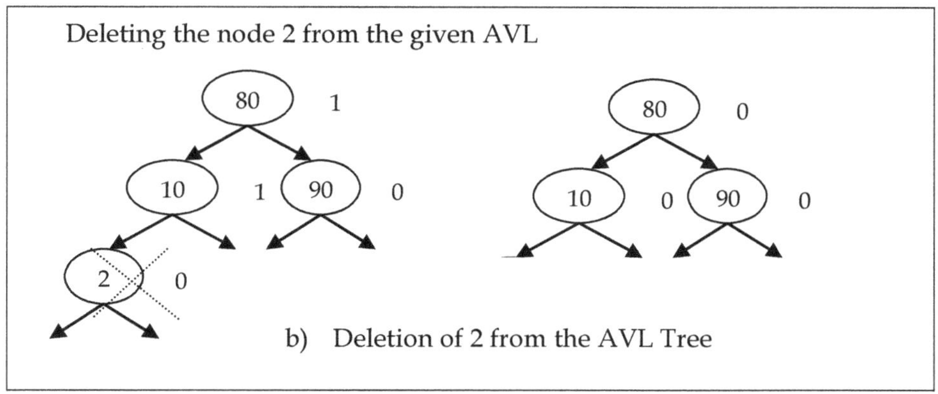

b) Deletion of 2 from the AVL Tree

Program to this effect has been given in the explained as follows.

Problem: To compute the balancing factor after deletion. Balance the AVL, if becomes unbalance.

8.10 Exercise

A. **Descriptive type questions**

1. What is the AVL tree? What is the significance of balancing factors in the AVL tree?
2. What are the advantages that can be leverages if the user is applying the AVL data structure in his application? Justify.
3. What are the different types of rotations applicable in AVL tree?
4. Discuss in detail when the left-right-left (LRL) rotation is needed in the AVL tree?
5. How the traversal in the AVL tree is different from that of BST?
6. Discuss the various conditions applicable during the deletion of the node from an AVL tree.
7. What are the various drawbacks of the AVL tree?
8. Compute the complexity of inserting a node in an AVL tree.
9. Discuss the cases during insertion when no rotation is taking place.
10. Discuss the number of levels above it will be effected once the AVL tree becomes unbalance during the insertion of the elements.

B. **Short answer type questions**

(Follow the instruction as solve the given questions)

i. AVL tree is also a BST [True/False].

ii. AVL tree yields better performance relative to BST [True/False].

iii. AVL Tree is slow in relative to BST during:

a. Traversal
b. Display
c. insertion time
d. None of these

iv. AVL yields good performance during:

a. Searching
b. Insertion
c. Deletion
d. All the above

v. It is possible to give left-left-right rotation in an AVL tree [True/ False].

vi. It is possible to give left-right-right rotation in an AVL tree [True/ False].

vii. It is possible to give right-left-right rotation in an AVL tree [True/ False].

viii. Traversal in an AVL tree is similar to that of BST [True/ False].

ix. Rotation is needed during traversal of an AVL Tree [True/False].

x. Rotation may be given, if needed, during the following operation.

a. Traversal c. both a and b

b. Insertion d. none of these

Chapter 9
Multi way tree

Chapter Objective

- Defining the multi-way tree
- Describing the various application of multi-way tree.
- Defining and describing the B tree.
- Insertion and deletion in a B tree.
- Describing the B* tree and B+ tree.
- Describing the various application of B tree.

9 Multi-way Tree

Binary tree is performing profoundly well in cases where the depth is less. However, with the increase in the depth of a binary tree performance deteriorates. To address this issue, multi-way tree can be utilized. In multi-way tree, instead of having only two children we can have 'n' number of branches. Multi-way tree always remains the balance, which is the significant advantage of Multi-way tree. Consequently, yields better performance relative to the binary search tree.

9.1 Meaning of Multi-way tree

There are various application of a multi-way tree, for instance, B tree, B+ tree and B* trees are the various implementations. All these trees are having their own pros and cons. Therefore, it depends upon the implementer to opt the multi-way tree that is well fulfilling for his specific requirement. Each of these trees has been discussed in the following section.

9.2 B Tree

B Tree is an example of a multi-way tree. This data structure is widely used for storing the data into the storage device, for instance hard disk. B Tree organizes the data at almost at the same level and depth can also be controlled. A 'B' tree having the *n* child will follow the following rules:

i) In a B tree, keys are arranged in sorted order

ii) Root node will have at least two nodes, if it is not acting as the leaf node.

iii) Each non-leaf node will have at least n/2 child at each level. However, it is not applicable in the case of root node.

iv) Total number of keys in a tree should be less than n. For instance, if a tree is of 'n' order, total number of keys cannot increase n. The B tree of order n can have maximum n-1 keys.

v) All the keys in the left nodes are less than the parent keys whereas the keys to the right are more than the parent key.

vi) All leaf nodes are at the same level.

vii) All the nodes consist of at-least (n/2) -1 keys, except the root node that can have one key.

The number 'n' taken for the B tree should be odd.

Structure of a B tree is depicted as follows:

```
const int n=5;
class bnode
{
int keys[n-1];
bnode *next[n];
};
```

A. **Creation of B Tree**

To understand the B tree, consider the following series.

78, 5, 56, 90, 12, 25, 10, 45, 98, 100, 88,

Consider that we have a B Tree of order 5; therefore total number of keys which it can have is 4. Initially, 78, 5, 56, 90 can be inserted as illustrated in the figure 9-1(a). However, on the arrival of 12, condition (maximum four key) will be violated. Therefore, [5, 12, 56, 78, 90] branching will take place and 56 will be acting as root node and the node less than 56 will be connected to the left node whereas the keys having the value greater than 56 will be connected to the right. Resultant tree is illustrated in the figure 9-1(a).

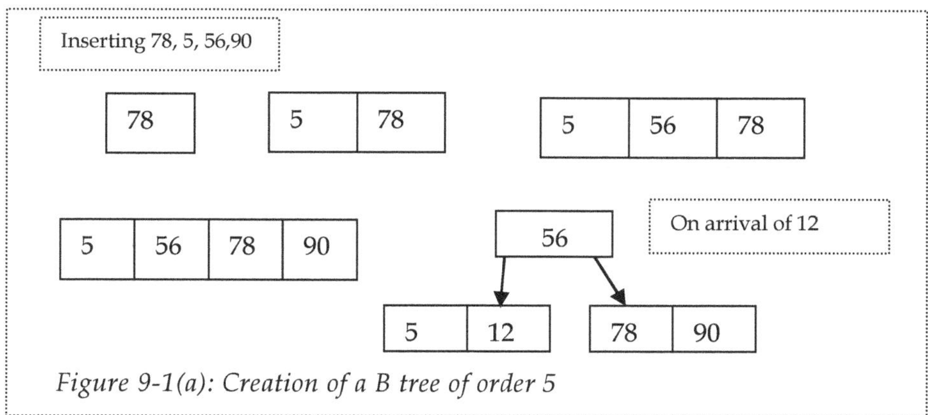

Figure 9-1(a): Creation of a B tree of order 5

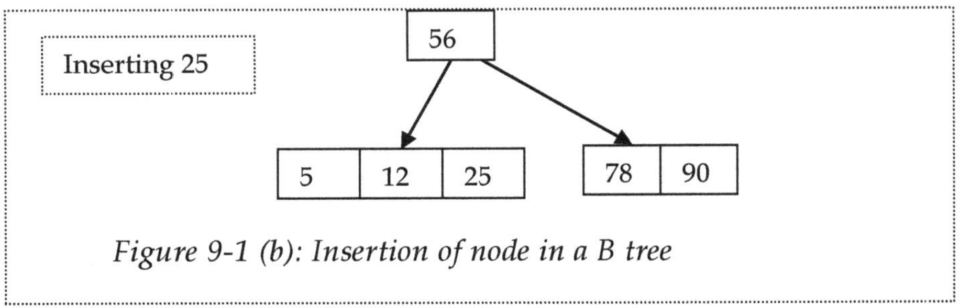

Figure 9-1 (b): Insertion of node in a B tree

After that we would like to insert 25, this will be going towards the left of 56 and will result in the B-tree as illustrated in the figure 9-1(b). On the arrival of the item 10, it will head towards left of 56. Resultant B-tree is illustrated in figure 9-1(c).

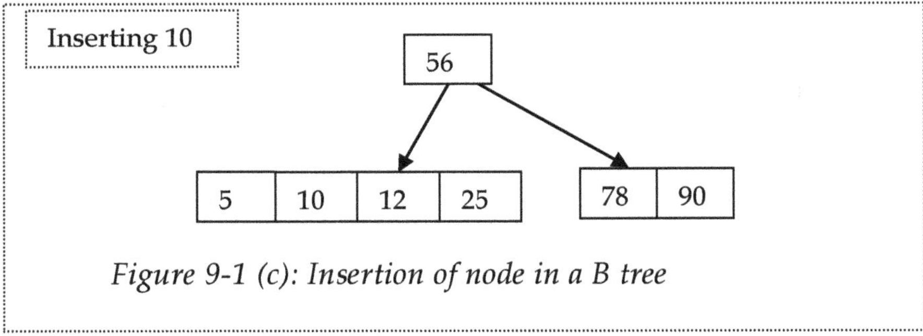

Figure 9-1 (c): Insertion of node in a B tree

On the arrival of 45, it will be directed towards the left branch. Left child is already full to its capacity; consequently, it will split the node in two branches. Resultant tree is illustrated in the figure 9-1(d).

In the above, consider a case; if number of keys in the parent is four in that case it won't be able to include all the five keys. As a result, it will split. Finally, the parent will also split to accommodate the key.

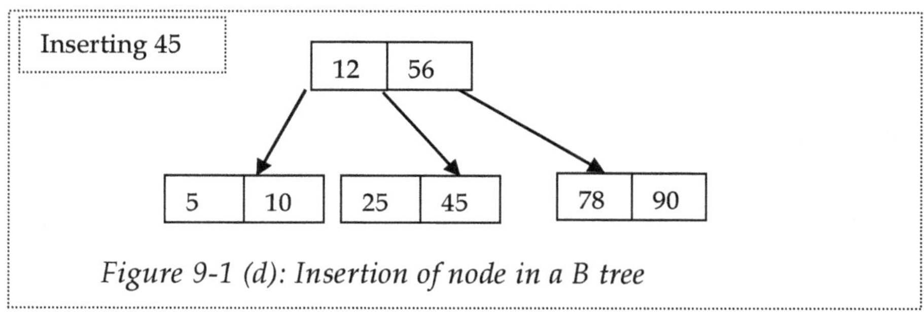

Figure 9-1 (d): Insertion of node in a B tree

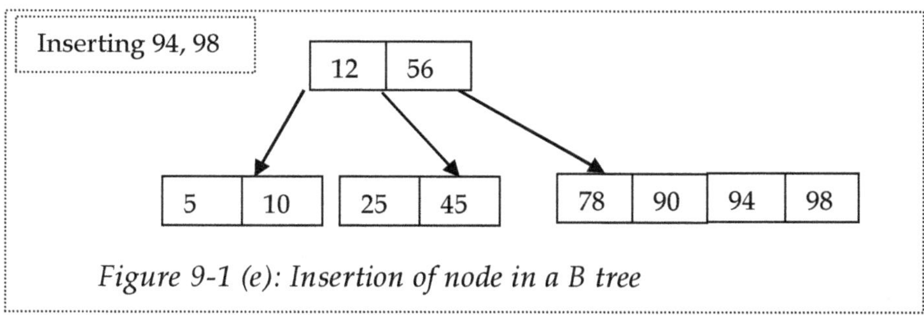

Figure 9-1 (e): Insertion of node in a B tree

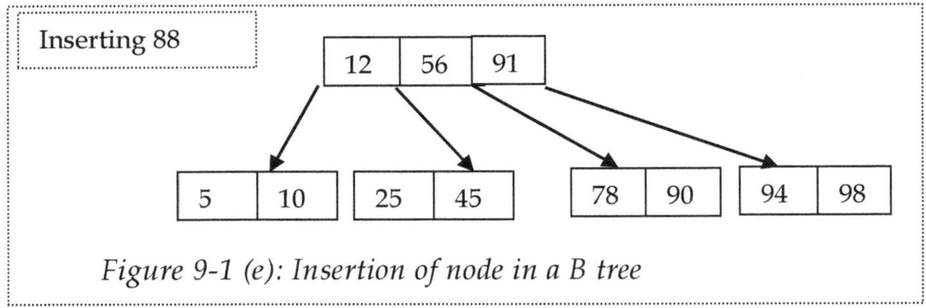

Figure 9-1 (e): Insertion of node in a B tree

Finally, the B tree is illustrated in the figure 9-1(e). Sometime split also propagates to the upper level. Consider the B tree illustrated in the figure 9-2. Due to the insertion of 33, the second branch will split, consequently, the mid element i.e. 33 will go to the upper node.

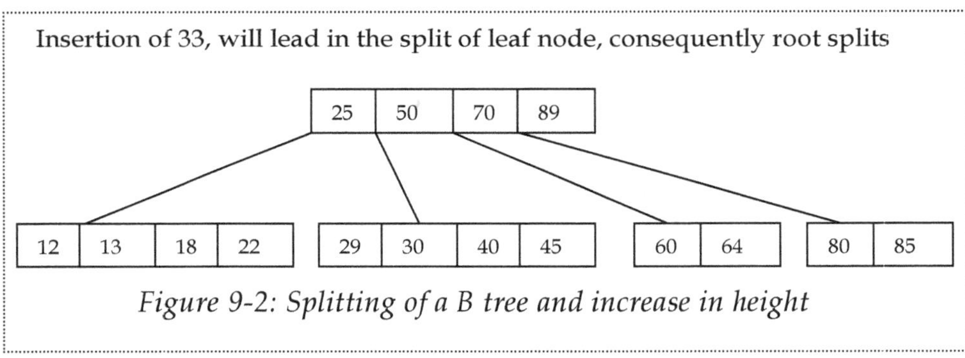

Figure 9-2: Splitting of a B tree and increase in height

However, the upper node is also full to its capacity. As a result, another split will occur on this level. Resultant tree is illustrated in the figure 9-3.

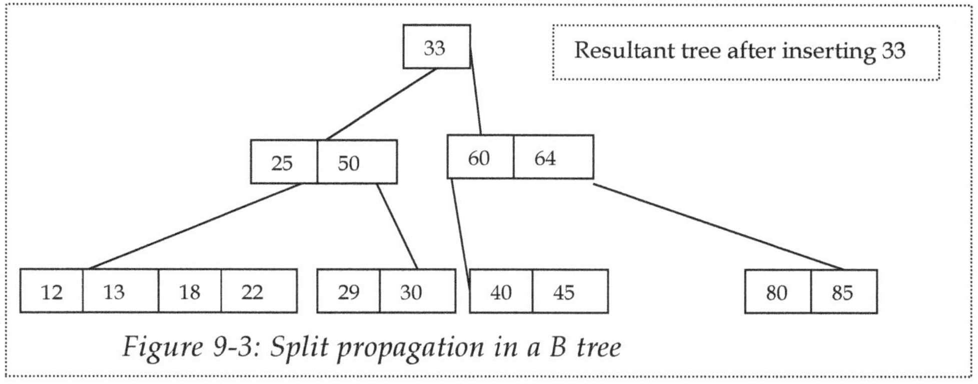

Figure 9-3: Split propagation in a B tree

B. **Deletion in a B tree**

Deletion in a B tree is profoundly complex relative to the creation of a B tree. Since during insertion key is inserted at leaf, correspondingly, key is to be removed from the leaf. Complexity in the B tree lies in the merging when the underflow occurs in a B tree.

During deletion of the B tree, following four cases can occur:

1. During deletion of a key, if the numbers of keys remaining are not violating any condition (n/2-1) then B tree is allowed to be as it is.
2. If the key is not in the leaf node in that case it is guaranteed that its predecessor or successor will be in a leaf node in that case we promote the predecessor or successor to the leaf node.

During the above two, if the condition of minimum number of keys to be maintained is violated in that case, we look for the neighboring nodes (sibling) that are required to be merged.

3. If one of the neighbors has more than the minimum key in that case, one of the key is promoted in the leaf node and the parent node is shifted in the leaf node.
4. If both of the neighbor nodes do not have more than the minimum node in that case both the nodes are merged together.

All the above cases have been illustrated in the following figures.

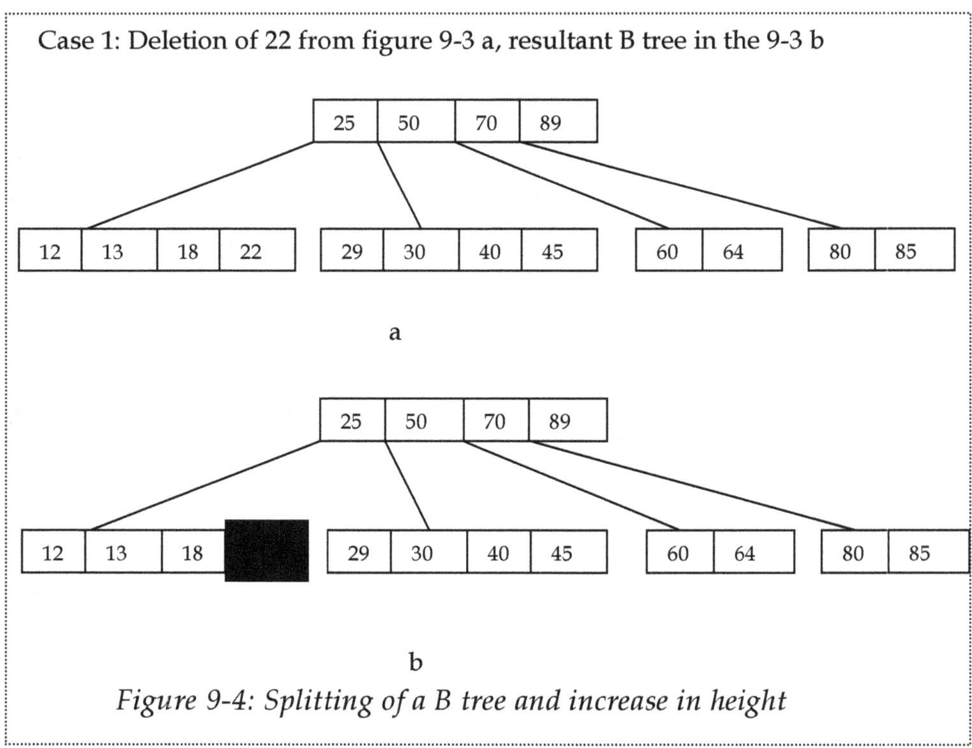

Figure 9-4: Splitting of a B tree and increase in height

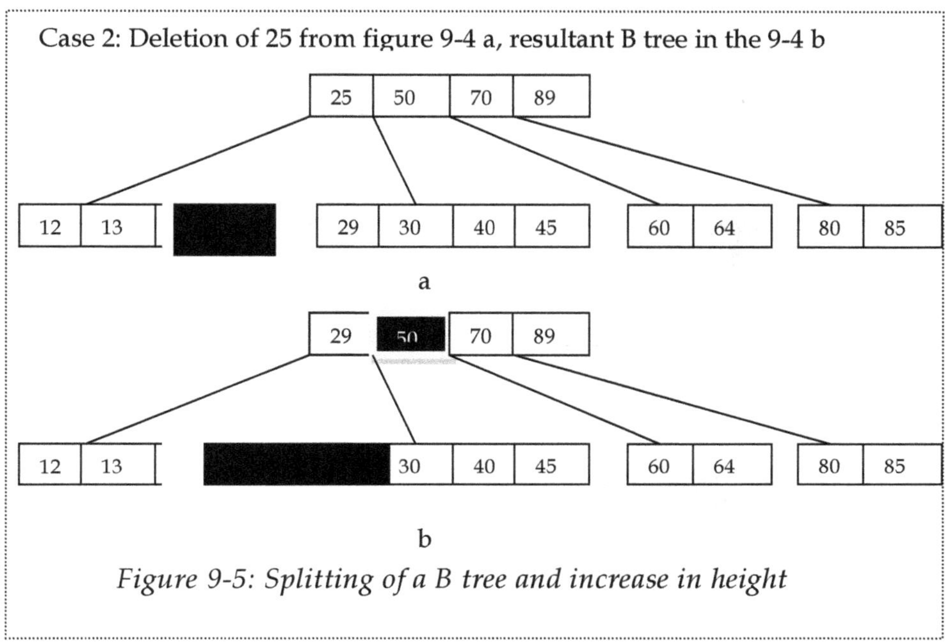

Figure 9-5: Splitting of a B tree and increase in height

Case 3: Deletion of 12 from figure 9-5 a, resultant B tree in the 9-5 b

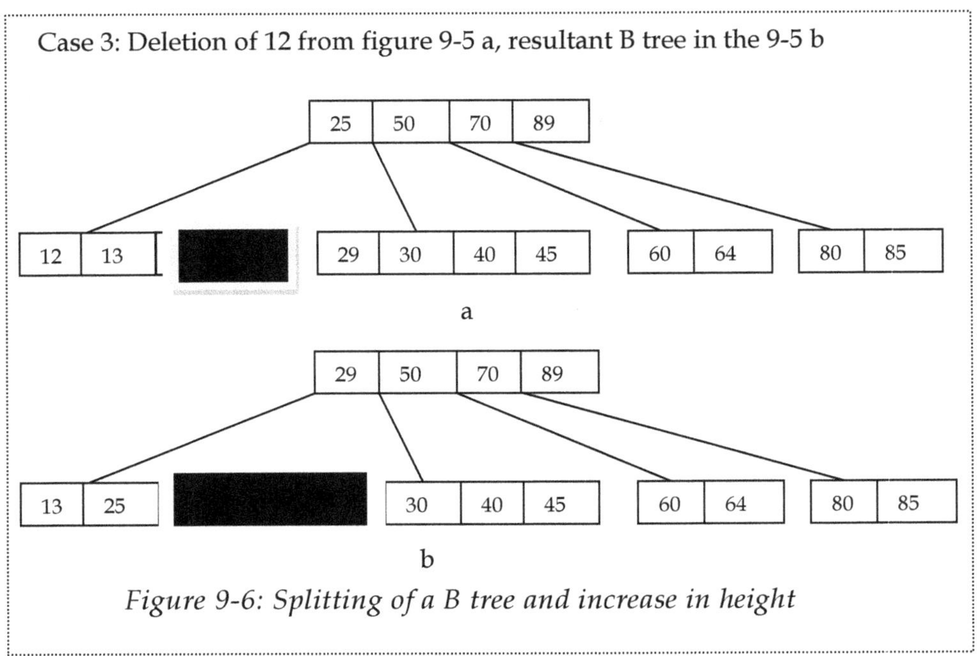

Figure 9-6: Splitting of a B tree and increase in height

Case 4: Deletion of 80 from figure 9-6 a, resultant B tree in the 9-6 b

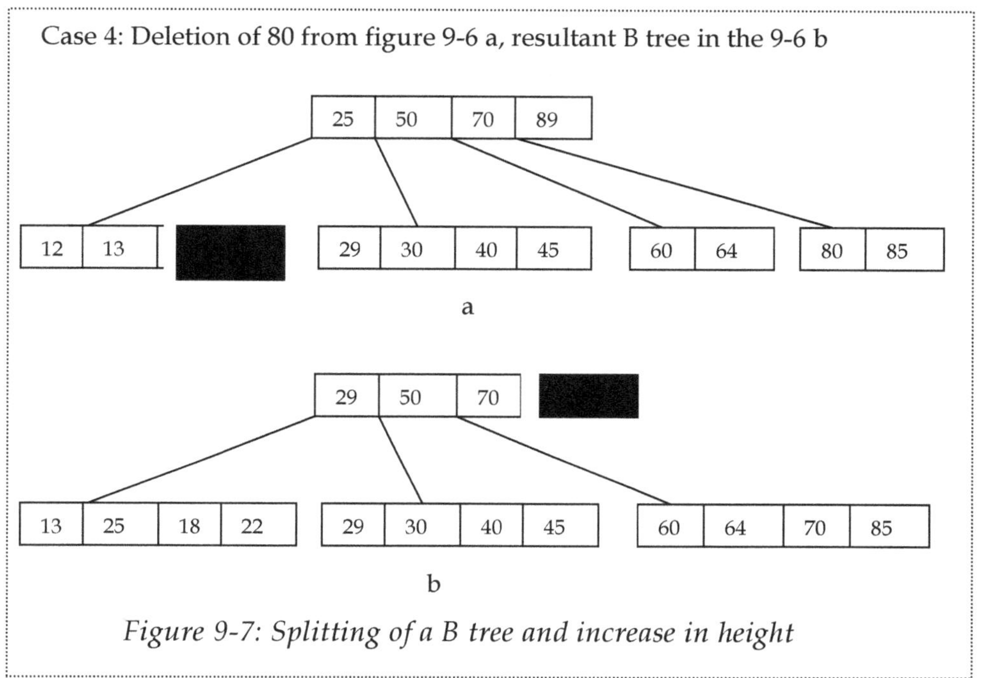

Figure 9-7: Splitting of a B tree and increase in height

9.3 B* Tree

Node of a B tree represent the block to be traversed for searching the information. Consequently, seek time will increase. To address this new version of B tree known as B* tree is used.

In a B* tree, splitting is delayed till all the nodes are not filled to 2/3 of its capacity. Therefore, fewer the nodes mans less seek time. The other measure is related to the number of split taking place. In case of B tree, one node splits into 2. However, in case of B* tree 2 nodes split into 3. Therefore, this split is also minimized.

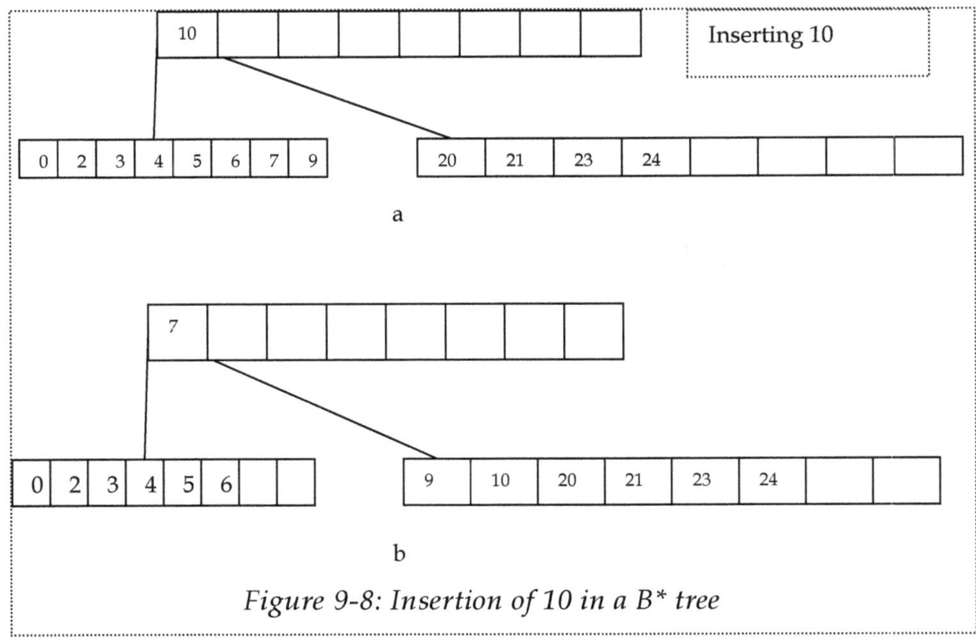

Figure 9-8: Insertion of 10 in a B tree*

Consider a B* tree of order 9. In a B* tree of order 9, maximum number of keys that can be accommodated are 8. In the above figure 9-8 a, B* tree is illustrated. If the next element that need to be inserted is 10, it will be directed towards the left side. Since, left node is already full to its capacity. Therefore, inserting 10 will result in the split of the node. However, it has been observed that its right sibling is not fill. Consequently, in the B* tree the split will be deferred till all the nodes of considered level are not full to 2/3. Since, in considered B* tree, its right node is not 2/3 full. Therefore, all the nodes will be linearly arranged, mid element of the linear order will be inserted at the top, whereas less will be arranged in the left and more will be placed in the right.

Similarly, if the nodes of the B* tree are full, in that case it will split. For instance,

9.4 B+ tree

B+ tree is the special case of a B tree in which data is organized at the leaf of the tree. Interior nodes maintain only the reference. All the leaves are connected together to form a link list. Consequently, sequential accessibility is possible in the B+ tree.

For a tree, to qualify the definition of B+ tree it should need the following properties.

Consider a B+ tree of order n:

- Root act as a leaf node if it is having at-least one element.
- Each node contains not more than n child and n-1 keys.
- Non leaf consist of (n/2)-1 keys in any node.
- Leaf nodes are connected to each other.

B+ tree is the widely used data structure for the storage, due to the availability of the data at the leaf node. Reference available at the top provides the routing capability.

Consider the series

9.5 B* Tree

9.6 Exercises

A. **Describe the following answers**

1. What do you understand by multi-way tree? Explain when a tree can be classified as a multi-way tree? Justify.
2. Distinguish the multi-way tree and a Binary search tree.
3. What are the restrictions applicable to a B tree?
4. Define the B+ tree. Explain the significant advantages of B+ tree.
5. Define the B* tree. Discuss the significant advantages and disadvantages of B* tree.
6. Write down the 3 major uses of the B tree. How the performance is governed by these multi-way trees?
7. Distinguish between B+ tree and B* tree.
8. Consider that you have been given a problem after analysing the problem, you could ascertained that you need to apply the multi-way tree. Which multi-way tree you will like to apply. Justify your answer.

B. **Short answer type questions**

1. B tree is also a BST [True/False].
2. All the BST can be termed as B Tree [True/False].
3. Tree having............can be termed as multi-way tree.

a. n number of children c. n number of keys.

b. Both a and c d. None of these

4. In a B tree of order N, it can have............minimum children:

a. N c. 2^N

b. 2^{N-1} d. None of these

5. In a B+ tree number, of order N, total number of leaf node would be

a. N/2 c. 2^N

b. Cannot be predicted d. None of these.

6. In the B tree, split may take place if the number of node is less than n/2 [True/False].

7. In a B+ tree, split is deferred till the children are not filled to ....

a. 2/3 c. ½

b. Both a and c d. none of these.

Chapter 10
Searching and sorting

Chapter Objective

- Defining the searching and its significance
- Describing the various types of searching
- Defining the sorting and its various types
- Describing the simple sorting methods
- Describing the complex sorting

10 Searching and Sorting

Sorting and searching are the basic operations for any collection of records maintained by the business entity. Query or record requested should be accessed in the minimum time. Delay in the accessibility may cause unpleasant reaction from the user. Sorted arranged data facilitates in fast accessibility/searching of the records. These two operations are complement to each other. The upcoming sections highlights the many of the prominent searching and sorting techniques that have significance for this topic.

10.1 Searching

Sorting and searching are profoundly significant in data structure. In case of query, we need to search the record from the existing database. Searching time will be minimum in sorted list, relative to the list that is un-sorted. According, searching is categorized into the following types.

10.1.1 Linear Search

In the linear search, data are randomly placed. In this method each element of the list is matched with the item to be searched. This process continues till element is not searched or the list is not exhausted. Linear search is simple method to implement but takes more time in searching.

Program: To search the element from the given list and return the search status

```
int search(int list[], int element)
 {
int i=0,found=0;
while(list[i])
 {
if(list[i]==element)     // if the element is found, terminate
  {
found=1;
break;
}
i++;
}
return found;
}
```

We can also return the value of index, instead of returning the status of flag. In the search method, if more than one elements are having the same value, While searching such element the item accessed first will be returned. To return the index from the above program, it can be modified as depicted in the following program.

Program: To search the element from the given list and return the index where item is found

```
int search(int list[], int element)
 {
int i=0, index=-1;
while(list[i])
 {
```

```
if(list[i]==element)      // if the element is found, terminate checking
 {
index=i;
break;
}
i++;
}
return index;
}
```

The performance of the above search is based on the number of comparisons needed to find out the element. If the searched element is found at the first comparison itself then its complexity will be O(1). Similarly, if it is found at the last position then it's complexity will be O(n).

In the worst case, linear search is having the complexity of O(n). That is huge in today's world and will take much time, if the data list is huge. **If the item is not found**, in that case also all the elements to be compared with the item to be searched. Due to search of all the items, here the complexity will be again O(n).

List that is arranged in sorted order gives the better performance in comparison to the non-sorted list. It is also observed that in a given list 20 % items are frequently accessed. If we can identify these 20 % item and arrange them at the beginning then the performance of the linear search can improve significantly. Therefore, it is required that the list be arranged for the better performance.

10.1.2 Binary search

Binary search is another method that is used for searching. However, it is much efficient relative to Linear search. Arranging the items in sorted order is the pre-requisite for a Binary search. In binary search, we do not check the element to be searched with each element of the given list; Instead, we follow the approach similar to our dictionary, where we open the random page, look for the word, if word is on the same page then start searching the word. Otherwise we are moving left if the alphabet is more or right if the alphabet is less to the word searched. In binary search, we follow the same approach. To achieve the above objective, we can follow the recursive and non-recursive approach to search the element.

A. **Recursive approach**

In the recursive approach, we determine the mid element of the array. If the mid element is equal to the item to be searched then we terminate here itself else we recursively call the function. If the lower index becomes more than the higher index in that case it can be inferred that the item to be searched is not available in the list.

```
//function for the recursive search
int rec_bsearch(int x[],int l,int u,int num)
{
int mid=(l+u)/2;
cout<<" l ="<<l<<" u="<<u<<endl;
 if(x[mid]==num)
 return 1;
```

```
if(l>u)
return 0;
if(num < x[mid])
 return rec_bsearch(x,l,mid-1,num);
 else
 return rec_bsearch(x,mid+1,u,num);
}
```

B. **Non-recursive approach**

In the non-recursive approach, we initialize the lower and the highest element and follow the same approach as followed in recursive method, but using non-recursive technique. In this method, we break the searching of the item as soon as the item to be searched is found in the list. We have used the variable 'flag' to determine whether the item has been searched in the given list or not. We consider that the item does exist in the list, correspondingly, we set the value to 0. Once the element is located, in that case flag is set to 1.

```
// Non-recursive function to search an element
int bsearch(int x[],int num)
{
int lower, upper, mid, flag=0;
lower=0;
upper=9;

while(lower<=upper)
{
```

```
mid=(lower+upper)/2;
if(x[mid]==num)
 {
 flag=1;
 break;
 }
 if(num < x[mid])  // Element may be at left hand side
   upper=mid-1;// move the highest to the left side
   else          // Element may be at right hand side
   lower=mid+1;// move the lower to the right side
 }
 return flag; // Finally, return the flag
}
```

10.2 Sorting

Items arranged in a list in random order give lower performance during searching. Although, if we compute the complexity sorted or unsorted array, it gives the same result. However, practically sorted array gives better performance relative to the unsorted array.

Sorting can be broadly categorized into two:

- External sorting
- Internal sorting

Sorting in which all the elements are not loaded into memory instead are available in secondary storage then such type of sorting is known as **external sorting**.

The other type of sorting is known as internal sorting in which elements are stored in the memory for sorting. Due to the memory usage for items storage, internal sorting is fast relative to the external sorting. Sorting techniques that are discussed in this book are example of internal sorting.

A. Bubble Sort

Bubble sorting functions similar to the bubble that has the characteristics of coming up due to light weight or heavier elements are remaining downwards. Bubble sorting using this technique. In the first pass the heaviest element is arranged at the right position. In the second pass, second highest element is arranged at the penultimate location of the list and so forth.

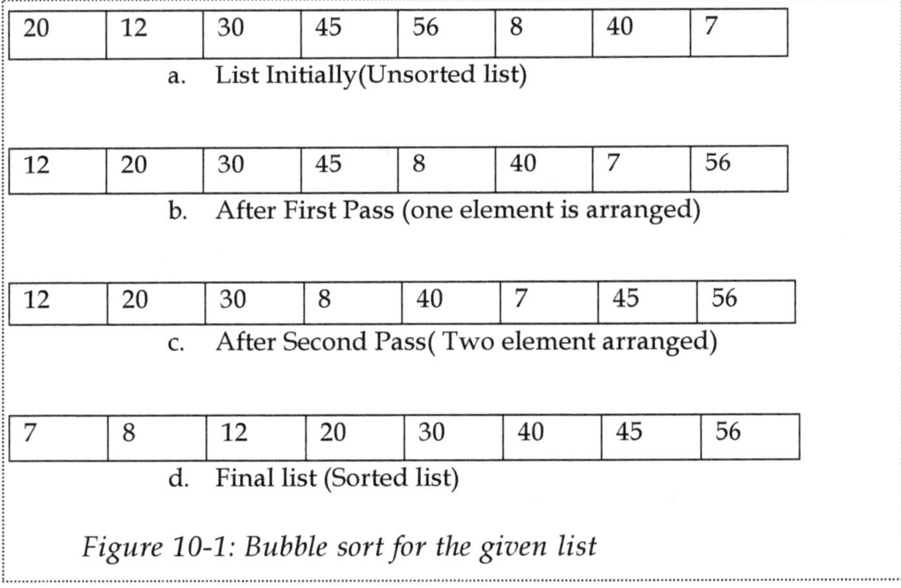

20	12	30	45	56	8	40	7

a. List Initially(Unsorted list)

12	20	30	45	8	40	7	56

b. After First Pass (one element is arranged)

12	20	30	8	40	7	45	56

c. After Second Pass(Two element arranged)

7	8	12	20	30	40	45	56

d. Final list (Sorted list)

Figure 10-1: Bubble sort for the given list

In the bubble sort, loops are controlled by the items that are arranged. Since, on each pass, one element will be placed at the appropriate place therefore in the second pass this item do not need to be disturbed.

Other case may be that the array given is already sorted. In this case no items will be swapped. Therefore, for the efficient program writing we have to also check whether the swapping of the element is occurring or not. If it is not occurring then it denotes that the elements are sorted. We terminate the loop here itself. Working of the program has been demonstrated in the following program.

```
// Problem: Program to sort the series using bubble sort
void bubble(int a[])
{
int i,j,temp;
for(i=0;i<8;i++)
{
for(j=0;j<7-i;j++)
 {
 if(a[j]>a[j+1]) // if item is more than the next item
  {
  temp=a[j];   // swapping if the right element is more
  a[j]=a[j+1];
  a[j+1]=temp;
  }
 }
 cout<<endl;
}
}
```

To determine the complexity of the bubble sort, we observe that for first pass the inner loops run for n-1. For the second pass, it runs for the n-2. Therefore, we can conclude that the complexity of bubble sort is O (n^2).

B. Insertion sort

In the insertion sort, initially we consider that the first element is in the sorted order. Sorted elements are arranged in the list known as left hand side. After that the first element, we consider the second element and compare it with the items available in the left hand side. During the scanning of the items, it is placed at the appropriate place. All the remaining items are shifted toward the right hand side. Working of the insertion sort is demonstrated in the following program.

```
// Program to sort the array
void insert(int a[])      //function to insert the array
 {
 int k,index,temp,item,i;
 for(k=0;k<n;k++)        // Starting from the first to n element of the array
  {
  item=a[k];    // storing the current element at item
  for(i=0;i<k;i++)        // To determine the position
   {
   if(a[i] > a[k])        // if the large elemen is found
        {
        for(int t=k;t>i;t--)        // shift all the elements to the right
        a[t]=a[t-1];                // element by element
        a[i]=item;                  // Place the item at right position
        break;                      // Stop the inner loop
```

```
        }
    }
  }
}
```

The outer for loop is used to sort all the elements of the array one by one. It is followed by the inner loop that runs from the 0th index to the position under consideration. For instance, if the index/location under consideration is 5. In that case, element has to be inserted between the 0th to the 4th location. Consequently, element is to be inserted at the position where the element having the value more than the current element is encountered. Third loop that having the variable t, starts with the last index and moves the element one by one. This results in creation of the space for the item under consideration. Eventually, element is placed at the hole created.

C. Selection sort

In the selection sort, smallest item is selected in each pass and arranged at appropriate place. In the first pass, we find out the smallest items from all the available items in the array. Once it is traced then we can place it at first position. In the second pass, we try to find out the smallest items from the remaining list (other than the first item that is already smallest), once it is traced then it is placed on the second position and so forth. Here we have to note that once we place the item at first or the second position. Item already exist in these positions, therefore we have to know the index of the smallest element then only we can swap the smallest element from the number in consideration. Working of the selection sort is demonstrated in the following program.

Program: This program sorts the array using selection sort. It swaps the item wherever less item is encountered.

```
void selection(int a[])
 {
 int i,j,temp;
 for(i=0;i<=7;i++)
  {
  for(j=i+1;j<=7;j++)
   {
   if(a[i] > a[j])
     {
     temp=a[i];
     a[i]=a[j];
     a[j]=temp;
     cout<<" a[i] "<<a[i]<<"  i="<<i<<endl;
     }
   }
}
}
```

Program: This function also sorts the item using selection sort, but it identifies the minimum item. At the end swap it with the array element.

```
void selection2(int a[])
 {
 int i,j,index,min;
 for(i=0;i<=7;i++)
```

```
{
min=a[i];
index=i;
for(j=i+1;j<=7;j++)
 {
 if(min > a[j])
  {
  min=a[j];
  index=j;
  cout<<" Min "<<min<<"  index="<<j<<endl;
  }
 }
 if(i!=j)//item is not the minimum
  {
  a[index]=a[i];
  a[i]=min;
  }
}
```

10.3 Efficient Sorting Algorithms

All the algorithms that are discussed above worked on the principle of exchange as a result, the algorithm were less efficient . All of them were having the complexity of $O(n^2)$. Their efficiency having compared here as

N= / efficiency	1	100	1000

Therefore, we need algorithm that should result in better performance. Algorithm discussed below give better algorithm.

A. Bucket sort

In the bucket sort algorithm, we arrange the items in groups based on the category. These categories of item are decided by the start value. For instance, consider the series 28,17, 40, 99, 27, 22, 96, 98. In this series, items are arranges as per their weight in a group. Series starts with the digit 1 with be grouped in one bucket, similarly numbers start with the 2 will be grouped into 2nd group. Process will continue up-to the value of 9. For the given series, bucket has been demonstrated in the following figure.

Elements after completion of phase 1		
17,		
22,	27,	28,
40,		
96,	98,	99

Initial list
28,
17,
40,
99,
27,
22,
96,
98

Figure 10-2: Bucket sorting

Within the bucket the elements are arranged in sorted order. For instance, if the number starts with the number 2 and it is having 3 elements as 28,22,27. These numbers will be arranged in sorted order as 22, 27, 28.

B. Count sort

Count sort is another sorting method that is profoundly efficient. In the count sort, we consider the n elements which ranges between 0 to m. we find out all the elements that are less than the particular element. Here in this case, we have considered that the numbers are equal. Here first count the number of particular digit. Which is followed by commutation of the numbers. To solve the count sort, we would consider two arrays, one consisting of the elements whereas the other stores the count of particular number. Consider a series consisting of 10 numbers. All these numbers are ranging from 0 to 7. Series and the working of count sorting has been illustrated in the following figure 10-3.

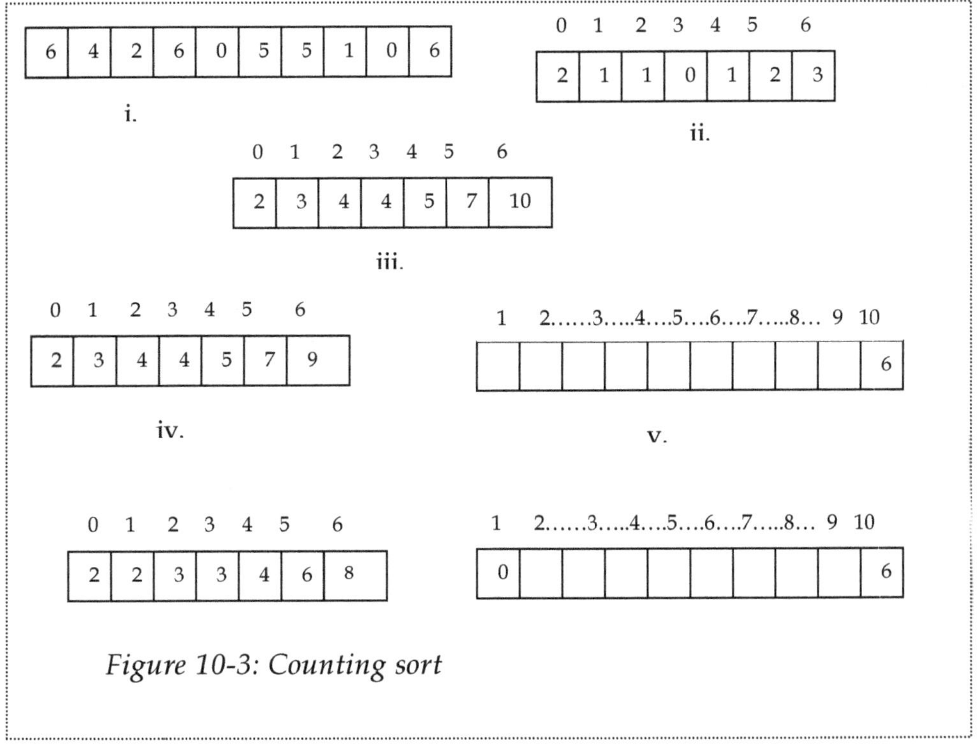

Figure 10-3: Counting sort

In the considered case:

n=10

Range=0-6

Therefore, we will count the numbers which are equal. Correspondingly, the count is written as illustrated in figure ii. Finally the count is commutative that assist in determining the number of elements less than the current number. Refer the list given in the i. again. Element is 6, Go to the 6th index of iii. In this case value is 10. Consequently, 6 is to be placed at the 10th position of the sorted list. Since, one item is already placed. Reduce the sum by 1 at the index position considered. This is followed by propagation of (-1) till the last element is not reached. In the considered example, since the last item is considered therefore, there is no propagation of reduction in value.

C. Radix sort

In the radix sort, numbers are arranged based on the radix. We define the radix as base. For instance, in the decimal number radix is 10. Now numbers are arranges first on the most significant value, and move towards least significant value. In each pass, we arrange them based on one positional value. At the end, whole series is available in the sorted order. This series make the usage of count sort and arrange the series based on the count method.

D. Quick Sort

Quick sort is the widely used technique to sort the element. In this method we divide the list in two. To determine the position from where the list to be divided is ascertained by the pivot element.

Pivot element is the first element which is move towards right if the element encountered are less than the pivot element. Movement terminates as soon as item encountered is more than the pivot element. Index of this element is stored. After that pivot element is moved from the extreme right to the left, till the elements are more than the pivot element. As soon as the item less than the pivot element is encountered than we terminate here itself, if lower index is less than the upper index than both the item are swapped. We again start comparing the element from the left hand side. During the complete process, the pivot element is placed at exact position. Items to the left of the pivot will be less and the items right of the pivot elements will be more. Consider the series of figure 12-2.

34	20	45	12	89	78	30	66	98

Figure 10-4: sorting the series using quick sort

In this series there are total 09 elements. Therefore, lower will be 0, whereas the upper will be 07. In the given series, the first element is 34, this element is known as pivot element. This element is compared with the other elements of the series (starting from the left series) one by one. This comparison starts from left/right, in our case we have considered the left hand side as starting point. During movement towards the right, we ensure that the element encountered are less than the element that is pivot. If the element is not less, our traversal terminate and we have to check from the right side. From this side, we continue to move towards the left till elements encountered are less the pivot element. The moment element that is less than the pivot is encountered, we halt the movement, here we exchange both the elements (bigger of the left side to the smaller of right side) the element with the highest number to the smallest. .

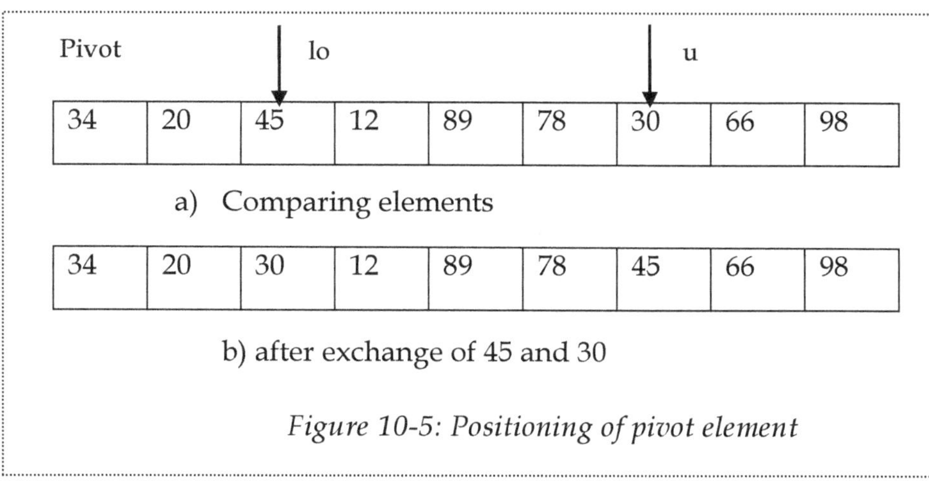

Figure 10-5: Positioning of pivot element

```
// program for the quick sort using recursive method
void quicksort ( int ar[], int lower, int upper)
{
int i;
if(upper > lower)// number of elements are more than 1
{
i=partition(ar,lower, upper);
quicksort(ar,lower, i-1); // quicksort for the left half
quicksort(ar, i+1,upper); // quicksort for the right half
}
}
```

Partition function is given as

```
// function to partition after placing the pivot element at the appropriate
place.
int partition(in ar, int left, int right)
{
int l, r, temp,  i;  // l for the left, r for right
l=left;
r=right +1;
while( r>= l)
 {
while( ar[++l] < i); // move right till elements are smaller than pivot
while(ar[--r] > i); // move towards left till elements are more than pivot
if( l > u)
  {
t=ar[l];
ar[l]=ar[r];
ar[r]=t;
}
}
t=ar[lower];
ar[lower]=ar[r];
ar[r]=t;
return r;
}
```

E. Merge sort

In the merge sort, we follow the divide and conquer method. In this series, first we divide the series into individual number, then we conquer them we arranging the items of the series. Finally, we follow the merge method to create the complete list. Therefore, merge sort is the popular example of the divide and conquer method. Functioning of the merge sort is dependent upon the count and radix sort. It is considered as one of the most efficient algorithm and proved asymptotically as one of the best algorithms. In the given series of figure 12-4, the total number of elements are 8, therefore it will be divided into two group.

28	17	40	99	27	22	96	98

Total number of elements are 8
Divide them in two series, each of 08/2=4 elements

(28, 17, 40, 99) (27,22, 96, 98)

Total number of elements are 4
Divide them in two series, each of 4/2=2 elements

(28, 17) (40, 99) (27,22) (96, 98)

Figure 10-6: Divide and conquer in quick sort

One list will consisting of first four elements, while the second series consisting of the rest of the four elements. Now both of the series are (28, 17, 40, 99), (27, 22, 96, 98). In divide and conquer method, we go up-to the lowest level, it means that the series have to be divide further. Since, now in each series consisting of 4 elements therefore they have to divide into the group of 02. (((28, 17), (40, 99)), ((27, 22), (96, 98)). Finally, we divide into the group of 1 as (((28),(17)),(40), (99)), ((27),(22), (96), (98)). Now they are divided into the lowest component. Here, each series is consisting of one element therefore, it is considered as sorted. Afterwards, elements are grouped in two and they are sorted as (17, 28) (40, 99) (22, 27), (96, 98). After that they are merged into the group of four and sorted among them as (17, 28, 40, 99) (22, 27, 96, 98). Now both the series are in sorted order. Finally, we group both the series and sort them. Consequently, the series obtained will be in the sorted order as (17 22 27 28 40 96 98 99). This approach is known as bottom up approach method. Program to merge sort has been given as follows.

```
// Program to sort the array using mergesort
void mergesort(int ar[], int lower, int upper)
{
int mid;
if(upper > lower)
{
mid=(lower+upper)/2;
mergesort(ar, lower, mid);     // divide the series into two (left side)
mergesort(ar,mid+1,upper);  // divide the series into two (right side)
merge(ar, lower, mid, mid+1, upper); // merge the half
}        // end of if
}        // end of function
```

F. Heap sort

Heap is a data structure that is widely utilized in priority queue.

Heap is defined as follows:

i. A large dynamic area of memory that can be utilized by the programmer and same may be de-allocated when not needed.

ii. A balanced, left justified binary tree in which no node has a value greater than the value in its parents.

Heap sorts follows the second definition.

In sorting, Quick-sort is usually gives the performance of O (n log n), however, in the worst case it slows down to O (n^2). New sorting method known as heap sort guaranteed O (n log n). Consequently, it is widely used in the critical application where the time is a significant factor.

To know the heap sort, we need to know certain definitions.

Heap Property

It can be defined as follows:

Node in a tree follows the heap property if its root is more than the children

All the leaf node follow the heap property.

If a tree does not follow the heap property, an operation known as shift operation is to be applied, that enable the given tree to qualify as heap. Once this operation is applied at one level, node at the upper level may violate the definition. Therefore, shift-up operation is repeatedly applied till it does not follow the heap property or it has not reached the root node. Tree fulfilling the heap sort has been illustrated in the following figure.

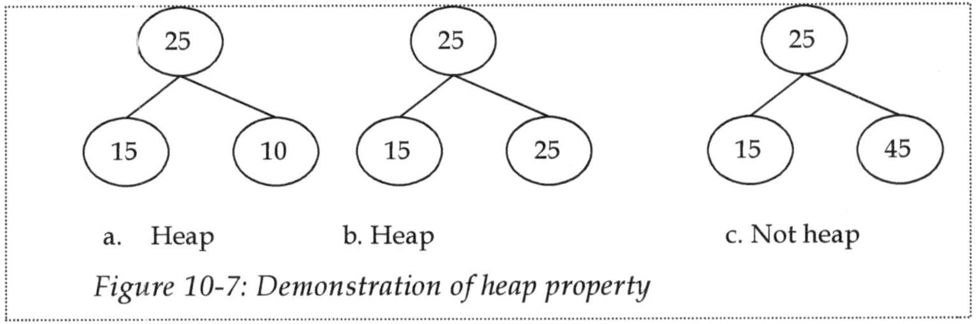

Figure 10-7: Demonstration of heap property

Constructing the Heap

Now, we would like to learn about the heap with the help of an example. Consider the series, 20, 9, 40, 70, 56, 34, 90, 12, 76, 80, 33 for which heap is to be constructed that is to be followed by sorting the given series.

On the arrival of 20, since no root is existing, consequently, the root will be created. On the arrival of 9, it will be routed to the left and will act as the left node of the heap tree. Since, attachment of the 9 does not violate any condition. Therefore, it will remain to the left of the existing tree as illustrated in the figure 10-8(b). On the arrival of 40, it will be attached to the right of the node, since the heap definition violates, consequently, shift-up operation is to be carried out. During shift operation, its parent node (i.e. 20) will occupy its position whereas the new node 40 will act as parent node. Same has been illustrated in the figure 10-8(c).

On the arrival of 70, it will be inserted at the extreme left as illustrated in the figure 10-8 (d). insertion of this node will violate the definition of heap. Consequently, shift-up operation is to carried out till it does not adhering to the heap definition. On shifting on level up, we observe that it still the tree is not following the definition of the heap. Consequently, it is shifted-up again. Here it is acting as the root node. Since, no upper level is available, therefore it is allowed to remain there. It is also observed that now it is not violating any heap definition.

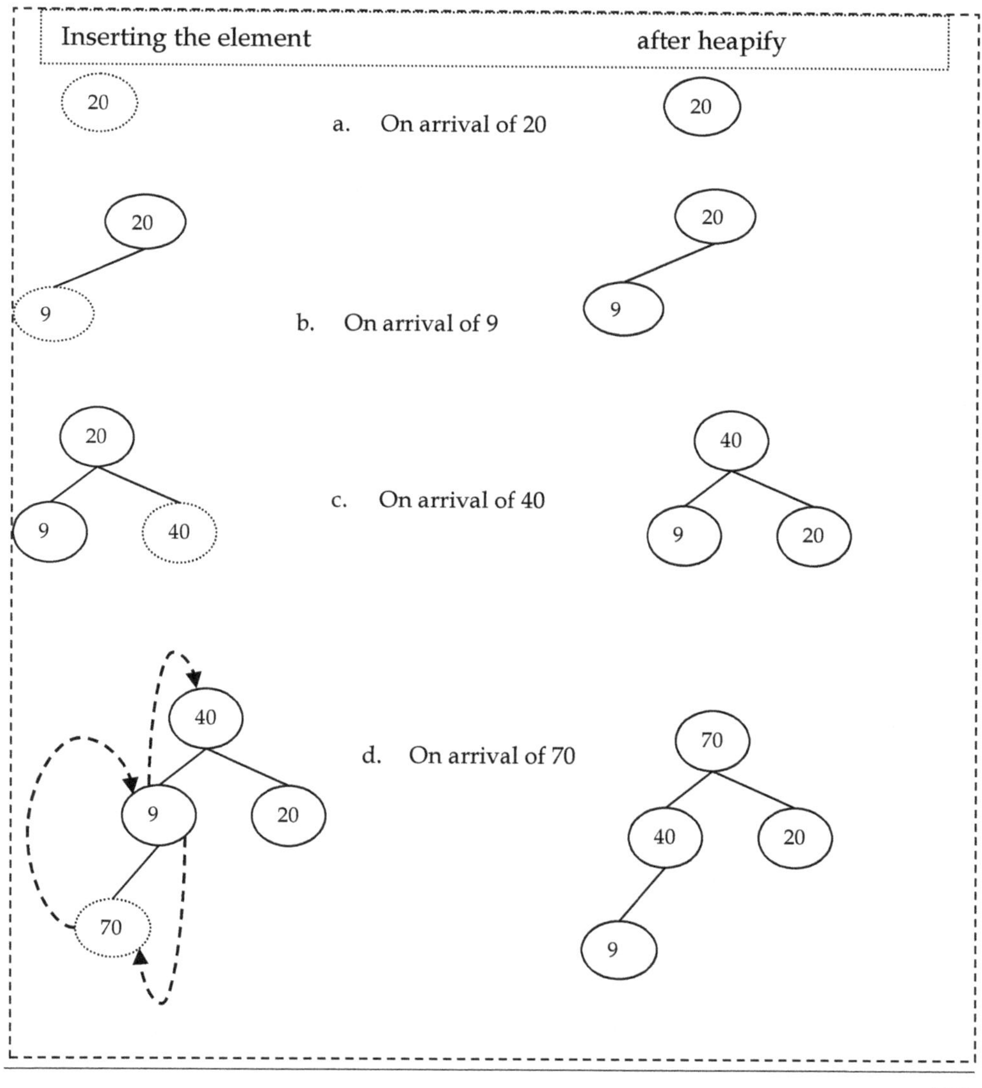

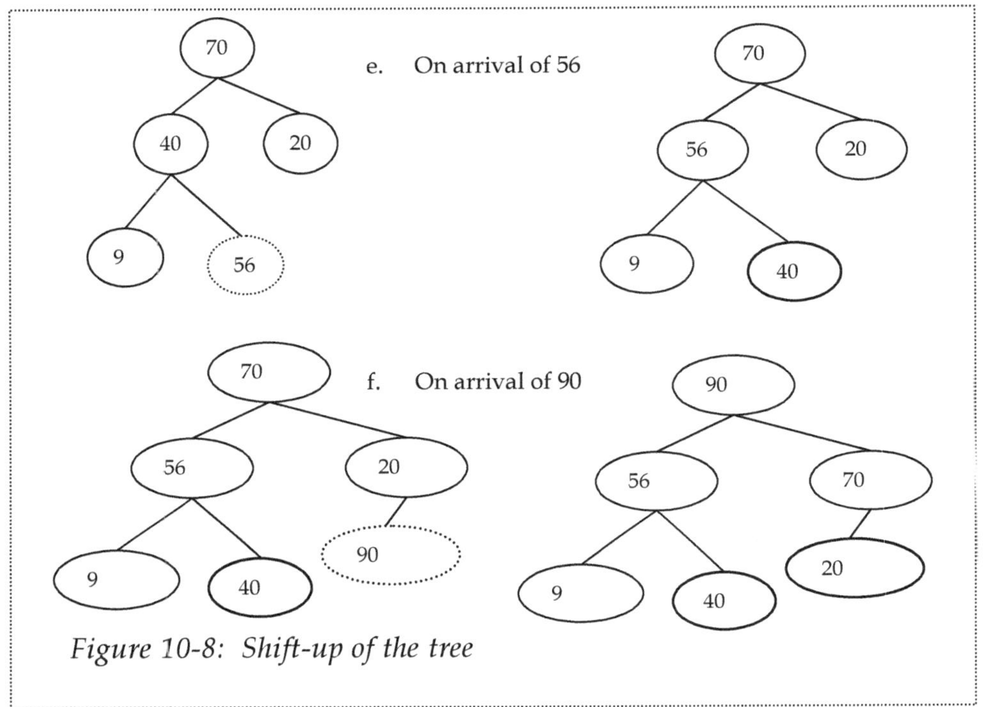

Figure 10-8: Shift-up of the tree

This process continues till all the elements are not inserted in the heap. Complete heap is illustrated in the figure 10-8.

To store them in the array so that they remain in sorted order. We take the root element, this element is element having the maximum value. Based on the array, it is placed at the last index of the array, as illustrated in the figure 10-10.

This is followed by determining the right most node of the lowest level of the tree. If the rightmost is not available than the left node of the same parent is considered for replacement with the root as illustrated in the 10-9 (b).

Replacement of item may lead to the violation of heap definition. Consequently, again all the elements are checked for their values. If element is more, shift up operation results.

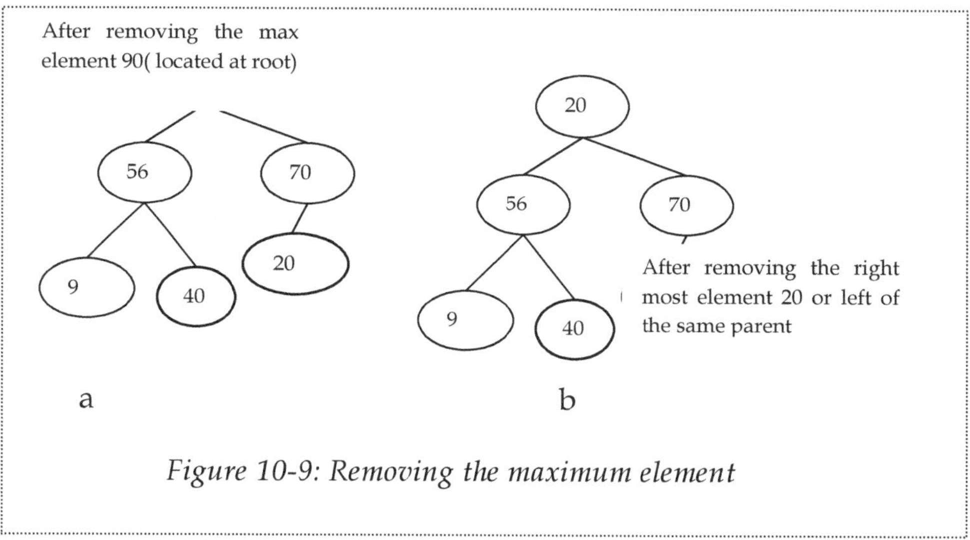

Figure 10-9: Removing the maximum element

Since, in the resultant tree of 10-9 (b) heap definition violates due to the availability of items more than the root node. Consequently, shift up operation is to be applied. Resultant tree is illustrated in the figure 10-11.

Similarly, we would remove one element from the heap, place it in the array (at the first position available at the extreme right of the node). Examine the remaining tree for the adherence of heap, if it is violated, shift up operation is carried out to avoid any error.

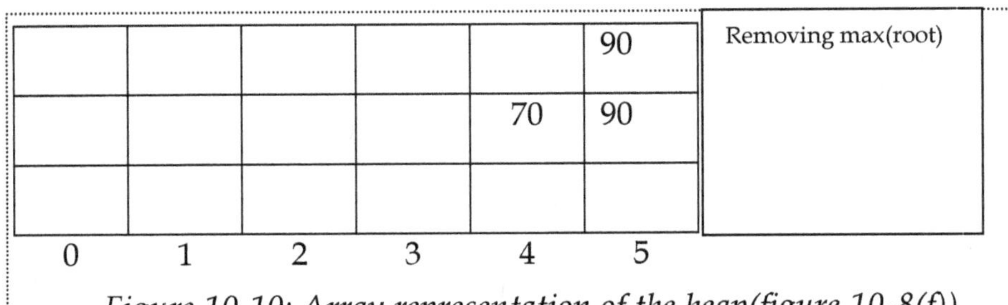

Figure 10-10: Array representation of the heap(figure 10-8(f))

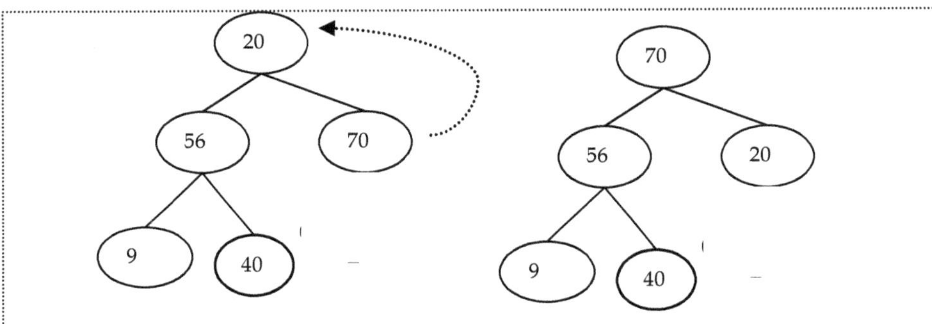

Figure 10-11: Shift up operation after removal of max element

10.4 Exercise

1. A series has been given as 34, 6, 12, 90, 33, 86, 76 what will the output of the given series after 3rd pass in
   i) Insertion sort
   ii) Selection sort
   iii) Bubble sort

2. For the given series, 34, 6, 12, 90, 33, 86, 76 which algorithm (insertion, selection, bubble) will be best algorithm. Justify your case.
3. In the bubble sort, is it possible that the series is already sorted before completion of final pass?
4. If the answer of the above question 2 is yes, How to resolve the issue so that the overall performance can be improved.
5. In all the discussed sorting algorithm, which is giving the best performance.

Chapter 11
String

Chapter Objective

- Defining the string in C++
- Defining the various function on string such as upper, lower, mid, left.
- Searching of pattern in a string
- Discussing the brute force, KMP and Rabin karp algorithm

11 String

Strings are having much significance in data structure. In languages like C and C++, it is represented with the help of character array. To manipulate the string, a number of functions are already existing in the string header file. However, we may need more functions to accomplish many of the routine task such as extracting the string, searching for the specific pattern, conversion from one case to another case, etc.

In string to achieve a single task there are many functions exist representing various approaches of their experts. However, usage of these method depends upon various factors, including processing time, ease of use and resources capability.

Many string functions needed in our variety of needs have been described in the upcoming sub-section.

11.1 Significant function of string

To accomplished any task related to string, either we have to use the functions that are already defined in the string header file or we have to create our own function. However, this section describes some of the complex functions that are widely needed for the string.

11.1.1 Converting the string into other cases

Due to variety of reasons, we need to convert the string text in upper, lower or sentence case. Therefore, function must exist that should facilitate the conversion from one case to another case. Various popular case conversion functions such as in lower case, upper case, sentence case, etc. have been defined as follows.

A. **Upper case conversion**

Upper case conversion function is used to convert the string character from lower case into upper case. To accomplish this purpose, we have used the ASCII values of character. If the character is not falling within the range of capital letter, it is converted into capital letter by subtracting 32 from the character value. Upper function has been enumerated in the following function.

```
// Program to convert the given string into upper characters
// function to convert the string into upper case
void toupper(char str[])
{
int i=0;
while(str[i]!='\0')// continue till end of the string is not encountered
{
if((str[i]>=97) && (str[i]<=122))
str[i]=str[i]-32;          // change it into corresponding upper case
i++;
}
}
```

B. **Lower case Conversion**

Similar to upper case conversion, we can also convert the string into lower case, if the user have entered into the capital letters. Corresponding to upper case conversion, we have used the ASCII table to convert the string character into lower case, if it does not fall under the category of lower case. The following program describes the conversion from the upper case to the lower case.

```
// Program to convert the upper case letter in lowercase
//function to convert into lower case
void tolower(char str[])
{
int i=0;
while(str[i]!='\0')
{
if((str[i]>=65) && (str[i]<=92))
str[i]=str[i]+32;
i++;
}
}
```

11.1.2 Extracting the substring

In addition to converting the string from one case to another case, we can also extract the group of characters from the string. These characters may be from the starting of the string, from the mid of the string or from the end of the string. In addition, there is a need to truncate the leading spaces entered by the user.

Correspondingly, various functions to accomplish the above objective have been defined as follows:

A. **Removing the leading space**

At the time of string input, user may inputs the spaces in a string. These leading spaces are undesired and effect the length of the string. Even worst, on various occasion does not give the correct result due to the presence of leading spaces.

To remove the leading space, we have defined the function trim(char[]) that accepts the character array(string), and removes the leading spaces.

To remove the leading space, we have used the flag 'start' that denotes that this is the start of the string. To figure out that the present character is space, we have again used the ASCII table where the space has the value 32. Correspondingly, we have used the logic that if it is start of string and it is space, string should continue to move to the next character. Once any other character is arrived then it is copied. At the same time 'start' will be set to false, since the characters have started. Finally, the NULL character is also copied.

```
// Function to remove the leading space from a string
void trim(char str[])
 {
 int i=0,j=0,start=1;
 while(str[i]!='\0')
  {
  if((str[i]==32)&& (start))      // if space at the beginning
```

```
  {
  i++;
  //cout<<"blank found ";
  continue;
  }
  str[j]=str[i];
  start=0;        // Now if the space exist, it is in-between
  j++;
  i++;
 // cout<<"in trim"<<endl;
//  cout<<endl;
}
str[j]='\0';
 }
```

B. **Extracting the character from the start**

We can extract the character from the start of the string. To accomplish this task, we have created a temporary array with the name 'temp'. We read the given string character by character upto the character intended by the user. For instance, if the user is intending to extract the first 4 characters, then it should start from the 0th index and should continue upto the 3rd index (Now total will be 4 characters). The entire program is enumerated as follows.

```
// Program to extract the first n character from the given string
// given string is st and number of characters are n
void left(char st[],int n)          {
  int i=0;
```

```
  char temp[20];
  while(i<n)//copying the string into temp
   {
   temp[i]=st[i];
   i++;
   }
   temp[i]='\0';
   strcpy(st,temp);//copying the temp string back to the st
  }
```

C. **Extracting the character from the middle**

We can also extract the string from the middle. To accomplish this task, we have used the mid function. Here it is significant that the difference of indexing and the user supplied position should not have any mismatch. Consider that user is aiming to extract from the 2nd position to 5th position. In the array, index of the supplied argument will be 1st and 4th. Consequently, argument has to be indexed to hide the difference between the indexing and the user's perception of character location.

```
void mid(char str[],int start, int last)
  {
  int i=start-1,j=0;
  char temp[20];
  while(i<last)//copying the string into temp
   {
   temp[j]=str[i];
   i++;
```

```
  j++;
  }
  temp[j]='\0';
  strcpy(str,temp);//copying the temp string back to the st
 }
```

In the above program, we have extracted the character from the start till the end into a temp string. **Eventually, the temp string is copied into the original string by using the strcpy() function, defined in the string.h header file.**

D. **Extracting the string from the end**

Extracting the string from the end is relatively complex than other extraction methods discussed earlier. During extraction of a string from the end, we can use the logic described in the following program.

```
// Program to extract the 'n' character from the end of a string
void last(char str[],int n)
{
int len=strlen(str);// determine the length of the string
int sp=len-n; //find out the starting position from where the...
// string extraction start
char temp[30];
int i=0;
while(str[sp]!='\0')
{
temp[i]=str[sp];
i++;
sp++;
```

```
}
temp[i]=str[sp];// copying the NULL character
strcpy(str, temp); // copying the extracted string back to the original
                   // string
}
```

In the above program, first we determine the length of the string, which can be determined by the string function strlen() defined in the string.h. Afterwards, we have computed from last where we have to start extracting. To accomplish this objective, we have subtracted the 'n' value passed by the user from the string length already computed. For instance, if user is aiming to extract the last 4 character from the string. First we determine the length of the string, consider it is 15. Based on the available data, starting point of an array can be computed by subtracting 15-4=11. It signifies that we have to start from the 11th index and continue upto the end i.e. 14th index.

11.2 String Matching Algorithm

In the String matching, we compare the string with the given pattern to figure out, whether a particular pattern exist in the considered string or not. If the pattern exist then it should give the suitable message, otherwise message for non-presence of the pattern should be flashed. Popular string matching algorithms are discussed in the upcoming sub-section.

11.2.1 Brute force string matching

In the brute force string matching algorithm, we try to recognize the presence of a pattern in the given string. In this method, string is examined for the presence of a pattern from the starting index '0', if the first character of the string and the pattern matches then we compare the next character, if any of the character of string and pattern is not matching further examination is terminated. Afterwards, examination starts from 1st index of the string with 0th index of the pattern to examine the presence of pattern. We continue till pattern is not exhausted or the string is not exhausted. If the pattern is exhausted it indicates that the pattern exist in the given string. Program for the brute force has been described as follows.

```
// Program to find out the pattern based on brute force algorithm
int bforce(char st[], char pattern[])
 {
int i=0, status=0;
int index;
while (st[i]!= '\0')
 {
j=0;
index=i;
  {
  while ((st[i]!='\0')&& (pattern[j]!='\0'))
{
if (st[i]==pattern[j])
{
i++;
```

```
j++;
}
}// end of inner while loop
if(pattern[i]=='\0')     // if the pattern is exhausted
{
status=1;                // change the status as successful
break;
}
i=index;        // set the i with the value as before inner while loop
i++;    // increment the index so that next element can be checked
}       // end of outer loop
return status;
}// end of function
```

We have used two loops in our program, outer and inner while loops respectively. Outer loop is governed by the length of the string whereas inner loop is governed by the pattern and string to be examined. If the matching is continued then the inner loop continues. After the exit of the inner loop, pattern is examined for whether it is exhausted or not. If it is exhausted, further checking is terminated.

If the pattern is not exhausted, in that case, we restore the value of i with the index that represents the value of i before the starting of the inner loop. Finally, i is incremented so that checking can be started with the next element. This examination will continue till pattern or string is not exhausted. If the pattern is exhausted it represent the status as 1, otherwise status will be 0.

11.2.2Knuth Morris Pratt (KMP)

Brute force algorithm is suffering from the major limitation that it is evaluating the string from the beginning and continues to match till mismatch does not occurs or the string is not exhausted. In case of mismatch, it will start checking the 1st index (or the next address from where the last time it has started). It never consider that possibility of pattern existence will be less from the 1st index once the matching already taken place upto 4th or 5th character. Consequently, it is termed that brute force algorithm never applies any intelligence. For instance, consider a case that we have started comparison from the beginning, first character of the string and the given pattern is matching, second is also matching, and third is also matching. However, mismatch has occurred at the fourth location. In this case there is no probability of string existence from the second element. Any probability of matching will start from the 4th character only. However, this case has not been considered by the Brute force, instead it will start searching from the next (here in this case second) character.

The above limitation has been addressed by the Knuth Morris Pratt or (KMP). In this algorithm, we start from the beginning and compare the pattern with the string by also applying the intelligence. Working of KMP has been depicted as follows:

```
// Program to display the KMP
int KMP(char str[], char patt[])
{
int sl=strlen(str);
```

```
int pl=strlen(patt);
cout<<"String length ="<<sl<<endl;
cout<<"Pattern length ="<<pl<<endl;
int index=-1;
int i=0,j=0;
while(i<=sl)    // Check till the i is less then string
 {
j=0;
while((str[i]==patt[j]) && (j<=pl))      // if string and pattern is matching
{                                        // at the same time, less than pattern
i++;                          // go to the next character of string
j++;                          // go to the next character of pattern
}
if(j>=pl)                     // if pattern completely found in the string
{
index=i-pl;     // first index of the string where matching found
break;
}
i++;     // if no matching found, go to the next character
}
return index;  // return the starting index if found, otherwise return -1
}
```

In the above KMP algorithm, first we determine the length of string as well as of the pattern. The outer loop is governed by the total length of the string whereas the inner loop by the pattern length. If the matching character is found in that case index of both the string and the pattern is increased. If the pattern is completely checked (no more character exist) in that case further comparison is to be prevented, this is considered with the statement if (j>=pl). The used conditional statement signifies that the pattern is exhausted. To stop the further comparison 'break' statement is used that prevents any further comparison. Eventually, string index from where the pattern start is returned.

In case, if the pattern does not have the matching character next character of string is to be evaluated. This is achieved with the help of i++ statement available just before the closing of outer loop.

Exercise

1. What is the objective of Brute force string pattern matching algorithm?
2. How the KMP works? Determine the complexity of KMP.
3. What is the difference between the brute force algorithm and KMP?
4. How the efficiency is achieved with the usage of KMP.
5. Take a String RAMAYAN, corresponding to the string consider the patterns "RAM" and "MAY". Carry out the dry run for pattern matching using Brute force algorithm and KMP. Also find out the comparison needed in case of Brute force and KMP algorithms.

Chapter 12
Hashing

Chapter Objective

- Defining hashing and significance of hashing
- Describing various hashing function.
- Describing the collision.
- Describing the various collision handling techniques in hashing.

12 Hashing

In the linear search or the binary search, performance is the major challenge. To overcome this challenge, we have another method known as hashing that allows to create and access the element on the basis of index, therefore, the performance of the algorithm will be O(1), instead of O(n) or O(log n). To organize the element in the hashing we use hash functions.

12.1 Hashing function

Hashing functions are the function that determines the unique index for the element. Correspondingly, elements are allocated to this new index/address. It is desirable that the function selected should generate the unique index so that elements can be placed at this unique address only. Prominent hashing functions have been discussed in the upcoming section.

12.1.1 Division method

The key purpose of this function is to generate the index so that items can be allocated at suitable position. In the division method, there are two numbers:

i. Key to be allocated an index.
ii. Total number of elements that can be allocated (size) to a given table.

In this method, we divide the key by the size and find out the remainder. The computed remainder act as an index of the given key (K mod size). For instance, consider that the total number that need to be allocated are 100. Number (Key) for which we have to allocate the address is 34. In this case remainder will be 34. Consequently, 34 will be allocated the index 34. Now, consider the number 254. In this case, 254 mod 100 remainder is 54, therefore, 254 will be allocated the index 54. Therefore, a number may be sufficiently large, however, the remainder will be between 0 to (size-1).

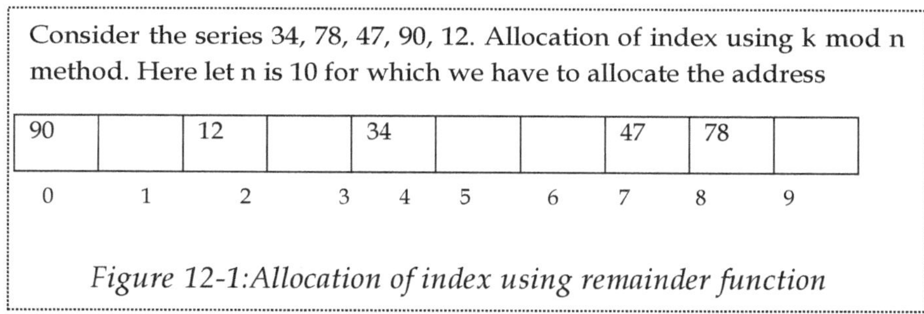

Consider the series 34, 78, 47, 90, 12. Allocation of index using k mod n method. Here let n is 10 for which we have to allocate the address
90
12
34
47
78
0 1 2 3 4 5 6 7 8 9

Figure 12-1:Allocation of index using remainder function

In the figure 12-1, allocation of index using remainder method has been illustrated. In the considered series, for the first element, index is computed as 34 mod 10, therefore it's index result at 4th location. Correspondingly, index for the remaining items can be computed and would be result at the index 8, 7, 0, 2 respectively.

Hashing function does not always provide the unique address. For instance, consider a new number 154, applying the rule, the address '54' will be generated. However, 54 is already occupied by the another number. If same index is allocated for more than one element then this phenomenon is known as collision. It is always undesired to have the collision. Correspondingly, it is suggested to take the size that should be the prime number. It is believed that if the size is prime number then it will generate less repeated index. However, collision is not altogether eliminated. To address the collision, numerous methods exist and some of the prominent of them have been discussed in the section 12.2.

12.1.2 Mid Square method

It is apparent from the above discussion that the division method results in excessive collision, since, we are directly operating on the key itself. Index can also be computed with the help of mid square method. In this method, instead of directly applying the rule, we square the given key. Once the square of a key is known then we take the mid of this number based on the length of index. For instance, consider the number 311. First we square the considered key, it will result in 96721. From the result computed, we take the mid of this number, based on the size of the table. In our case, consider the size of the table as 1000, then the mid number is 672. It can be written as H(311)=672, In this case the index 672 will be the index of the number. The index computed is entirely different from the considered number that we compute from the direct method. In this method, probability of the same index has been reduced significantly.

12.1.3Folding method

In this method the numbers are folded so that computation can be performed. We can apply two types of folding methods:

- Shift folding
- Boundary folding

In the folding method, the number computed is divided by the size to know the index of the key. It is considered as the hashing since it involves division and grouping of the number. Consider the number 254/32/6547/251, for this number we can apply two types of folding methods. In the **shift folding**, the number may be shifted in other group as well. Consider the number is divided into the group of 03, then the resultant number will be 254, 326, 547, 251. This is followed by adding these three number. In the case of on-going discussion, it will be 1374. To compute the index, we can use the division method as (number mod size). In the above function, the index generated are not unique instead more than one elements are having the same index.

In the folding method, we divide the number into the groups of equal part and then fold the given number as with the folded paper. Afterwards, the number obtained are added, result thus obtained is performed with the modulo size. For instance, consider the number 123674 987, Here the number is divided into the group of three 123, 674, 987. We carry out the addition on the number thus obtained i.e. 123+674+987=1784. Finally, modulo size is carried out on the resultant number, in this case it is 1784.

12.1.4 Extraction

In the extraction method, we extract only part of the key to compute the address, whereas remainder digits of the number are omitted from the key. For instance, if the number is 785/897/345, we can extract the first three number or the first six, or four number or any other combination considering the part of the key. This extracted number is acting as the index for the given number. It has been observed that the index thus generated give good result and minimizes the collision, if carefully chosen. For instance, consider the employee_id assigned to an employee of an organization, where few digits/character are common for all whereas few digits are unique. Consider that the employee_id is CB_KNP_208010. In this case the initial number/character are common, therefore these common characters are omitted(CB_KNP). Correspondingly, in India, account number is allocated considering the location id that is dependent on state and district then branch id. Now digits representing these items will be common for the majority of the customer, specifically in the same city and brach. Consequently, these common values need to be omitted.

12.1.5 Radix transformation

In the radix transformation method, we change the radix of the given key. Afterwards, number is divided by modulo size. The number computed act as an index of the key. Consider, a key $(101)_2$ is the given number, since it is in base 2 therefore we will change it in the base of 10. The resultant number thus produced in decimal, in the considered case it is 5. Afterwards, to compute the index (address) we compute the index as 5 module size=5, after considering 5 as the size of the total element can be stored. In our case, the address computed is 5.

12.2 Collision Handling Technique in Hashing

In the above hashing function, we have witnessed that hashing function(s) are not generating the unique index of the considered key. Instead, more than one key may result in the same index. During the allocation of index, if more than one elements leads to the same index, then it is known as collision and undesired phenomenon. Consequently, collision leads to reduction in the performance of hashing and need to be resolved at appropriate level. Following are some of the popular methods that can be employed for handling of the collision.

- Chaining method
- Coalesced Chaining method.
- Bucket method

Method to handle the collision is known as collision handling techniques. Following are the methods which can be employed to handle the collision:

A. **Linear probe method**

In the linear probing method, when two or more elements leads to the same index in that case to allocate the unique index to the second element we start probing the next cell from the point of collission that is empty. Consequently, element is allocated to the new available cell. Although, this method is simple and gives a good result. Howevr, performance degrades with the increase of number. For instance, if the number for which the cell may be the appropriate position arrives, in that case it will be shifted to new location. Consequently, collision increases with the increase of the number. Items that are allocated the shifted cell are known as clustered elements.

Consider a case in which the number of a series is 21,42, 14, 65, 32. All these numbers are arranged using the x mod 10, where x is the number whereas the 10 is used for the remainder. Index of the various number including the 32 have been illustrated in the figure 12-2 a. On the arrival of 32, this will also result at the 2nd Index, however same may not be permitted as the number of that index already exist. To resolve the collision, In the linear probe method probing for the unallocated cell will start from the cell of collision. In the considered list, the next available cell is $3^{rd,}$ therefore the number will be allocated at 3rd index and same has been illustrated in the figure 12-2 b.

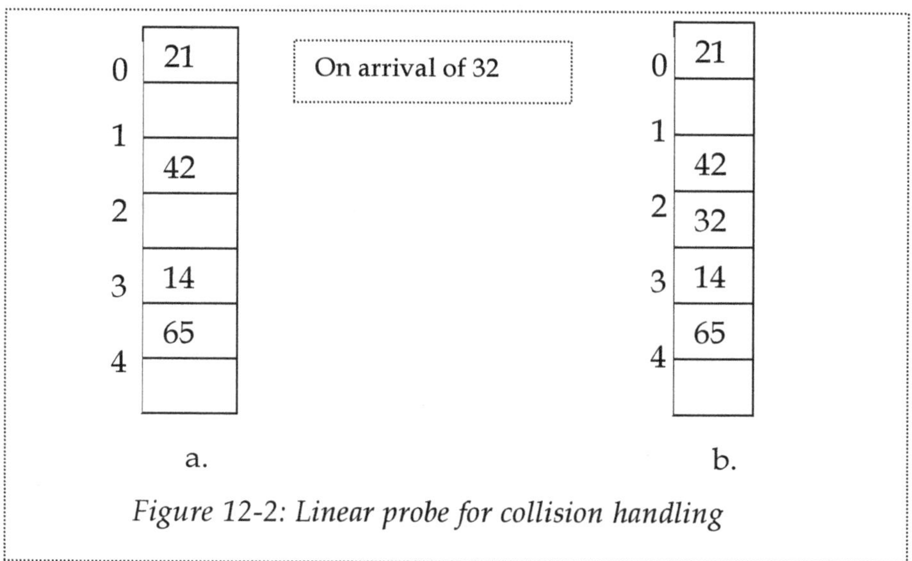

Figure 12-2: Linear probe for collision handling

B. **Chaining method**

In the chaining method, when the second item result in the same address, a link list is created that is also known as chain. All the elements that are leading to the address where the element is already stored, such elements are stored at the node of a link list. On the arrival on any other element at the same address, again a new node is created where the item is stored. Therefore, elements are arranged in an un-order form. During the accessing of the element, we continue to search the element till the item is not found or the considered list is not exhausted. This method of collision handling results in better performance relative to the linear probing method. However, major overhead lies at the time of chaining.

Consider the list as illustrated in the figure 12-3, a node will be created similar to link list node that will have the link at the starting index. All the other nodes that will result in the same index will have the node connected with the existing link list. Chaining method has been illustrated in the following figure.

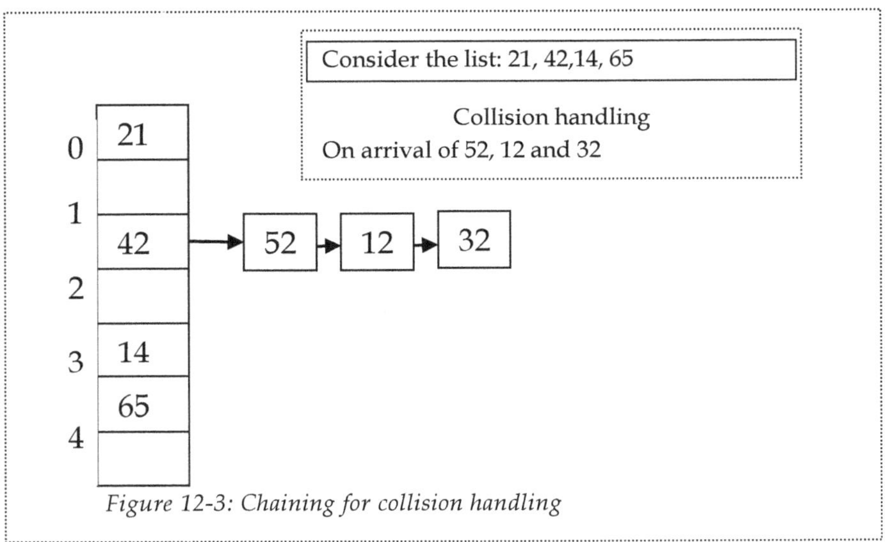

Figure 12-3: Chaining for collision handling

On the arrival of 52 it will be allocated the second index, since that index is already allocated therefore, collision will occur. To resolve it, a link node will be created where this new item will be allocated. Correspondingly, on the arrival of new item 12, the new node will be created at the index 2, where the number will be allocated, refer figure 12-3.

C. **Double chaining method**

In the chaining method, elements that are leading to the same index are connected together with the chain. In this method, a new node is created for all those element that result in the same index, similar to that of link list. While arranging the items in this method, we can any of the type of the list so that the elements are stored in the sorted order. Due to the sorted element arrangement performance can be improved profoundly.

Exercise

Descriptive type questions

1. What is hashing? How it is different from the other method of finding out the indexing?
2. Can be defined the hashing as search? Justify
3. What are the various methods of Hashing defined the advantages and disadvantages of each of them?
4. What is collision? How it occurs in hashing? Justify with suitable example.
5. Discuss the various methods to resolve the collision? Discuss their advantages and disadvantaged.
6. Study the various real implementation where hashing is used. Enumerate its advantages and disadvantages.

6. What are the major limitation of the linear probe method? How it is has been resolved by the subsequent methods.
7. Differentiate between the linear probe method with the chaining method. Discuss their strength and weakness.
8. How the limitations of the chaining methods have been overcome?

Chapter 15
Elementary Graphs

Chapter Objective

- Defining the graph and its terminology.
- Discussing the various types of graph
- Representing the graph
- Traversal in a graph
- Minimum spanning tree in a graph
- Shortest path in a graph

13 Elementary Graphs

In previous chapters, the majority of the portion was focused on tree data structure. Tree forms one to many relationship from parent to the child. At the same time, it does not forms the cycle. Even though, tree is one of the widely used data structures, yet does not fulfills many of the objective. For instance, consider the case if the data need to be send to the shortest path and acknowledge of success or failure need to be returned. In these requirement where the cycle is formed a new data structure known as Graph is used.

13.1 Basic Definitions

A graph consist of vertex (similar to node of a tree), various vertex are connected together with the help of a path known as edges. In any graph we have collection of vertex and edges.

A. **Graph**

A graph 'G' can be defined as a data structure consist of finite set of non-empty vertices(V) and set of edges 'E'. Graph 'G' is represented by a tuple (V,E). In a graph, vertices have names and can represent the other properties. In graph, edges are used to represent the relationship between two objects. For instance, distance between the two vertices. Figure 13-1 consist of 08 vertices namely 'a', 'b', 'c', 'd', 'e', 'f', 'g', 'h'. Each vertices are connected to the pair of vertex.

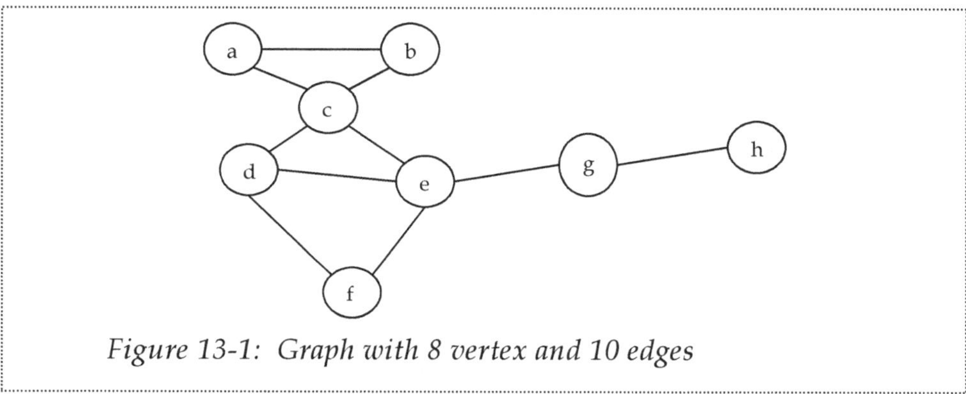

Figure 13-1: Graph with 8 vertex and 10 edges

B. Directed Graph

In a graph, if we denote the direction of the edges then it is known as directed graph, it is illustrated in the figure 13-2. Such kind of graph is also known as ordered graph. In the directed graph, the edge 'ad' is not same as 'da'. We can distinguish the edges from one another with the help of the direction given.

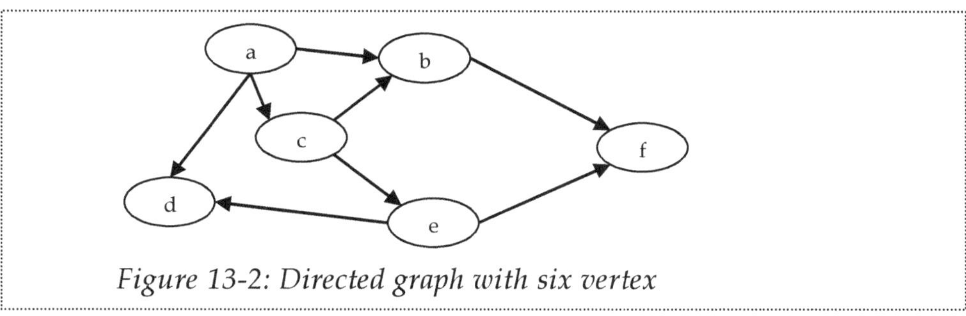

Figure 13-2: Directed graph with six vertex

Consider the case, if there is a need to visit from vertex 'a' to 'f'. In this case one path is 'ac', 'ce', 'ef' and the other possible path exist is 'ab', 'bf'. On the other hand, if we intend to reach 'a' from 'f' then it is not possible. Since, edges directed towards the destination 'a' are not existing.

In a graph, if the edge V_i and V_j exist, at the same time the edge V_j to V_i also exist. In a graph, if all the edges follow the above type of edges then such type of graph is known as symmetric graph. Otherwise it is known as asymmetric graph. The graph illustrated in the figure 13-2 is not symmetric since the edge V_i and V_j exist while the edge V_j to V_i does not exist.

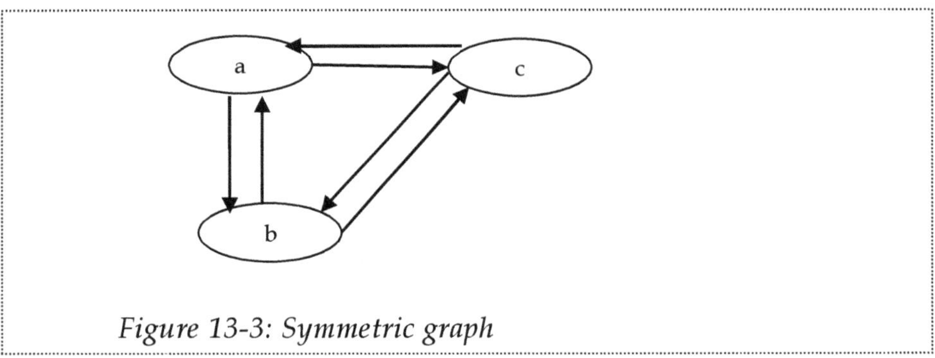

Figure 13-3: Symmetric graph

C. Undirected graph

In the figure 13-1, direction of edges are not denoted. In such type of graph order does not have significance, therefore they are known as unordered. When the edges of a graph are unordered pairs then the graph is known as undirected graph. In the undirected graph, the edges ac, ca are undistinguishable.

D. **Degree**

In a graph, degree of the vertex is governed by the number of edges and the type of graph(symmetric or asymmetric). In the case of undirected graph, all the edges are the part of the degree. Whereas, in the case of directed graph, degree is categorized into in-degree and out-degree. Vertex having the edges with direction towards it known as In-degree. In the out-degree all the edges are directed away from the vertex. In the given figure 13-2, in-degree and out-degree of the each vertex has been enumerated in the table 13.1.

Table 13.1: Degree of various vertex of graph of figure 13-2

Vertex	In-degree	Out-degree	Degree
A	0	2	2
B	2	2	3
C	1	2	3
D	2	0	2

E. **Incidence**

In a graph, the edge connecting the adjacent vertex is known as incidence. Consider the graph of figure 13-1, the two vertex 'a' and 'b' are connected together with the help of an edge. This edge is known as incidence of 'a' and 'b'.

F. **Adjacency**

In an undirected graph, if an edge 'e' is connected with the help of two vertices V_i, and V_j then both the edges are known as adjacent. Consider the graph illustrated in the figure 13-1, the edge 'ab' and 'ac ' both are adjacent.

G. **Path**

Path in a graph is a set of vertices used to reach from the source to the destination. For instance, consider the graph of figure 13-2 the path between the source 'a' to the destination 'f' is ac, ce, ef.

The graphs in which the path consist of all the vertices of the graph then it is known as Hamiltonian path.

H. **Cycle**

In any graph, if we start from the source vertex and return to the vertex where we have started(source vertex), such path is known as cycle. In the directed graph, we may have path from source to destination that may not formed the cycle. However, in the undirected graph probability of cycle is more since it does not involves the direction.

I. **Weighted graph**

A graph in which edges are assigned the weight are known as weighted edges. Weighted graph is illustrated in the figure 13-4. In the illustrated figure, weight of the edges E_{12}=7, and E_{13}=5.

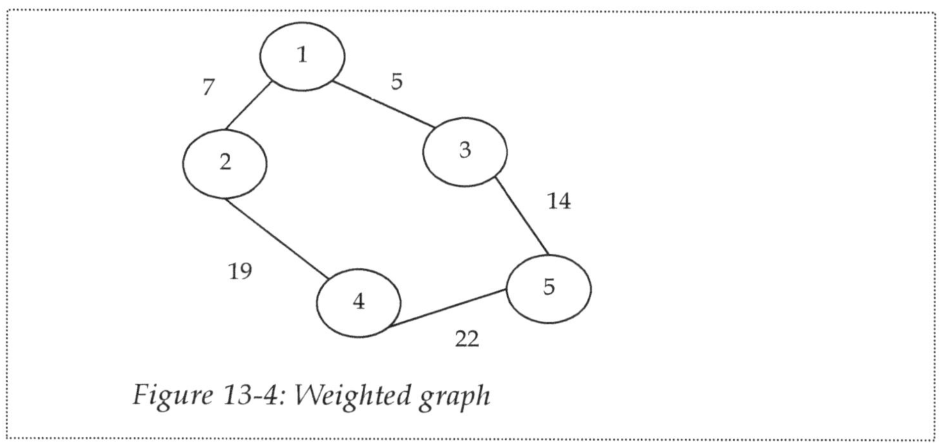

Figure 13-4: Weighted graph

13.2 Representation of Graphs

Once the graph has been created, then they need to be represented in the computer, this is known as representation of a graph. Following are the various method that can be used to represent the graph.

13.2.1 Adjacency matrix

In a matrix, adjacency matrix is used to represent the edges between the two vertex. If the vertex V_i is connected to the Vertex V_j with the help of a link known as edge then we represent this edge as one. In case if it is not connected then it is represented as '0'. We have enumerated the adjacency matrix of the graph of figure in the following table.

Table 13.2: Adjacency matrix of the figure 13-1

	a	b	c	d	e	f	g	h
a	0	1	1	0	0	0	0	0
b	1	0	1	0	0	0	0	0
c	1	1	0	1	1	0	0	0
d	0	0	1	0	1	1	0	0
e	0	0	1	0	1	1	1	0
f	0	0	0	1	1	0	0	0
g	0	0	0	0	1	0	1	0
h	1	0	0	0	0	0	0	0

In the undirected graph, if the edge exist between the vertex A_i to the Vertex A_j then 1 is to be placed in the edge A_{ij} as well as the edge A_{ji}, since direction does not have any significance in undirected graph. Adjacency matrix obtained for the undirected graph is symmetric that implies that if the edge exist from the vertex A_i to A_j then it also applies for the A_j to A_i. Degree of any vertex can be determined with the help of adjacency matrix. **Degree of any node is the sum of all the 1 in a particular row of the vertex**. In table 13.2, we can determine the degree of vertex 'c' is 4. Correspondingly, degree of other vertex can be determined.

In the directed graph, adjacency matrix is significantly different to that of undirected graph. In the case of directed graph only those edges are considered that represent the edge between the two vertexes of the graph. For instance, if we say 'ab' it means we assume that the edge will be directed from 'a' to 'b'. if we consider 'ba' it is significantly different from the 'ab' where the direction is from source 'a' towards the destination 'b', whereas in the 'ba' edge is from the 'b' to the 'a'.

Table 13.3: Adjacency matrix of figure13-2

	a	b	c	d	e	f	g
a	0	1	0	1	0	0	0
b	0	0	0	0	0	1	0
c	0	0	0	0	1	0	0
d	0	0	0	0	0	0	0
e	0	0	0	1	0	1	0
f	0	0	0	0	0	0	0

In the directed graph, an edge may exist from the vertex V_i to V_j, however, that may not be true from the V_j to V_i. Therefore, adjacent matrix for the directed graph is not symmetric.

Degree of directed graph can be defined as sum of in-degree and out-degree of any vertex. In-degree of any directed graph is the total number of '1' in that column, whereas out-degree in a directed graph is the total number of '1' in the row. Consequently, degree of any node can be computed as:

Degree of vertex (V_i)= *in-degree of vertex* (V_i) + *out-degree of vertex* (V_i)

13.2.2 Adjacency list

In the adjacency list, we create the link list for the vertex and all the nodes adjacent to it. For instance, each vertex represents the link list having the nodes which are represented by the adjacent vertex. Therefore, all the nodes that are adjacent can be accessed from the particular node is taken into the single adjacency list. Adjacency list of figure 13-1 is illustrated in figure 13-5.

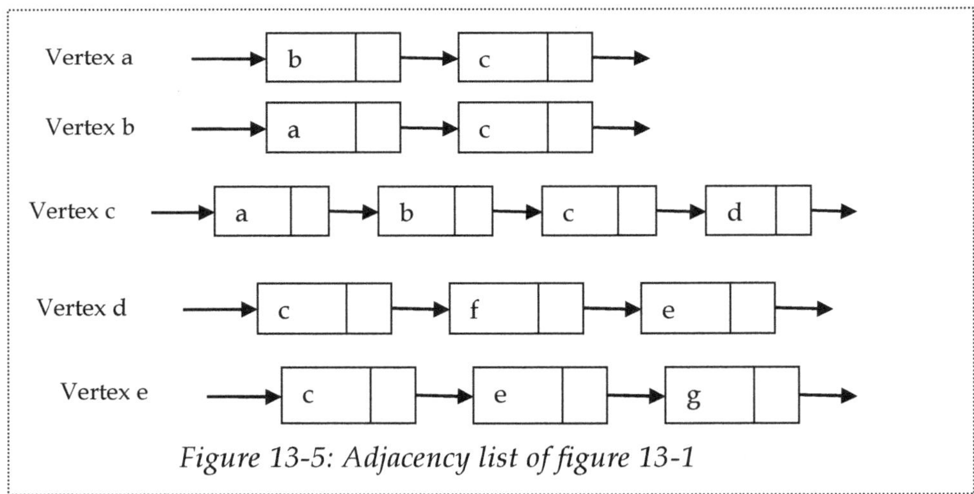

Figure 13-5: Adjacency list of figure 13-1

Adjacency list can be created using the link list program.

Adjacency list for the directed graph can be created similar to the undirected graph. However, there is a minor difference that is attributed due to the direction component of the directed graph. Adjacency list of the directed graph as illustrated in the figure 13-2, has been illustrated in the following figure 13-6..

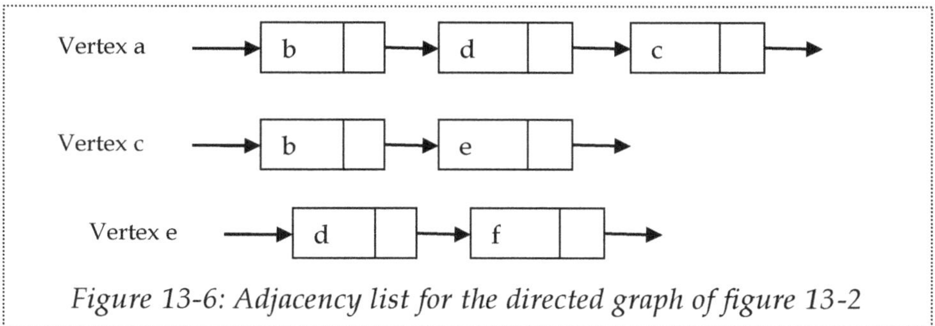

Figure 13-6: Adjacency list for the directed graph of figure 13-2

In the adjacency list, vertex 'b' and 'd' does not have any adjacency list consequently, they will point to the NULL.

13.2.3 Incidence matrix

Consider the graph 'G' with "n" vertices and "ne" edges but does not have any self-loop. Consider the matrix $A=(a_{ij})$ with n x ne, where n is the number of vertices and ne is the number of edges as follows.

$A_{ij}=1$ if "ej" is incident to the vertex "v_i"

=0, otherwise

Such a matrix is known as the incidence matrix of a graph. **In other terms incidence matrix are the edges that are incident on the particular vertex**. Therefore, we write all the incidence edges and all the vertex. If the incidence edge belongs to the particular vertex then 1 is placed otherwise 0. Consider the graph of the figure 13-7, In this graph, incidences are (1,2), (2,3), (2,4) (3,5) (3,6) (3,7)

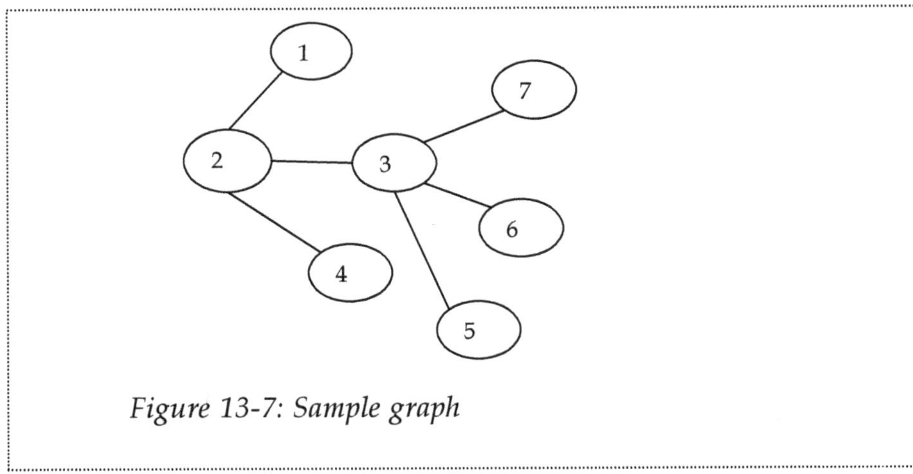

Figure 13-7: Sample graph

Incidence has been depicted in the following table.

Table 13.4: Incidence matrix for the figure 13-7

	(1,2),	(2,3)	(2,4)	(3,5)	(3,6)	(3,7)
1.	1	0	0	0	0	0
2.	1	1	1		0	0
3.	0	1		1	1	1
4.	0	0	1	0	0	0
5.	0	0	0	1	0	0
6.	0	0	0	0	1	0

7.	0	0	0	0	0	1

Adjacency incidence matrix for the directed graph is different from the undirected graph. For any edge a_{ij} of a graph, incidence matrix is derived as per the following rule.

A_{ij}=1 if "e_i" is the incident out of V_i.

=-1 if "e_i" is the incident into V_i

=0 if "ei" is not an incident to V_i.

13.3 Minimum spanning tree

A graph "G" has been illustrated in the figure 15-8, this graph is forming the cycle. Graph is significantly different from the tree, the topic that is already discussed. However, that is not the case, tree of the figure 13-8 (a) has been given in the figure 13-8(b). Tree of the figure 13-8(b) is similar to that of the tree that has been discussed in the previous chapter with the difference that it does not have a root. In the undirected graph, parent child relationship is also not apparent. Consequently, we can term tree as a graph which does not have a cycle.

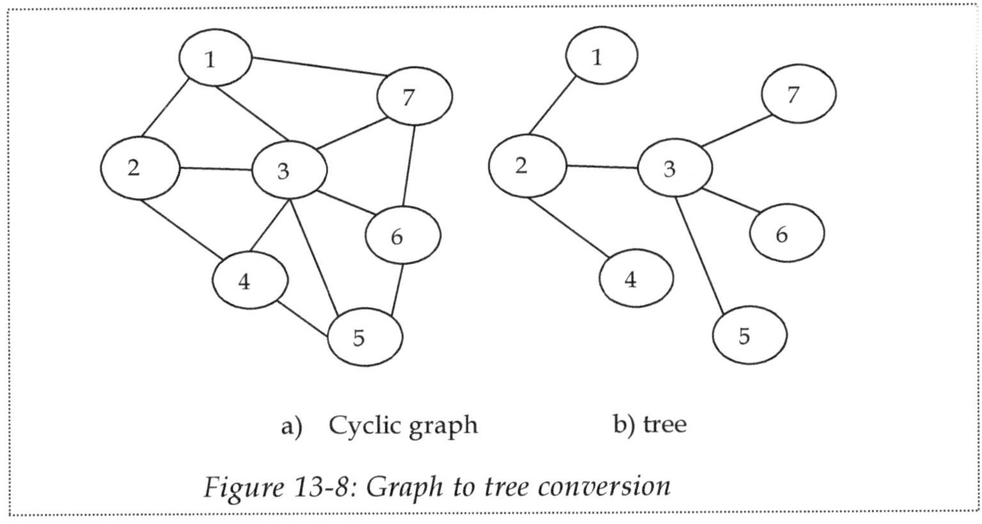

Figure 13-8: Graph to tree conversion

A sub-graph of figure 13-8(a) that consist of all the vertex and not forming the cycle has been illustrated in the figure 13-8 (b). A minimum spanning tree is the sub-graph (tree) of a graph that forms a tree by selecting the minimum weight of a sub-graph.

There are various minimum spanning tree algorithm existing, and defining the minimum spanning tree in their own way. Some of the prominent of these algorithms have been discussed in the upcoming sub-section.

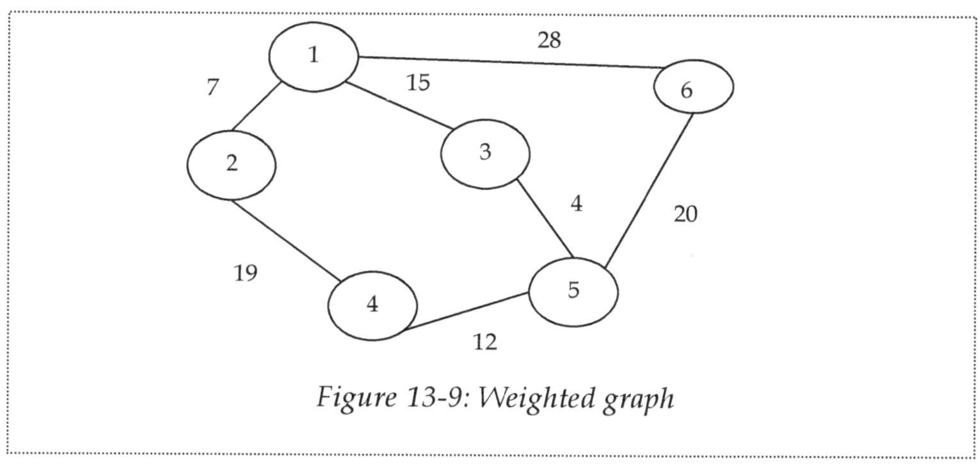

Figure 13-9: Weighted graph

13.3.1 Kruskal's Algorithm

In the Kruskal's algorithm, to determine the minimum spanning tree, weight are considered in the increasing order. A graph having 'n' vertex will have a forest of 'n' tree. In each step, one edge is considered that is minimum from the available edges. Minimum edge is considered if it is not forming the cycle in a tree.

In the graph of figure 13-9, the edge that will have minimum weight will be selected. In the considered graph the edge of vertex $V_{3,5}$ is having the minimum weight, i.e. 4. Consequently, it will be selected first. Same has been illustrated in the figure 13-10 (b).

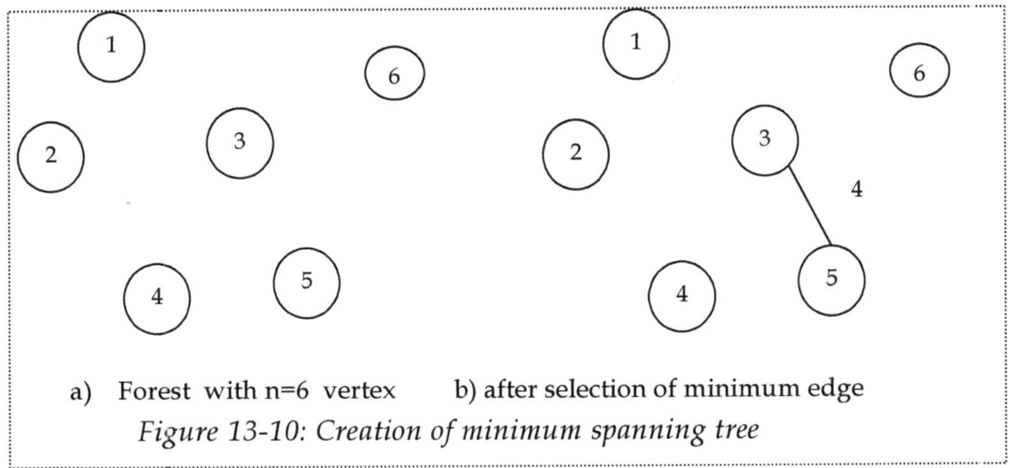

a) Forest with n=6 vertex b) after selection of minimum edge

Figure 13-10: Creation of minimum spanning tree

In the next step, the other minimum edge is considered from the available edges. Now, the minimum node among the available set is 7, that is the edge connecting the vertex $V_{1,2}$. Resultant spanning tree will be as illustrated in the figure 13-11. Similarly, other edges are considered in the increasing order. The other edge that will be considered is $E_{1,3.}$, weight associated with this vertex is 15.

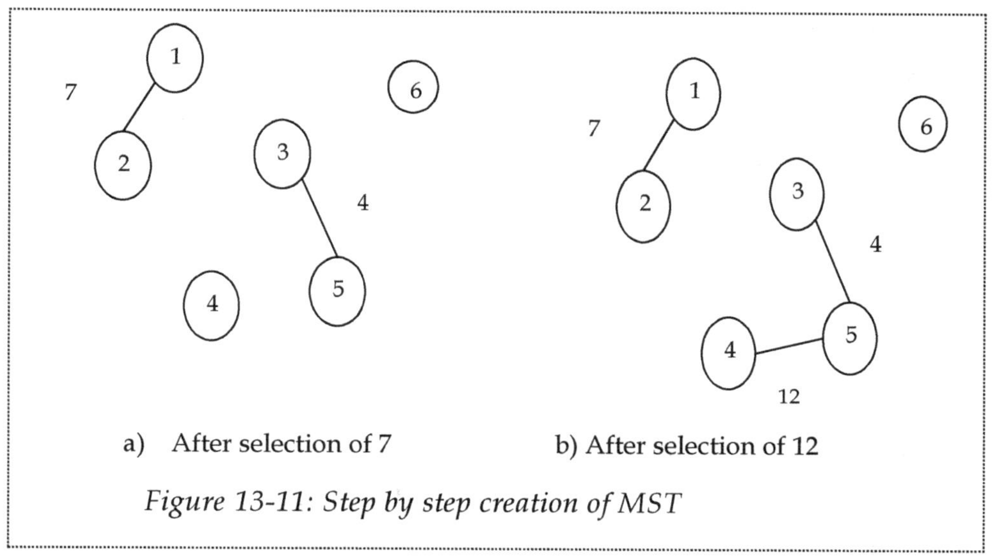

a) After selection of 7 b) After selection of 12

Figure 13-11: Step by step creation of MST

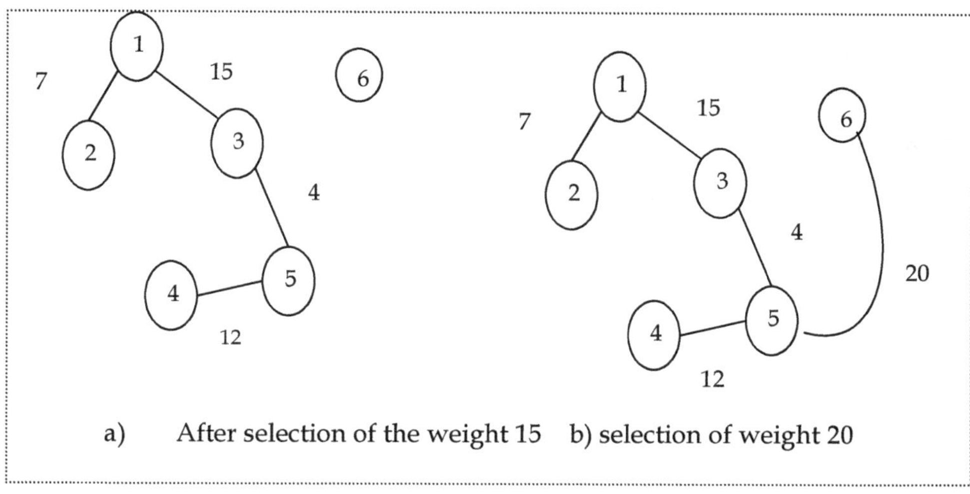

a) After selection of the weight 15 b) selection of weight 20

After selection of 15, the next edge is $E_{2,4}$ which is 19, but if this edge will be selected the cycle will be formed, therefore, this edge will be dropped. The next weight is 20 that is related to the edge "$e_{5,6}$" is selected. Even though, other edges are left but they cannot be selected as they will result in the cycle. Finally, weight associated with this graph (MST) can be computed by adding all the weight of the MST thus obtained.

Total weight=4+7+12+15+20

=58

13.3.2Prim's Algorithm

Prim's algorithm is the other method utilized to determine the minimum spanning tree (MST). Unlike the Kruskal's algorithm, in the Prim's algorithm, we select any of the edges from the graph. This is known as arbitrary selection of edges from the graph. From this edge, we can select the edge from the available edges. However, the edge with the minimum weight is selected. This process will continue till all the vertex are not traversed. The entire method of prim's is depicted in the following figures.

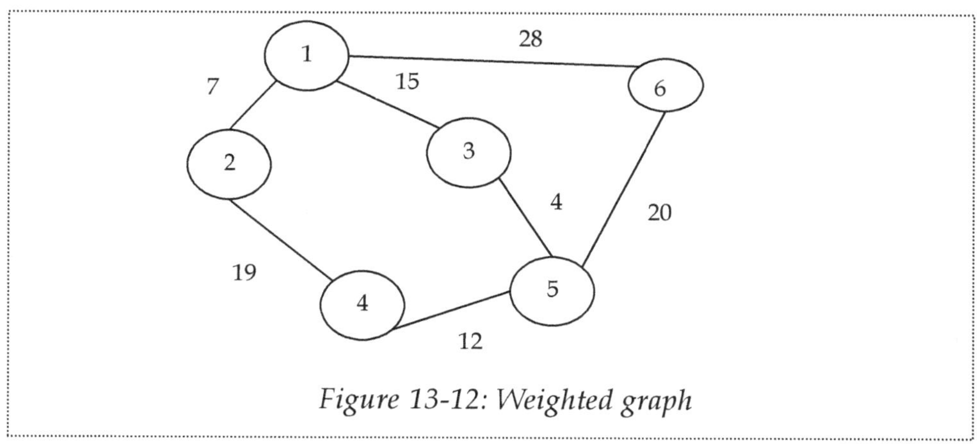

Figure 13-12: Weighted graph

Consider the graph of figure 13-12 from which we have to determine the minimum spanning tree. In this method, we will opt for any arbitrary edge, in our case we have considered the edge "e_{13}" and having the weight of 15.

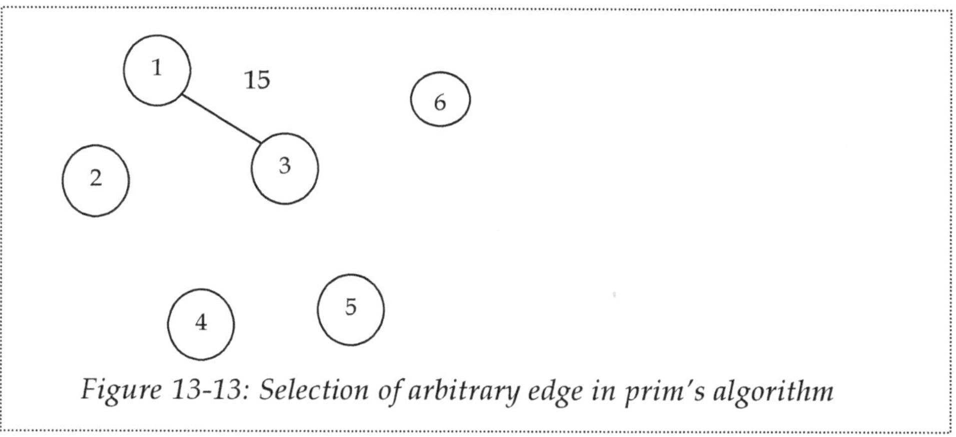

Figure 13-13: Selection of arbitrary edge in prim's algorithm

Now the available edges of the graph are E_{12}, E_{16} and E_{35}, these edges are having the weight 7, 28 and 4. Since, in the available weight 4 is minimum that is of the edge $E_{3,5}$ therefore, the next edge that will be selected isE_{35}. Consequently, the new spanning tree will be as illustrated in the figure 15-14. Afterwards, we will check for the available edges which are E_{12}, E_{16}, E_{54}, E_{56} having the weight 7, 28, 12 and 20 respectively. Among the available edges and their respective weight, the edge E_{12} is having the minimum weight i.e. 7.

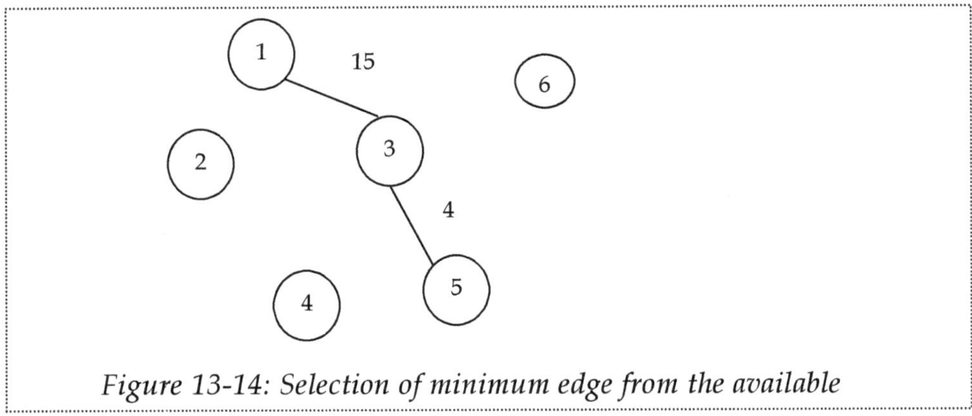

Figure 13-14: Selection of minimum edge from the available

Now the available edges are E_{56}, E_{45}, E_{12}, E_{16}. In the available edges weight associated to them are 20, 12, 7 and 28 respectively. Among the available weight edge E_{12} will have the minimum weight. Consequently, the next edge E_{12} will be selected. Same has been illustrated in the following figure.

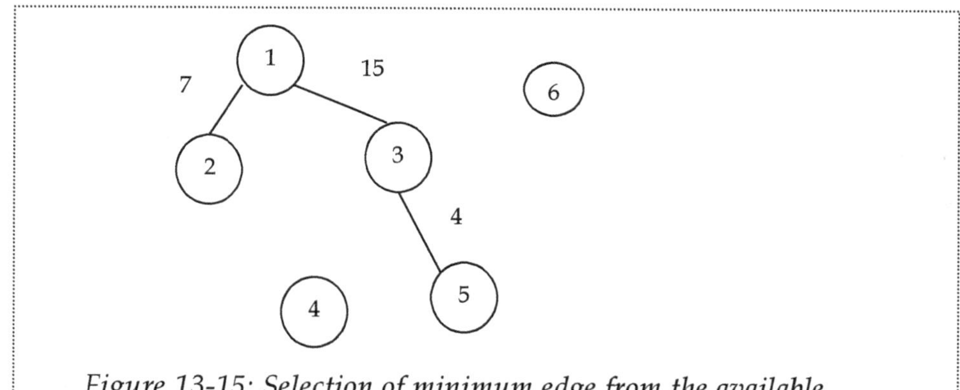

Figure 13-15: Selection of minimum edge from the available

After this step, now we are left with the E_{56}, E_{45}, E_{24}, E_{16}, Weight associated to them are 20, 12, 19 and 28 respectively. Therefore, the minimum weight available is 12 and the edge associated to it is E_{45}.

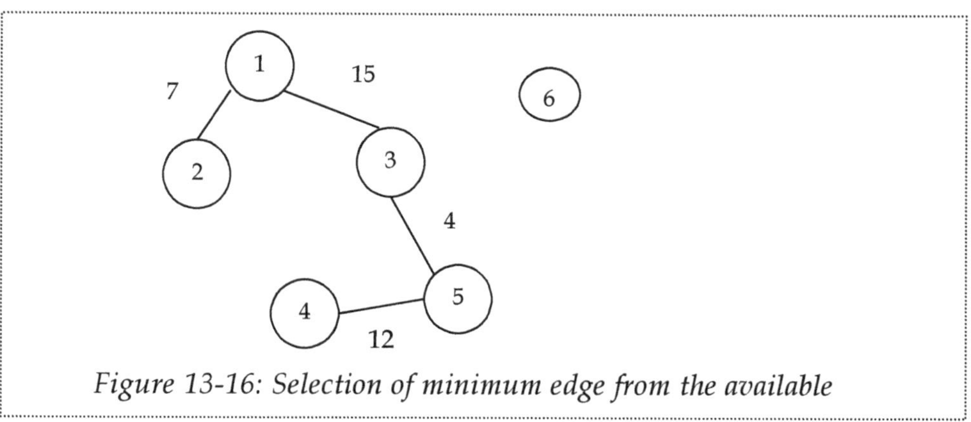

Figure 13-16: Selection of minimum edge from the available

Afterwards, only the edges are available are E_{56}, E_{24}, E_{16}, among these edges E_{24} cannot be considered since it does make the cycle. Therefore, edges that are left are E_{56}, E_{16}, and the weight associated to them are 20 and 28 respectively. Among them minimum is 20 therefore, it will be selected. Finally, minimum spanning tree is illustrated in the figure 13-16. Since, edges that are left are forming the cycle, consequently they cannot be considered. Total weight associated to this graph can be computed as:

MST =*4+7+12+15+20*

=*58*

It is apparent from both the method that the minimum spanning tree is having the same value 58. Consequently, it signifies that the MST does not change with the change of algorithm.

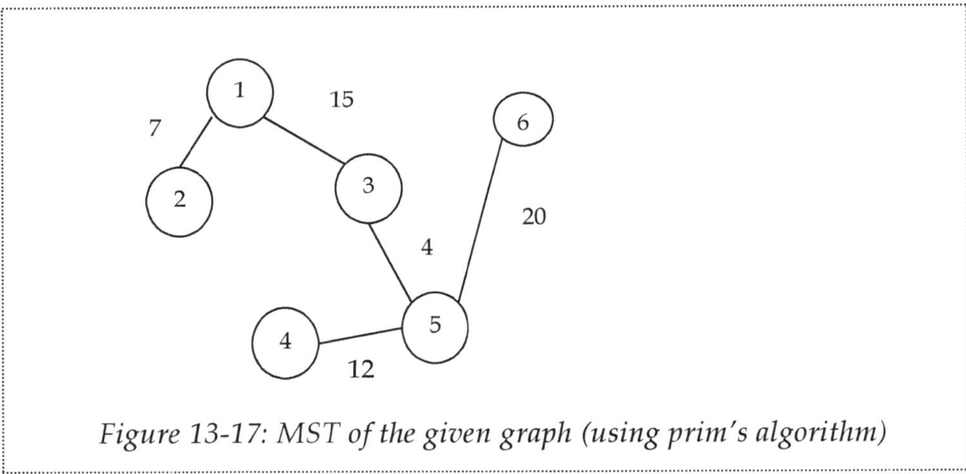

Figure 13-17: MST of the given graph (using prim's algorithm)

13.4 Traversal in a Graph

Visiting each and every node in a graph once is known as traversal. In the graph traversal, none of the node should be visited more than once and none of the node should remain unvisited. In graphs, there are two prominent traversal techniques that are widely used. Each of them has been discussed in the upcoming section.

13.4.1 Depth first search

In the depth first search method, we start from the one Vertex and continue to traverse up-to the deepest level. In the case of depth first traversal, we traverse at the deepest level of the considered vertex. This allows to access vertex based on their depth.

Consider the case of the figure 13-18. In this graph, we can start from any of the vertex, however, we are starting from the Vertex-1. This is followed by all the nodes at the next level of this node, In this case, they are 2, 5, 6. Afterwards, we would like to traverse all the vertex of the other vertex directly to the vertex 2. In the figure 13-18, it is 3, since, visit to 6 is already accomplished. Afterwards, we again consider, the other vertex directly connected to vertex-1. In the considered figure, it is 4. We would not consider the node 6, since, it is already marked as visited. Therefore, the entire depth first traversal is 1,2,5,6,3,4. Readers are requested to refer the depth first search method explained and coded in tree traversal(section 7.4).

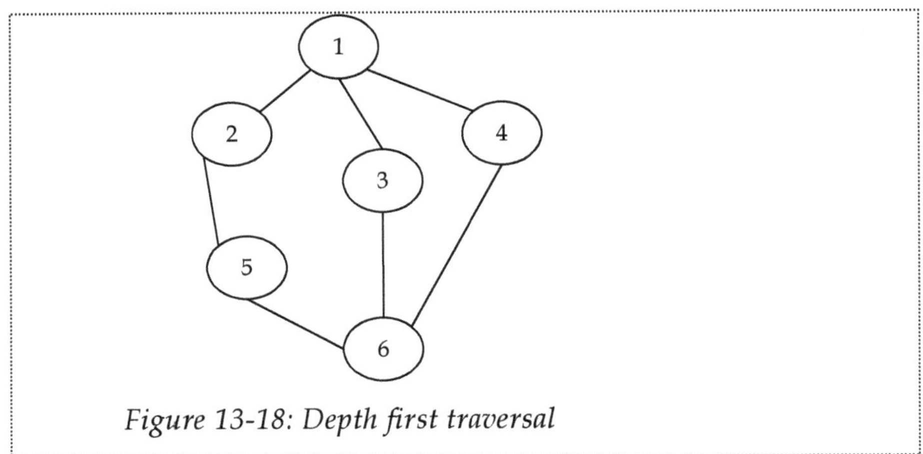

Figure 13-18: Depth first traversal

13.4.2 Breadth first search

In the breadth first search method, we start from the vertex Vi, Once all the neighbors of the vertex V_i is visited then we visit the neighbor of neighbors, and will continue till each node is not visited. During visit of the node due care is to be observed to avoid visiting any node twice. Breadth first search is similar to the BFS of binary tree. While traversing the vertex Vi, we identify all the neighbors of this vertex, once the neighbors are identified then they are inserted in the queue. Therefore, the edges inserted at the end are removed at the end. To enable the level by level traversal, we can use two queue. Consider the graph of figure 13-18, the breadth first traversal can be determine as follows:

i) Consider the first vertex visited is V1.
ii) Neighbours of the V1 are 2,3,4 therefore all of them are inserted into the queue. After insertion, one element from

the queue is removed (de-queue), the item available at first position of the queue is removed first. In this case, the first vertex is V2 therefore it is removed and visited.

iii) Neighbours of V2 are inserted at the rear side of the queue, in this case it is V5. Therefore, the resultant queue will be V3,V4,V5

iv. This is followed by de-queue of the neighbors already inserted i.e. V_3. It's neighbor is V_6, therefore, it would be inserted in the queue. Consequently, the resultant queue would be V_4,V_5, V_6.

v. In the step, we would de-queue from the queue consequently, we would obtain V_4. Neighbour of this node is V6 that is already visited therefore, no more node will be added. Consequently, the resultant queue would be V_5, V_6.

vi. In the next step, again the next vertex is de-queued in this case it is V_5. Neighbour of the V5 is only V6, it is already visited. Consequently, no more nodes will be added in the existing queue which will have only vertex V6.

vii. Eventually, we would de-queue the V6 from the queue. Since, it does not have any neighbor, therefore, no more vertex can be en-queue. Since, the queue is also empty, therefore, the entire operation will be terminated. The resultant queue of the breadth first traversal is: V1, V2, V3, V4, V5, V6.

Readers are requested to refer the section 7.4, for the

implementation of the program. However, one more data member visited is to be included. By default it would have the value of '0' that represents the non-traversal of the vertex. Once the vertex is visited its value will be set to 1. This will prevent the repeated visit of the same vertex.

13.5 Shortest path algorithm

Shortest path algorithm determines the shortest path in a given from the source to destination. Many time, we need to know the shortest distance from the source to the destination to minimize the cost of traversing or to reduce the latency.

To determine the shortest path from source to destination numerous algorithms are existing. These algorithm can be significantly useful in reducing the overhead/Cost of traversal from given source to the destination. Some of the prominent algorithm has been described in the following sub-sections.

13.5.1 Dijkshtra's Algorithm

Dijkshtra's algorithm is profoundly popular algorithm to determine the shortest path from the given and source. This algorithm is applied in wide applications. For instance, in networking where we need to select the shortest from the given source to the destination to minimize the latency.

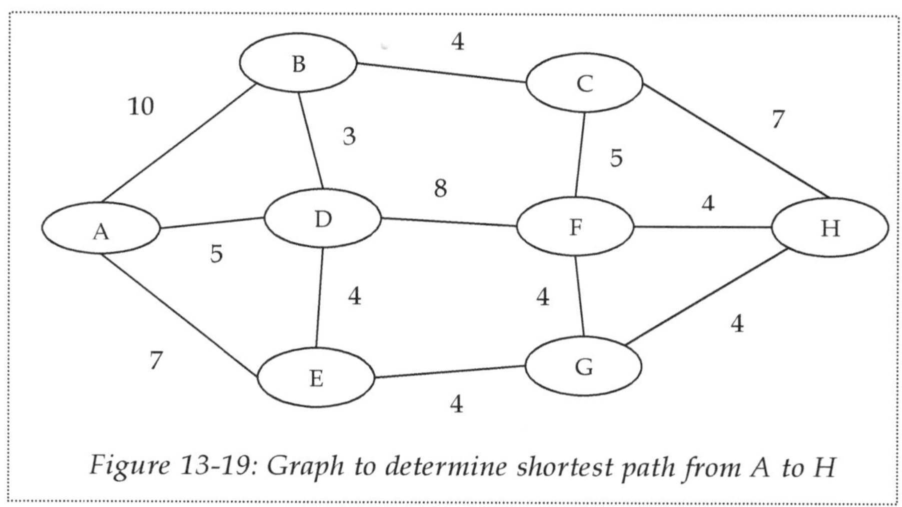

Figure 13-19: Graph to determine shortest path from A to H

In the Dijkshtra's algorithm other than the source we consider all the nodes are at the infinite distance. Consequently, they are assigned the infinity to all the nodes. Consider the figure of 13-19, we have to determine the shortest path from the source A to the destination H. Whole procedure has been depicted as follows:

1. Find out all the adjacent nodes from the source.
2. Figure out the minimum distance from source to the other adjacent node. Consider it as B.

Appendix A

TEMPLATE

14 Template

Templates are used for creating the generic classes and function. It is recently added features in C++. Templates offer the following advantages:

- Avoids re-writing the code again.
- Prevents the testing time for re-written code.
- Prevents any error that may creep due to re-writing of the code.

Due to the above advantages, templates have gained the wide popularity. We can understand the limitations that exist due to non-usage of template with the help of following program.

14.1 Need of a template

Consider a case in which user is intending to initialize the integer and float array and passes them as an argument. Consequently, to accomplish this objective, (s)he has to define the following program.

```
#include<iostream.h>
#include<conio.h>
const int size=4;
class one
{
```

```
int a[size];
float b[size];
public:
one(int[]);
one(float[]);
void sum();
void sum(float);
};
void one::sum(float s1)
 {
 float s=0.0;
 cout<<" In the float sum"<<endl;
 for(int i=0;i<size;i++)
 s=s+b[i];
 cout<<" Float sum"<<s<<endl;
}
one::one(int aa[])
{
 for(int i=0;i<size;i++)
 a[i]=aa[i];
 }
 one::one(float bb[])
 {
 for(int i=0;i<size;i++)
 b[i]=bb[i];
 }
 void one::sum()
 {
 int s=0;
 for(int i=0;i<size;i++)
```

```
s=s+a[i];
cout<<" Integer sum"<<s<<endl;
}
int main()
{
clrscr();
int arr[]={2,3,4,5};
float farr[]={4.2,6.3,4.7,9.4};
float s=0.0;
one a(arr);
one b(farr);

//one b;

// a=arr;
a.sum();
b.sum(s);
getch();
return 0;
}
```

It is apparent from the above code a number of redundancies that exist due to various types of data. Such redundancy not only requires re-writing of the code but also increases the effort of re-writing the code. In addition, error may creep in during the re-writing of the code.

14.2 Use of a template

To write the same code once, we can use the template, which is discussed in section ……. Template can be categorized into

- Class template
- Function template

Class template is used in the cases where we need to send the data type for the entire class as with the above example. Similarly, function template can be used as a template that accept the argument of any type and perform the function needed. It is followed by returning the value of the required type if needed.

14.3 Class template

Class template is used in the case where the data type is to be created that need to be accessed by many members of the class. To create the template we have to use the syntax

template<class type>

Here the type may be the build in type or the user defined type. In our case, we have represented it with the small t. consequently, the statement will be

template<class t>

we can defined more than one type in the argument. Correspondingly, class can accept more than one data type. Syntax for more than one data type is:

template< class t1, class t2,……., class tn>

However, we have discussed only for the single data type.

14.3.1 Class template single argument type

To write the class code for the program discussed in the section. , we can write the program as:

```
Program: Use of class template
#include<iostream.h>
#include<conio.h>
const int size=4;
template<class t>
class one
{
t a[size];          // declaring the t type
public:
one(t[]);
void sum();
};
template<class t>
one<t>::one(t aa[])
{
 for(int i=0;i<size;i++)
 a[i]=aa[i];
 }
template<class t>
 void one<t>::sum()   // defining the function outside the class
 {
 t s=0;
 for(int i=0;i<size;i++)
 s=s+a[i];                // adding the number one by one
 cout<<" sum of all numbers: "<<s<<endl;
 }
```

```
int main()
{
clrscr( );
int arr[]={2,3,4,5};
float farr[]={2.5,3.2,4.6,5.9};
one<int> a(arr);        // creating the template as integer type
one<float> b(farr);     // creating the template as float type
a.sum();
cout<<" Sum of float array"<<endl;
b.sum( );
getch( );
return 0;
}
```

14.4 Class template with two argument

In many cases, we need to create the template for more than two data type. This is accomplished in the template. To achieve the above cited requirement, we can use the following syntax.

template<class t1, class t2>

Consider the following example in which programmer is aiming to take two different type of arguments. In this case, we can use the template that can accept two arguments instead of one. Complete program for the above objective can be written as:

```
// Program to enumerate the use of two argument type in the class
template<class type1, class type2>
class one
```

```
{
type1 first;
type2 second;
public:
one(type1 o, type2 t);
void display();
};
template<class type1, class type2>
one<type1,type2>::one(type1 o, type2 t)
{
first=o;
second=t;
 }
template<class type1, class type2>
 void one<type1,type2>::display()
 {
 for(int i=0;i<second;i++)
 cout<<first<<"\t";
  }
 int main()
 {
 clrscr();
 one<char*,int> o1("jitendra",2);

 one<int,int> o2(30,4);
 o1.display();
 cout<<endl;
 o2.display();
 getch();
 return 0;
```

```
}
Output
Jitendra        jitendra
30      30      30      30
}
```

14.5 Function template

Function template is used to create the generic function. Consequently, same function can be used for wide variety of data types. To define that the function is template type we define it with the keyword, template similar to class type. Syntax for declaring the generic function type has been written as follows:

```
template<class t>
return-type function_name(class t);
```

14.5.1 Function template using one argument

Generic function of one argument will enable the user to support the single argument for various data type. Need of a function template can be realized by the following example.

Consider that user intend to pass character array or integer array along with the element to be searched. Since, both the data types are different, therefore, two different function has to be created as described in the following program.

```
// Program to search the element from the integer/character array
const int size=4;
```

```
//function to search the integer type element from integer array
void search(int a[size], int element)
 {
 int i=0;
 int flag=0;
 while(i<size)
   {
   if(a[i]==element)
   {
   flag=1;
   break;
   }
   i++;
 } //end of while
 if(flag)
 cout<<" item found";
 else
 cout<<"item not in the list";
 }//end of function
//function to search the char type element from character type array
void search(char a[size], char element)
 {
 int i=0;
 int flag=0;
 while(i<size)
   {
   if(a[i]==element)
   {
   flag=1;
   break;
```

```
  }
  i++;
} //end of while
if(flag)
cout<<" item found";
else
cout<<"item not in the list";
}//end of function

int main()
{
clrscr();
int arr[]={2,3,4,5};
float farr[]={2.5,3.2,4.6,5.9};
char a[]={'a','c','e','g'};
cout<<"integer result"<<endl;
search(arr,14);
cout<<"character result"<<endl;
search(a,'c');
getch();
return 0;
}
```

To avoid the re-writing of the same code, function template can be used. In the considered example, **we have taken the two argument, however, both of them are same type**.

```
// Program to search the element using generic function
const int size=4;
template<class t>
```

```
void search(t a[size], t element)
{
int i=0;
int flag=0;
while(i<size)
  {
  if(a[i]==element)
  {
  flag=1;
  break;
  }
  i++;
} //end of while
if(flag)
cout<<" item found";
else
cout<<"item not in the list";
}//end of function
int main()
{
clrscr();
int arr[]={2,3,4,5};
float farr[]={2.5,3.2,4.6,5.9};
char a[]={'a','c','e','g'};
cout<<"integer result"<<endl;
search(arr,14);
cout<<"character result"<<endl;
search(a,'c');
getch();
return 0;
```

```
}
```

In the above example, we have declared the function generic type. Consequently, in the call of integer type i.e. search(arr,14), it will get converted into integer type. Whereas at the time of character array i.e. search(a, 'c') it will converted into character type. Therefore, it is apparent from the above code that we can eliminate lot of re-writing of the code by using the template.

14.5.2 Function template using two argument

Similar to one argument type template function, we can create two argument type template type function. This will enable to pass two different type of arguments.

Consider the case that we are aiming to print the first argument based on the value of second argument. First argument may be any data type. Same has been illustrated with the help of following example:

```
// Function template type, accepting two different argument type
template<class type1, class type2>
 void display(type1 one, type2 two)
 {
 int i=0;
 while(i<two){
 cout<<one<<"\t";
 i++;
 } //end of while
 }//end of function
```

```
int main()
{
clrscr();
display("jitendra",5);
display(58,3);
getch();
return 0;
}
Output
jitendra      jitendra      jitendra      jitendra      jitendra
58      58      58
}
```

In the above program, first we pass the string and the number of times passed string is to be printed. Consequently, at the time of called function display("jitendra", 5), it will display the name jitendra 5 times. In the second call we pass the integer type by display(58,3), therefore, 58 is printed 3 times.

15 Salient Features

Data structure is the backbone of computer science. A number of books on this subject are available and are enriching the students as per their own methodology. However, this book is written to facilitate the readers in self learning. Other features of this book are:

- Use of simple language for coding.
- Major focus on link list, tree, stack, and queue.
- In majority of the cases, both recursive and non-recursive functions have been used for single operation.
- Object oriented approach using C++ to code the program.
- Objective of each chapter discussed in the beginning.
- Code is substantiated with ample of figures and description.
- All the written codes are tested and executed.
- Written considering the novice and experts.
- Each chapter is followed by case study.
- Inclusion of exercise at the end of the chapter to enable the student to evaluate themselves.

Indexing

D

E

F

G

H

I

K

L

M

N

O

P

Q

R

S

T

U

W

www.ingramcontent.com/pod-product-compliance
Lightning Source LLC
Chambersburg PA
CBHW080135060326
40689CB00018B/3800

* 9 7 8 1 5 0 0 9 4 9 0 5 1 *